Alan Valentine

Trial Balance

THE EDUCATION
OF AN AMERICAN

PANTHEON

CONTENTS

Preface

FOR many years I have been more devoted to Angus than to any other man. His little successes and failures, and how he took them, have given me satisfaction, amusement, and dismay. We have shared close intimacy and unpopular opinions, and in recent years have indulged in mutual speculations in what we could learn by looking backward over our earlier experiences. Angus sought in his more confident past the explanation of his present confusions, and although few of his conclusions are original they interest me as a man's reactions to himself and his times.

Angus never thought of his life as material for biography: what can be told is unimportant and what is significant cannot be told. Personal experiences are worth recording only if they throw some light on those of others. His own exposure to the forces of our times was in some ways characteristic of a twentieth-century American and in others unusual. Whether his reactions are typical or unique, they may amuse the psychologists, or possibly console other men that they are not alone in their uncertainties.

Because he had lived chiefly in academic circles, Angus evaluated all his experiences in terms of his education. He was attracted by the idea of carrying forward the story of the education of an American from the point where Henry Adams left off. Adams had written of himself as a nineteenth-century American aristocrat educated to eighteenth-century concepts; Angus would try to present himself as a wanderer in the twentieth, who had been inculcated with nineteenth-century values. He threatened to call his account *Gullible's Travels*.

What Angus wanted to do was to measure the events of his time in terms of their contributions to his understanding—to evaluate his earlier vicissitudes in later relative tranquillity, and trace the effect of twentieth-century forces on a man trained for the nineteenth. All but the most superior men damage their auto-biographical ships on the Scylla of egoism or the Charybdis of false modesty, and Angus had no hope of escaping both. He knew that no matter how objective he tried to be he would not avoid the outcome predicted by Benjamin Franklin in embarking on his own autobiography:

"In reality there is perhaps no one of our natural passions so hard to subdue as pride. Disguise it, struggle with it, beat it down, stifle it, mortify it as much as one pleases; it is still alive and will every now and then peep out and show itself; you will see it perhaps often in this history; for even if I could conceive that I had compleatly overcome it, I should probably be proud of my humility."

In justice to his closest intimate through life, Angus felt obliged to acknowledge his lifelong debt to his *amour-propre*. It often misled but never deserted him, and it had supported him staunchly through his worst moments. Take away men's egoism and, according to Emerson, you would castrate some of the greatest benefactors of mankind. It is the little persistent irritants of self-love that have goaded some men into their loftiest accomplishments.

Angus knew his egoism had not produced such happy results, but since he could not escape it he decided to offer it as an admonitory example to others. An account of the misadventures into which conceit had led him might serve as a whistling buoy to warn others off the dangerous ledges of self-complacency.

Any boy born in 1901 has seen the world of his childhood vanish and a new, disconcerting one take its place. American habits and values have changed more in the last fifty years than in the previous century. In spirit 1901 was closer to Hamilton than to Harry Hopkins, and the confusions and adjustments between the two worlds have been shared by nearly every man and woman of our generation. The more efficiently an American boy was inculcated with the attitudes traditional in 1901, the less happily he can cope with those of the mid-century. Every generation has met change, and reacted to it with enthusiasm or dismay, but no generation offers more material than our own for the study of human adjustment and frustration. We are living through a revolution in culture as drastic as that in mechanics, without much speculation where it is leading us.

Adams and Angus, so unlike in background and talents, had similar reactions to the changes of their times. Each thought he saw a decline in the quality of American ideals and values; each believed that the number of constants in human thought was decreasing alarmingly; each was depressed by the mounting confusions around him and within him. Adams in 1900 and Angus in 1950 saw unity and diversity at war with one another and were not sure which side to take. And each blamed modern society for his disappointments and spiritual malaise.

There the parallels end. Adams was brilliant and cultivated. Angus was intellectually his inferior, culturally limited, and emotionally naïve. Adams had fine perceptions and social sophistication; Angus was at times obtuse, stubborn, and as ignorant of how he looked to others as any crude schoolboy. His emotions were undisciplined and he was never good at concealing his irritations, though he usually justified them afterwards to his own satisfaction. His academic education had made his mind a useful instrument, but nothing could make it a first-rate one. He could recognize and desire intellectual quality, but he could not attain it. He lost his sense of humor under pressure and strained it under encouragement; in jokes as in arguments he could not let well enough alone. He charged ideas and people with his head down and his eyes closed. In short, he was more like the average American than he could bear to admit.

Because his native mediocrities were at war with the standards of high quality his unusual opportunities had given him, he was particularly bitter against all mediocrity and never forgave education for its failure to achieve the impossible. Yet despite his limitations he would not concede to the life and thoughts they ordained and was doomed to discomfort between his average talents and his excessive ambitions.

In offering this self-analysis, Angus tried to limit his account to his intellectual advances and retreats, but he was no more successful in painting a portrait by reason alone than in living by it. The man he pictures is not a rounded figure; it lacks perspective. His chapters are merely separate vignettes, and by ignoring the emotional experiences that should have taught him most of all, they are only two-dimensional. He did not realize this mistake, in writing as in living, until too late.

A man stuffed with inherited inhibitions and cultivated cautions cannot write comfortably about himself. He seeks some device, no matter how transparent, to escape the embarrassment of the first person singular. He does not want to seem to take himself too seriously or to be another twentieth-century exhibitionist, and he knows that modern society regards public self-evaluation as the most indecent form of self-exposure. Try as he will to be honest about himself, he is aware that the man he is writing about is really another, created by the distortions of his subjective view.

Adams wrote of his own education in the third person; his artistry obscures from his readers how little he tells them of himself. A less skillful writer, trying to be less reticent than Adams, must separate himself a little further from the man he depicts. The perceptive reader will not be surprised when I confess that Angus is a fictional character—as much myself as I can make him, but still a figment of my rationalizations. He is only half a man at that—a print without color because a man without the personal history I have censored. I hope that the reader will not assume me as barren of warm feelings and perceptions of beauty as Angus seems to be. Angus cannot reflect, however, what his original may not possess: the ability to draw inspiration from friendships and exaltation from the arts. But it may be my own deficiencies, not his amputations of Angus, that make Angus seem so limited in heart.

Twentieth-century American culture and Angus did their best for each other. If the results are disappointing, that may not impair their usefulness to others who want to consider the forces that are making Americans what they are. As a person, Angus is not worth writing a book about, but as a product of America he illustrates its conflicts.

Kinsale, County Cork   A.V.

PART 1

EDUCATION BY

Plan

I

Tribal Origins

ANGUS entered the world almost simultaneously with the twentieth century, though somewhat less auspiciously. He apparently did not want to be a child of the century, and declared immediately a reluctance to accept its ways. Had he known what it would prove to be like he might have joined it even more ungraciously. It was only much later that he realized that being born in 1901 had given him at least a minor literary advantage—the right to claim some identity between his personal experiences and the events of the nineteen hundreds.

Five decades do not give a man full objectivity on his youth, but they provide him with some perspective on the circumstances of his earlier years. A boy himself is not a judge of his environment; he grows like a vegetable, and is too busy drawing whatever nutriment the soil and climate of his origin offer to consider their fertility and beneficence. Only when he has started to go to seed does a man speculate on his reactions to his beginnings and his tribal culture. Even then his conclusions are likely to be tinctured with the rationalisms of egoism and the syrups of self-approbation. Fortunately, such deceptions are usually obvious to his observers, who can make them a source of instruction or at least of amusement.

Looking back at the roots of his origin, Angus at fifty concluded that though they lay in somewhat stony and exhausted soil they were healthier than most. Wines of special flavor sometimes come from thin soil, if the plant is hardy enough. His roots were precious to him because they were his, but they also had qualities which, even in 1901, were becoming rare. If they did not produce good wine, the fault did not lie primarily in the stock.

To be born into the American middle class in the early twentieth century was to join the newly privileged of the earth. They enjoyed a world of freedom, comfort, security, and opportunity hitherto reserved for aristocrats. Angus had that good fortune, and special advantages as well, for few boys of the time could grow up on acres deeded to their ancestors by the Indians, or join a family tradition that was at once patriarchal and independent. He was most fortunate of all in his parents, who had none of the spiritual anemia and intellectual inertia that had begun to infect and devitalize the stock around them. Angus took all this for granted, so far as he understood it, and like any healthy young extrovert of five or six years was too busy exploring and tasting his environment to evaluate it. What his roots failed to give him he did not suspect until he was a man.

The world of which he slowly grew conscious was not the America of slums, racial inequalities, economic frustrations, and greedy aggrandizements that contemporary journalists and reformers were beginning to picture. Lincoln Steffens and the "muckrakers" of *McClure's* did not impinge on Angus' consciousness for many years. He vaguely recognized the existence of a society separate from his own stable and superior Anglo-Saxon one, for across the railroad tracks lay a district called The Orchard, inhabited by men and women who seemed to Angus to have come from another world. There Italian immigrants had

established a beach-head amid Long Island's prosperous bour-
geoisie—an extra-legal self-governing community of their own.
It was more squalid than picturesque, but to a small boy like
Angus it was filled with the glamour of the foreign and the
dangerous. From it came tales, doubtless exaggerated, of knifings,
of warfare between rival Sicilian societies, of marital Donny-
brooks, and of interesting establishments never described beyond
the single whispered word "houses." From it also came scores of
stocky, mysterious little men to do all the hardest and poorest-
paid work of the community. A boy who watched them digging
ditches, mending roads, and tending gardens found them more
colorful than pitiful, more docile than dangerous. Working alone,
each was silent but not unfriendly; laboring together in some
trench, their unintelligible conversations were as spirited and
continuous as the motion of their picks and shovels. No Americans worked so hard and long for so little, walked so far to work,
or laughed so much. No Americans would make a lunch of
sausage and hard bread unwrapped from red bandannas, then
refilled with dandelion greens hurriedly collected from the roadside.

Angus noticed with perplexity that when his elders talked of
these immigrants as a social addition they deplored their presence, but when there was hard work to be done they welcomed
their availability. It took him some time to learn the American
distinction between a citizen as an economic asset and as a social
liability. Politically the Italians of The Orchard were a dubious
intrusion. Some friends of his family instructed these newcomers
in the merits of democracy as exemplified by the Republican
party, and supported their teaching by small annual investments
in good government, discreetly exchanged, to make sure that if
these new citizens voted at all they voted right. Occasionally
the local Democrats would, by unethically high bids which in-
flated the value of Italian votes, challenge good government and
threaten to undermine the social structure. This was the only
whirlpool in the quiet current of local polity, and if any other

social and political problems existed in the community, Angus
was no more aware of them than his elders seemed to be.

To a Frank Norris or an Upton Sinclair, the world of young
Angus would have seemed unpardonably remote from the real
and more sordid America, but, allowing for a few variations in
geography and local mores, the society he knew was probably
more typical of the America of 1910 than the Chicago stockyards
or the Bowery. What he saw and how he reacted to it were not
very different from the observations and reactions of a farm boy
in Nebraska, a doctor's son in Pennsylvania, or a prosperous
groceryman's child in the quieter streets of Brooklyn Heights.
Comfortable middle-class Americans kept themselves to themselves; they had created a world they liked and did not look at-
tentively beyond it. Their world was the dominant world in
America, and they did not dream how soon and how completely
it would change.

Henry Adams wrote of the Quincy of his boyhood in terms of
a social nucleus unified by unique attitudes toward God, the
human race, and Boston. Brand Whitlock, Tarkington, Mar-
quand, and Bellamy later pictured communities in Indiana,
Massachusetts, and upstate New York as homogeneous units.
Such areas might have their discordant groups, but they were
only variants on the dominant themes played by an established
local society. Each area had its social pattern, generally recognized and generally accepted.

In the quadrant of Long Island Angus came to know, there
was no longer a clear and determinant social pattern. In that
sense Nassau County had no society, but only separate groups.
There was little left in the way of unity in the traditions, ends,
and values of its inhabitants: they met, transacted business, and
returned to the separate social particles of their origins. No force
of social gravitation held them to a common center except economic effort; the other forces were centrifugal. Their only sense
of mutual mission centered upon getting at least one's share of
the burgeoning prosperity, increasing the value of their real es-

tate, and improving the service on the Long Island Rail Road. Before Angus was twelve he began to sense the amorphous disparity of the social groups around him, and to wonder about the forces that pulled men together and pushed them apart.

Looking backward as a man, Angus realized that what was happening to Nassau County in his childhood was also taking place in many other towns and areas across America. The melting pot and industrial furnace of democracy were at work, and the old order was changing so rapidly that there was hardly time to be nostalgic. Change was more evident than amalgamation; if the ingredients of the pot were blending into a new unity they were doing so very slowly, meanwhile throwing some unattractive scum to the surface. The only apparent unities in the new America were those of the lowest common denominators. The hot flame beneath the pot was the common urge toward accumulation and comfort; freedom was the slogan but prosperity was the goal of new citizens as well as old. The spiritual and intellectual energy of democracy remained relatively inert while its economic energy boiled over. The atmosphere of society's judgments became more and more tentative and provisional, lacking in firm criteria, even while fortunes were being made, cities built, wars won, and horsepower multiplied—and the future of America was being determined by these events. As economic security developed, Americans became less spiritually secure.

Angus represented one of the older social groups that was fighting a rear-guard battle against this disintegration. His paternal heredity was a close intermixture of Yankee, Dutch, and Quaker founders of the local community—an intermixture so close that he could confidently address as cousin any Seaman or Underhill from Jericho, any Albertson or Hicks from Westbury, any Post or Mott from Roslyn, any Willits or Frost from Locust Valley, any Mudge or Coles from Glen Cove. Though these descendants of the original elite no longer controlled the politics, social standards, or wealth of the county, they still felt superiority and exerted influence. As these old families saw the newcomers take over the power, they acted defensively, preserving their old customs but not the physical energy or spiritual force that had created them. While reluctantly conceding, step by step, to modernism, they continued to profess the outward forms of puritanism and Quakerism without the deep convictions or material renunciations of the earlier founders.

Conservative and reasonably prosperous, they could still plow the straightest furrows when they had to, but did not trouble to compete with the Polish farmers who were turning the plains around Mineola and Jamaica into truck gardens and bank accounts. The scions of the early settlers preferred the less strenuous activities of local bank boards, real estate developments on their inherited farm lands, and cautious ventures into trade and investment. Caution was in fact their economic and social watchword; they were so careful not to endanger what they possessed that they seldom made investments more daring than government bonds and local land mortgages, though they watched with envy other men who made fortunes in business and private stocks. They rarely risked new friendships, either, outside the established clan boundaries. Fighting a losing battle against the greater enterprise of newer Americans with foreign names, they vacillated between sporadic efforts to rival the commercial devotion of invading Brigattis, Connollys, Cszkowskis, and Cohens, and withdrawal into a fading and not very lavender-like gentility.

Had their decline in physical and spiritual energy been balanced by an advance in intellectual acumen they might have held their own, but few of them had gone far in education or ever stretched their minds. They were more ignorant than they realized. The Quaker interest in schools and colleges came too late in the nineteenth century for most of Angus' older relatives to have profited by it, or to understand except in the vaguest ways the aims and values of higher education. The tradition that a boy should go to work when he finished school lingered on. Angus' father had yearned to go to college, and there was money to send him, but instead he was put to work in Brooklyn, and there

learned the loneliness and sterile amenities of a back-hall bed-
room where he secretly cooked over the gas mantle to supple-
ment the inadequate meals provided him by his respectable
Quaker landlord. The superiority the old Long Island families,
Quaker or not, professed had in most cases no foundations in
physical or intellectual capacity. As for morals, most of their
boasted virtue was outward virtue because it was vestigial.

The effect of all this upon an Angus in knickerbockers was to
make him very conscious of his separateness from most of society.
Whatever the rest of the world might say or do, his family and
the local Quakers would do something else—and do it with a
sense of moral superiority. The more the growing boy widened
his horizons the more he became aware of the psychic gap between the self-contained and backward-looking group that made
up his immediate society, and the fluid and forward-rushing humanity that was inundating it. These newcomers were as devastating to the aborigines as were the Visigoths when they descended upon some village of Latium, but because the modern
invasion was less sudden it was less apparent. There were few
outward differences between the work and play of the older elite
and the mixed population that submerged it; by 1920 they might
be partners in the same undertakings, play golf at the same local
clubs, take their wives twice a winter to the same "show" in
New York, and spend similar incomes in similar ways. Probably
the average Nassau County citizen was not one tenth as conscious of the old families as they were conscious of themselves,
but to a member, although a junior member, of Victorianism in
retreat, the difference was very great.

In the case of Angus' immediate home circle this attitude was
enhanced by the powerful sense of independence derived from a
strong-minded grandmother of Dutch extraction. She was so
much her own mistress that when she married a Quaker she not
only refused to join the faith but would never accompany her
husband to First Day Meeting. To be stubborn or reactionary
was to be strong-willed, and that adjective was not used in deroga-

tion. "As independent as a hog on ice" was a familiar phrase and a complimentary one. But individuality did not engender zest. To be gay or spontaneous was to display a lack of stability, and Angus' grandmother's conviction of the wickedness of gaiety was so strong that she complained she could never really enjoy having a good time. Throughout a long life she rarely committed pleasure. Nearly every aspect of Angus' environment conditioned him toward instinctive and humorless nonconformity.

Yet that environment, and especially his parents, exuded far more warmth and affection than its rather belligerent defensiveness revealed. There were devoted aunts and uncles eager to understand and encourage this rather promising small nephew. But even they, Angus decided after his eyes were somewhat opened to the wonders of the world, were unconsciously sterile in appreciation of the beautiful, and of aesthetic and spiritual values. They let him grow up as remote from the fine arts as if he had been the son of a North Carolina sharecropper or an unsuccessful Arizona rancher. Beauty, to many of his elders, was restricted to a striking sunset, a charming landscape (preferably including a cow or a bit of salt water), a full-blown rose, or a prize trotting horse. Sculpture meant nothing to Angus except gray busts of bearded men in elementary school corridors or darker bronze heads of Shakespeare in normally unused front parlors, or black-and-white prints of an armless and embarrassingly naked Greek woman in textbooks on the classics.

As for music, except for his mother's Mozart, it connoted his uncle's phonograph (which echoed Lew Dockstader's minstrels more often than the Red Seal opera arias), painful compulsory scales on the piano, hymns heard through open church windows or dutifully droned at school exercises, local bands at firemen's parades, and waltzes and two-steps by piano and inexpert violin at dancing school. The graphic arts were just as limited. The pictures around Angus were chiefly family photographs and sepia reproductions of Millet's reapers, Troyon's cows, and two small angels of Raphael sipping water from a scallop shell. It did not occur to him that there are exciting mysteries in color and messages in symbolism. In a friend's home there was a volume of Blake's illustrations which at once attracted his curiosity and offended his concept of what graphic art should be—pictorial scenery like the prints of Currier and Ives.

Literature was more familiar and far more rewarding. Poetry was an exalted expression, sometimes unintelligible but always to be admired, though of course one never expected to set eyes on a real poet. The favorite poet of his grandmother was Felicia Hemans, of his uncles James Whitcomb Riley, and though many home bookshelves held copies of Shakespeare, Wordsworth, and Longfellow, they were left unopened in favor of James Greenleaf Whittier and Edmund Vance Cooke. Fiction and history were sheer delight to Angus, and under his mother's guidance he explored the charmed worlds of Jason and Jim Hawkins, Huck Finn and Captain Hook, Rob Roy and Oliver Twist—as well as the Rover Boys, the Minute Boys, the Motor Boys, and the Submarine Boys in endless volumes. Richard Cœur de Lion and Robin Hood were his idols, and he spent hours in private daydreams populated by knights and burly friars, with himself as a promising squire. On many a quiet autumn evening Fresh Pond Lane would echo with shouted boy soprano defiances of Brian du Bois Guilbert and the thwack of a wooden sword against some villain disguised as a sycamore tree.

Angus tested his own conduct, not without rationalization, by what Richard or King Arthur would have thought of it. Among other challenging activities of knights were the vows they made. So Angus made vows too, with all the medieval trimmings he could remember or invent. Having made them he surprisingly kept them, though not without some disturbance to others. As a boy of ten he once vowed in a moment of un-Quakerly abandon to jump from the second-story window at the top of the front stairs. For logistical reasons this had to be attempted in secret, but once on the sill of the window fears of parental disapproval were dwarfed by fears of broken bones. The brown August lawn beneath looked very distant and very hard, but he could never face Ivanhoe or Lancelot, even in print, unless he kept his vow.

Great-Aunt Mary was plodding up the dusty lane that hot afternoon, modestly resplendent though overwarm in her calling-dress of russet bombazine, carrying a quart pail of fresh peach ice cream on one arm and a large candy box of warm chocolate brownies on the other. As she neared the house she saw across the meadow a small figure in yellow seersucker blouse perched perilously on the window ledge. She hurried her short steps as much as age, her burdens, and her long skirt would allow, and reached the entrance drive in time to see the diminutive Squire of Ivanhoe launch himself, land heavily on the ground, and, with what appeared to be the final spasm, roll under the rhododendron bush and lie still.

She rushed to him, sprinkling brownies on the lawn.

"Is thee badly hurt?" She came as close to shrieking as Quaker calm and shortness of breath would permit.

There was no reply, but a grass-stained arm reached out and gathered in a vagrant brownie. Thus fortified, and helped by a trembling arm, Squire Angus struggled to his feet and submitted with unusual docility to pattings and proddings in search of broken bones. There were only bruises, and the peach ice cream, intended for dinner, proved a sovereign remedy, as well as a sign that the gods smiled on those who kept their hazardous words. Having thus proved himself, the Squire was remarkably amenable for several weeks. He was not punished, but later his father pointed out that though keeping promises to parents was less glamorous than keeping vows to Ivanhoe, it was somewhat less dangerous and more helpful.

To Angus the literature he loved was a gift of the gods, and those who wrote it must have been beings far superior to anyone he would ever know. Someday he might meet a writer, and in his highest moments he even resolved to be one, but he never thought of meeting a painter, a sculptor, or a real musician, or particularly wanted to. Except for his reading and his parents, the world of the spirit was just as remote as the world of the arts. He knew the emotions of love, fear, happiness, and sorrow, but did not think of them as more than personal reactions to given personal situations. The idea that the spirit could be a link between all men, or that emotion is the essential medium of faith and religion, would not dawn on him for many years. There was nothing emotional about Quakerism, or spiritual about friendship, as he saw them.

His world had its emotional values, but they were mostly moral or mundane. His first theft, when he stole a five-cent candy bar in the Greek Candy Kitchen, troubled his spirit so much that the next afternoon after school he secretly replaced it, grubby but intact. That was morality, but morality was always stern and went no further than the Decalogue. The social morality he knew seemed even then superficial, and the social occasions often mildly hypocritical because of the display of false sentiment they involved. He developed a dislike, which lasted throughout his life, for large-scale social formalities; "occasions" were almost certain to be boring if not false in their professions. It was, of course, important to co-operate with society and to get on comfortably with other people, and that demanded social give-and-take, but there were many people he would have been rather relieved never to set eyes on again. Those one liked the best, or was most often thrown with, one called friends, but one did not go out looking for friendships or expect anything spiritually uplifting from them. Except for boys to play with, one waited quiescently for whatever human relationships circumstances would bring. No one suggested that there might be some wisdom or stimulus in every man and woman one met, if one could only find and extract it. Angus was like those around him in not trying very hard to understand other people. He preferred books for inspiration and activity for enjoyment; when one no longer wanted to read a book or play baseball one could stop, but human beings were less easily discarded. There were only a few people he loved and sought; to those he was without reservation devoted, but his instinct was not to love humanity in general or expect very much personal warmth from it.

The word values consequently meant very little to him except in material things, for those were the only values he heard about—except, of course, for the daily preaching of teachers and the more rare occasions when The Spirit moved someone to words at First Day Meeting—and those he discounted as conventions required by the event. Of the more familiar values the greatest were honesty, hard work, economy, helpfulness to parents, and (later) chastity, and if a boy observed those he was virtuous. To waste anything, even if one could afford it, was the sin most frequently stressed in daily life. Attics were filled with piles of carefully preserved and ordered copies of the *Farm Journal,* the *Friends' Intelligencer,* the *Woman's Home Companion,* and the Brooklyn *Daily Eagle,* to the despair of residuary legatees. Not poverty but principle so conditioned Angus that he always felt guilty if he did not clean his plate or took more than he wanted, or failed to turn out all the lights on leaving a room, or neglected to wear the oldest suit of clothes the occasion would allow. At his most prosperous he still read every menu from right to left, whether in Pavillon or a roadside lunch stand, and never got his hair cut until it was overdue. There was more emphasis on saving things and money than on saving other people's feelings, or the gifts of the spirit.

Had these been the only influences in his boyhood, Angus might have grown into the most insufferable prig on Long Island. But his immediate circle of watered-down puritanism was not, and did not try to be, wholly restrictive upon him, and his parents had a wider view. In any case no human power could have limited the scope and acquaintances of an independent American boy who was curious about the world, owned a bicycle, and was ready to play with anybody who would play. The new world might be full of dangers and temptations, but it was also full of interest and excitement. Angus explored it and made friends among the urban invaders as only a boy can do. His reactions to them and their ways were mixed, but they led him to the secret resolve that when he could he would escape forever from the restrictions of his tribal stockade. He did not want to leave his family behind him—only the trammels of their ways.

The physical changes the new world brought to his doorstep, over the decade of his youth, were to Angus spectacular. As a small tow-head in faded khaki pants, Angus could walk down School and Glen Streets and know and be known by almost everyone he met: the only grocery store was presided over by Cousin Sidney Bowne, who also led the conversations in the carriage shed after Meetings on First Days; across the street was the bank where Angus' father was Cashier and Cousin Frederick Willits was President; a few steps up Glen Street was the white frame building where Uncle Ellwood rested his three hundred odd pounds as Postmaster until Woodrow Wilson defeated the Republicans. Just beyond, skipping the Episcopal Church as out of bounds, was the hardware store of Cousin Samuel Seaman and then the garage of his son, both automatically patronized by all Quakers to renew their kitchenware and refill their Ford and EMF tanks at thirteen cents a gallon.

As a boy in yellowed flannel trousers home from college, Angus found the old landmarks and friends submerged among new faces and new names on mushroomed shops and branch stores. The bank was struggling to hold its accounts against two rivals; the old grocery store no longer bore the name of Bowne or held its former monopoly; a Federal fantasy in half-timber replaced the frame post office; next to it was the new movie palace, and several garages flaunted their orange tanks and plate-glass fronts. New York City had made Nassau County into its suburb and its citizens into cultural and economic satellites.

The change was exciting to a youth, though for the first time he knew the meaning of nostalgia. Older members of his family deplored the altered tone of their village, now a city, but their regrets were tempered by the rising value of their lands and by the tide of prosperity that ran up their own little inlets. If their influence was diminishing, their bank accounts were not, and even Quakers can be realists.

In this inchoate society another element had entered and remained distinct from the majority. It remained separate because it was peripatetic and because it was wealthy. The age of the millionaire estates was approaching its impressive climax. Before the century began, a few families with riches had established themselves on the hilltops overlooking the Sound, their gables and turrets standing in the splendid isolation of green lawns, groomed shrubbery, and landscaped woodlands. These first families of wealth had over the years become accepted and even boasted fixtures in the community. Though they were not numerous enough to affect its ways, they took a civic interest in the community and their children thought of it as home. One seldom saw them except in the tonneaus of Pierce-Arrows and Panhards en route to country club or station, but their children could be glimpsed in formal riding clothes, posting or bouncing beside their grooms along the choicer byways, and local shopkeepers found their wives usually courteous and uniformly profitable. Their comings and goings, their homes and yachts and relative riches, were matters of endless and rather prideful speculation among the lesser townspeople. They were to them what the local squire was to the English village, and to the more entranced their palatial homes were what the Cathedral was to the tradesmen of Chartres.

But to these original and well-bred grandees were rapidly being added newer and less conservative millionaires with ways more gaudy and manners less good. They came in numbers sufficient to make "the wealthy set" no longer only a decoration to the community but an essential factor in its prosperity, for more and more of its inhabitants became directly or indirectly dependent upon them. Local stores looked to them for profits, local workmen for employment, local society for its manners and mores, local youth for its models and values. The independence the local citizens had once possessed was giving way to economic and social imitation.

The fringe of this colony of plutocracy was a curious place for a Quaker boy to live, though Angus later conceded that it was a good antidote to a Quaker simplicity that had become Quaker narrowness. Some of the large estates lay on land that had been his family's farm, and this knowledge gave a youth half living with Robin Hood and Ivanhoe a sense of romantic melancholy and defiant equality. His was the elite of the Saxons and theirs of the conquering Normans, and although their ways might be different, both were nobility and his strain was the older. He felt justified in ignoring their no-trespassing signs and iron gateways, and spent many hours exploring alone their woodlands and outbuildings, peeping across their manicured lawns at their tennis and bathing, and talking with their Scottish gardeners and English grooms. Doubtless he knew their lands and some of their servants more intimately than they.

His glimpses of their luxuries and their libraries aroused his envy and ambition. Though he came to disdain the apparent softness of their overindulged and overwatched children, he determined to gain what they had, and to win his own place in the warm sun of power—preferably in some way more admirable and dashing than the accumulation of oil and textile stocks. On the few occasions when he was invited to play with the children of what his family when in the parlor called "the summer people," but when in the kitchen called "the rich folks," he felt he was the equal of most of them in intelligence, and their superior in staying power. They made him feel both imitative and scornful.

What they thought of him—that rather uncomfortable playmate more conscious than they that he came from a different world—he never knew, if they thought of him at all. Certainly they did not take him half as seriously as he took himself, for humor about oneself was not excessive in his family circle and he had very little of it. His visits to the local Valhallas might have taught him much in ease of manners and distinction of bearing had he imitated the best of the models he found there. He encountered from the parents of these occasional playmates a graciousness rather more tactful and polished than he was accustomed to elsewhere, and in time realized that this was not special attention to a small boy seen to be ill at ease, but routine courtesy born of relaxed success. It was not that what they had to dispense in food and toys was so magnificent that really impressed Angus, or even that they gave it more openhandedly, for they could afford to be generous without personal sacrifice. But when, on one occasion Angus never forgot, he was nervously sitting at a large and elaborate birthday dinner party for a child of Standard Oil, and found that he and he alone had been overlooked when the plates of soup were handed round by a footman, his host at the far end of the table saw that the error was remedied, and did it in a way that turned Angus' terror at being conspicuous into delight at a special compliment. Mr. Herbert Pratt simply said:

"This is a special soup a little stronger than I let these kids have. It's like my own and I want you to try it."

The episode was in contrast to one Angus' father had told him of his own boyhood, when he was invited to spend the day with the son or grandson of that eminent but cautious farmer, Gideon Frost, who left his estate to found a Quaker school. Angus' father came to play, but Gideon put the two boys to work in the barn, and kept them hard at it all day. When, late in the afternoon, the exhausted guest was about to leave for home, old Gideon said to him:

"Now, Charles, thee's worked well all day and I hope thee's enjoyed it, for work is the greatest joy of man. As a special reward I want thee to ask Ellwood here to take thee down into the cellar to the apple barrel, and pick thee out a rotten-specked apple to eat on thy way home."

In later years, when Angus listened to political diatribes against the selfish malefactors of great wealth, or read of the irresponsible power of some of the same families he had visited at

Red Spring and North Shore country estates, the portrait did not fit the reality he knew. He wondered whether those who criticized them would have worn their rich mantles with equal grace and social responsibility, and whether the New Deal denunciators would have preferred Gideon Frost to Herbert Pratt.

All this was only the setting of education. Its negative aspects were in striking contrast with the affirmative warmth of Angus' two greatest childhood influences, his mother and his father. When he came to understand in later years how desiccated were the spiritual austerities from which each of them derived, he wondered at the miracles of self-development that had made them what they were. Each brought to Angus, in very different ways, devotions and ideals rare in almost any setting. Their effort to free themselves from the narrownesses of their background augmented Angus' feeling of separation from the rest of the world and special loyalty to them. It was clear even to a boy that the Scottish inheritance and values of his mother were different from those of the family and environment into which she had married. She had been bred to traditions of gentility and love of the arts, even if little or nothing had been done to implement them. This made her something of an alien in the negative conventionality of her new surroundings. The refinements she sought and practiced as best she could seemed to her in-laws to be a reproach to their own ways. For many years she longed for a piano of her own and when, after drastic economies, Angus' father gave her a Steinway baby grand, his family deplored this sacrifice of his daily lunch to gratify a wife's expensive whimsey for mere music, especially as one of the new Edison phonographs would have cost less and offered more variety. The large crate in which the Steinway came was carefully carpentered by Angus' father into a playhouse for him. To the small boy it seemed more than ever that he and his parents were an inseparable trio against an unsympathetic world.

If that isolation put Angus more on the defensive than he should have been, it repaid him by the affectionate intensity of his home life and the benefaction of music there. All the hours his mother could spare from housework she spent at the new piano, and Angus never forgot the delight of lying on the bear rug before the open fire and listening, while autumn crickets chirped outside, to the blending chords and liquid ripples of Chopin's sonatas. He could not understand the magic of music, but it was clearly a miracle from heaven vouchsafed specially to him. If having to be different from others could bring such a reward, nonconformity was a joy as well as a virtue.

Then Angus fell ill with mastoids and meningitis, and the doctors gave up hope. Seeking some escape from her spiritual frustration, his mother had, a year or two before, embraced Christian Science, to the open disapproval of all the family except her husband and her sister. Now in this crisis she defied local medical laws and family opposition and sent for a Christian Science "practitioner." Doctors and certain relatives walked angrily from the house, but Angus' father, who had no faith in Mary Baker Eddy but limitless devotion to his wife, supported her. Angus made a sudden and complete recovery, and when he learned the story it seemed another miracle achieved by nonconformity, assisted by God and his parents. His home was unity, and the rest was an uncomprehending and incomprehensible diversity.

Angus knew his mother only with the mind and heart of a child, but the perceptions of a child are more unalloyed than those of a man. What he sensed about her as a boy he saw in retrospect to be true. She was a woman of emotional depth and spiritual hunger, whose life and environment provided little food for her eager and sensitive spirit. Her questing desires, driven inward, found their outlets in devotion to religion and to her son. Devotion demands devotion in return, and though Angus gave all he had, he was sometimes aware that it was not enough. Eager that her son should be and have all that had been denied her, she saved her tiny income toward his college education, and poured over him all her idealism, her veneration for literature and the arts, her yearning for beauty and spiritual understanding. This was far more than Angus could absorb. Had he been more sensitive he might have gained more that was precious, but then the intensity of her influence might have overwhelmed him. She was a noble woman but not a happy one, and she created high ideals but not high spirits.

The finest teaching Angus ever received came from his father, whose mind and heart were in the most perfect balance the boy ever knew. He was cheerful by temperament, and capable of giving and receiving endless enjoyment; firm in his standards but humane in his judgments. His instruction was chiefly by example—never dogmatic, never unjust, and unsympathetic only when some cruel or selfish act of Angus' made righteous wrath the best pedagogy. He had little formal education but was well-read, quick-minded, and wise from the heart. Humility and self-respect were in balance too, and so were a maturity of mind and an ability to enjoy anything a boy enjoyed. With those endearing qualities he understood and influenced Angus more than any other person in his life.

Angus had no need, as Henry Adams had, to discover a thirteenth-century Chartres as a fixed point by which he could measure men and motives; that had been given to him by his paternity. Only after years of being taught and teaching did Angus grasp the full educational lesson of that gift. Human wisdom is based on understanding, and understanding on affection. The teaching of humane values, which is the essence of human growth, must be based on example, on humility in the presence of truth, on a sense of partnership in its pursuit, and on a joyful savoring along the way. It is an obvious truth, but Angus was not the only professional educator who often forgot it. It was the son's saddest failure that having experienced such wisdom from his father he could not apply it better to his own children and his dealings with others.

II

Initiations

FROM the age of seven until his graduation at sixteen Angus attended almost continuously a small private school near his home. He was reasonably happy there most of the time, and even in moments of distress it never occurred to him that he had anything to complain about. But those years which made him happy did not make him very wise. In retrospect he concluded that though he had learned a great many useful things he learned almost nothing about those at the heart of living. He remained ignorant of what he needed most—an understanding of the give-and-take of human relationships.

Perhaps no school could have developed a generous and perceptive spirit in so self-centered a boy; when Angus came to know other schools he found none that tried harder than his own. Teachers are busy shoving factual worms down reluctant throats and preparing young fledglings for economic flight. They have little time and energy, even if they have the desire and the skill, to break through the tough shells of young egos and cultivate the embryo tenderness within. Angus learned enough of the

prescribed facts and techniques to get him into college; the classroom gave him some adolescent skills and ambitions, and the
playground finally instructed him in the more elementary of the
arts of getting others to tolerate and even like him. What he
learned of the arts of mental reproduction and social ingratiation was superficial, and his understanding of the human scene
went no deeper.

On the whole he was fortunate in his schooling. Though in
intellectual atmosphere and classroom instruction it was not first-
rate, it stimulated effort and set worthy goals even if they were
limited ones. In ways less obvious but equally important Friends
Academy was a good school. Though its cultural climate was
arid its social climate was healthy. It was a community of
teachers and students well above the average in sanity of mind,
freedom from prejudice, good will toward one another, and generous instincts toward mankind. Its teachers believed with simple faith in the ideals defined by Jefferson, Lincoln, and the more
restrained poems of Walt Whitman, and saw no need to explore
democracy or philosophy beyond them. This made their instruction more efficient than had it been more profound. They left
their pupils in no doubt that the democratic and Christian ideals
could ultimately be attained if each generation would do its part.
They practiced simple democracy and ethics more instinctively
and thoroughly than most academic and social microcosms.

The moralities the school fostered were old-fashioned, but they
were useful benchmarks for a young generation that would find
few other fixed guides to conduct in their later lives. Its boys and
girls pretty generally accepted its late Victorian ethics, and that
was better for them than the only available alternative, which
was the morality of expediency. The canons of puritanism had
grown threadbare, but they protected that first generation of the
new century, for a few formative years, from the ethical chaos
that was to come.

Angus went to Friends Academy a well-read but rather
spoiled only child, physically large and mentally precocious for

his years. He adjusted easily to his schoolwork, for he soon found that if he did what his teachers requested the classroom had few pains and terrors. His success in classes awakened his ambition to excel wherever he could, and he soon won the reputation for being "bright." That was misleading, since his talents were superior only in competition with the intellectually lazy or mediocre. His early precocity led him to overestimate his capacities and ignore his weaknesses. His school successes were due chiefly to the head start his mother had given him by home instruction, plus docility, ambition, and above-average effort.

From the beginning he was happy in his work, but it was several years before he was happy in his play. He had had no practice in getting on with other boys, and wore a little too openly his consciousness of his superiority. He needed the hard discipline of intolerant contemporaries, and he got it with a vengeance.

Part of Angus' difficulty was inevitable. He was a year or two younger than his classmates and ignorant of the mores of the schoolyard. It was a strain to keep up with them physically and socially, and yet his ambitions made him try to associate with older boys because he admired them and felt their intellectual equal. They resented his rather boastful classroom superiority and were delighted to exploit his futility in games and his naïveté in schoolboy ethics.

Even had there been no bullies in the school, the ways of adolescence would have given Angus his come-uppance. There were two or three older boys with a taste for minor sadisms, and they soon selected Angus as the deserving object of their best attentions. He learned to dread the lunch-time play hour and the ending of classes at three. He knew that he would be the last one, chosen with obvious reluctance, to be included in any game. He could be confident that one of the older boys would soon turn on him with cuffs and punches. He was the one who would be kicked in corridors, have his lunch stolen, and be made to stand against the gymnasium wall as the target for tennis balls, or put "through the mill" of straddled legs and swinging pad-dles. He spent many hours flat on his back in the dirt, his arms held down, while older boys took turns sitting on him and drop-ping spittle on his face because, even *in extremis,* he would not say "uncle."

Under the schoolboy code, the selection of Angus for popular torture involved no personal animus but was to maintain the standards and unity of the tribe. Every boy was put through it in proportion to his stubbornness and his inability to defend himself. Angus was cocky and, at the beginning, physically un-skilled. The sensible thing to do was to accept the tribal code and join the tribe. Angus knew this, but something in him would not let him yield. He would try to make himself inconspicuous, or to escape, but when the strong-arm squad caught up with him he was defiant. He bore very little personal resentment against the general persecution and persecutors. He understood the code and even admired some of his severest disciplinarians, but he never forgave the bullies who used the system to gratify their distorted ideas of fun.

The experience had its compensations, for little by little it made Angus durable in body and spirit. It also gave him an understanding of the underdog, a respect for the minority, and a strong distaste for college hazing and any form of mob rule. The discipline was invaluable in making him at least outwardly an acceptable and conforming member of society. His bad luck lay in undergoing the drastic treatment a few years too early. He was too young to know how to cope with the roughing-down process of social conformity in such crude forms, or to throw off its ef-fects on his spirit.

He was unlucky, too, that the boys of his school had not come from homes where gentleness and social tolerance were more emphasized. Other boys and other schools might have given him in ways less brutal the discipline he needed. As it was, his spirit was hardened in being made durable. Sensitivities which if cul-tivated might have made him more generous in his judgments,

more cordial of heart, and more perceptive of the feelings
of others were atrophied by the tribal initiation. He built up a
hard shell around his inner feelings which few of his intimates
were ever able to break down, and which in time he himself
could not penetrate. Whatever embryo of spiritual growth was
initially within that shell remained stunted for want of air and
nourishment. The discipline did not even humble his pride but
only drove it under cover, and fortified his distrust of men in
masses. Perhaps his later defensiveness against organized society
was derived from the badgering and bruises he received from the
first organized society he ever met. Throughout his life his
hackles always went up against even the suspicion of social co-
ercion.

Yet it is easy to magnify the effects of a little schoolboy hazing,
and make it the whipping boy for all Angus' emotional difficulties. Bullying may have left its scars, but what education in
realism does not? Until a child experiences grief, fear, and discipline he is living in an unreal world; it is only in excess or dis-
tortion that they warp the spirit. But who can say what is excess
to the psyche of a child? Youth has unguarded sensitivities, and
few griefs of maturity are as poignant, few pains as sharp, few
fears as devastating as those of childhood—sometimes without
the slightest awareness of elders. A boy has not had years
in which to build up emotional reserves to fall back upon in
times of disaster. He is not able to say, in the spirit of the Anglo-
Saxon poet: "Worse than this I have endured and can endure
again." If a child's securities seem to vanish, he is lost.

Though Angus sometimes had that emptied spirit at school,
it was refilled with love at home. But love, too, leads to suffering.
When Angus was thirteen his mother developed pneumonia. She
refused to see a doctor and sent for a Christian Science practitioner, but this time there was no miracle. Before Angus realized his mother was seriously ill she had died. For months he
felt as hollow as though he had no physical substance between
his chest and his knees. He often woke at night from

happy dreams in which his mother was present, to go once again through the pain of realizing she was no longer there. The worst blows have their compensations, and Angus and his father were drawn close together in an understanding that transcended both friendship and filial love. They became inseparable, not from lack of other resources but because each was happiest with the other.

These griefs of home and school merged in Angus' mind and gave him a bad year or two. Never in later life did he experience such sadness as in the combined loss of his mother and his sense of being unwanted by his schoolmates. He never again knew the total insecurity of entering a room with the conviction that every known face was unfriendly and every unknown a potential enemy, of being unpopular without knowing why, or the festering fear that he would commit the blunder that would lose an important school game or make him the laughingstock of his contemporaries. But even those were only the occasional nightmares of a boy who could call his daily life rewarding if not always sunny. Miseries were quickly forgotten, and recalled only in conscious reminiscence.

After all, youth has special remedies to cure or balance the dark hours. The remembrance of happiness re-creates it in some measure, but the recollection of pain no longer hurts, once the pain itself has gone. The worst fears of childhood seldom materialize, and are rarely as bad in reality as in imagination. Moments of despair are offset by heights of elation seldom if ever reached in later years. Age that tempers joy also tempers grief, and the deeper wounds of youth heal more rapidly.

And yet who knows whether the healing is complete? Beneath the cicatrice Angus' unconscious may have retained the inner lesions of childhood suffering. As a young man in college he used to wonder whether his classmates ever awoke at night from reliving in their dreams the worst moments of their school days. If they too had undergone similar ordeals in some form, they did not show it, and Angus was sure he bore no psychological after-effects of his early years of school. As I observed him in later years he seemed as free from them as most men.

It was probably the isolation of being an only child, more than anything else, that made him so avid for friendship with other boys of his age, and so grateful for it when it came. He learned early to be self-sufficient, but he longed for the reassurance that comes with personal intimacy. Even while he resisted the schoolboy tribe he hung about its fringes like a shy but hungry stray dog. He even nurtured hero worship for several of the older boys who had kicked him about, and when one of them was kind or generous to him he was as grateful as any puppy. Unfortunately, the quality of his idols was as limited as his choice, for the big boys at Friends Academy included only two or three worth admiring. They were farmers' sons, who drove to school in ancient buggies and stabled their horses beneath the crude gymnasium, or children of only moderately cultivated local parents, plus a handful of not very attractive boarding students from New York and New Jersey. A few of them were interesting, but as Angus matured he found them less so.

Angus was never a member of a boys' gang, but he had two or three close friendships with boys his age. One was the sturdy plodding son of a Glen Head farmer. He and Angus shared a determination to excel in games, a compact for mutual defense against attacks by older boys, and a shy attraction toward the same girls. It was a relationship in which each could both lead and lean upon the other: Alfred was the older, stronger, and more experienced in the practical arts of schoolboy coexistence; Angus had a quicker mind and a more venturesome imagination. For the last five years of school they were inseparable, and roomed together during the first year of college. The friendship never ended, but as they developed dissimilar interests, they followed them into separate worlds. Their devotion had been based on common needs of youth, and when these had been met there was no link except loyalty to the memory of a deeply satisfying alliance.

Angus' friendship with Alfred had been based on common efforts, ambitions, and defiances. His devotion to Charlie involved none of these. It made no demands and exacted none, and though it flourished over many years it was relaxed and sporadic. Charlie was a small, puckish boy with no apparent talents or ambitions. His sole objective was to escape from all obligations so that he could enjoy in slightly saturnine spirit whatever turned up. He was wholly indifferent to schoolwork and shamelessly behind in it; he did not care for team games, popularity, or girls. Perhaps Angus was drawn to him by a perverse attraction to one who did not scorn but simply did not care about nearly everything that Angus valued, and ignored politely all the effortful endeavors that seemed to Angus so important. Perhaps it was simply because Angus discovered in him what few others ever saw—a pixy imagination. Though Charlie never read and apparently seldom thought, he could create picaresque heroes from a fourth-dimensional world—humorous animals unlike those of reality or fiction, and remarkable events never romantic but always vivid and slightly fey. Without a drop of Irish blood, he peopled his days and those of Angus with leprechauns of his own invention, whose bizarre misadventures became entwined with the daily lives of the two boys. They were never written down, for Charlie wrote only painfully and illegibly and could not spell, and in any case would have thought recording such lightly constructed stories absurd, but his elaboration of this private and fantastic other world continued for years. Angus contributed to it nothing but the stimulus of admiration; he got from it a taste of the lighthearted and fantastic, remote from the rest of his experience. Charlie specialized in perceiving unconscious eccentricities in the people about him, and then personifying them into his own imaginary beings. He and Angus shared secret delight in identifying a sycophantic teacher with Raphael the webfooted unicorn who lived in the Principal's coat closet, or a pompous uncle with a malodorous but playful trunkless elephant named (because Charlie had heard the word at church and liked the sound) the Crested Concubine. Family lunch with Charlie was a delightful ordeal of wisely repressed hilarity, as family manners and conversation offered opportunities for immediate identification with his fourth-dimensional world. Charlie had to be groomed for the management of a large family estate, and the process damped out a talent that might have rivaled Thurber's. When Angus last saw him, only a fleeting twinkle and a repressed unorthodoxy remained of the friend of boyhood. The pixy had become the broker, and it was now the formerly serious young Angus who was the irregular member of society.

Friends Academy was a Quaker school, which meant that its trustees and a few of its teachers were members of the Society of Friends. The influence of this strategic minority was dominant but not exacting. School exercises were brief, low-church, and only mildly religious. The single denominational event was on Sundays, when the boarding students were herded across the road to Matinecock Friends' Meeting, but there they heard little that would have offended a Cardinal or a Hindu—if they heard anything at all, since most of the Meetings were entirely silent except for the impatient shuffling of schoolboy feet. There was no pressure to embrace Quakerism, although the school's atmosphere implied that its simplicity and integrity were worth imitating. Friends did not proselyte; indeed, it was difficult for Angus in boyhood to imagine anyone being a genuine Quaker who had not been born one.

Apart from this routine exercise, which even then seemed to Angus slightly vestigial, religion was as much ignored as if the Academy had been a public school. Beneath a cheerful but firm emphasis on morality and good works lay an undercurrent of polite agnosticism and just a touch of unconscious hypocrisy. The simplicity of the school's life and the spareness of its equipment were not derived so much from devotion to austerity as to Quaker economy, rationalized into an educational virtue.

But the school was as free from conscious pretense as any

nursery of education Angus would ever know. In that sense it had intellectual integrity, and that was its greatest merit. Its atmosphere and values were remarkably at one with those of the homes from which most of its pupils came, and this made up in consistency of family-school influence for its lack of intellectual quality. Its code had a reality and naturalness which seemed reasonable and intelligible to its students, who were never in doubt about why they were there and what was expected of them. They were not confused by phrases like "self-expression," "education for citizenship," "vocational orientation," "integration," or "psychological adjustment." They simply knew that there were certain things that had to be learned and that it was in their interest to learn them, whether they were going to college, or to offices, or back to farms.

The philosophy of the school was plain and convincing, and that made instruction efficient if unimaginative. It was wholly devoted to what it believed basic in education: the inculcation of habits of alertness, industry, cooperation, deference, and honesty. In fostering these it did not shrink from old-fashioned discipline, though never by physical force. So far as facts were concerned, it stuck to the traditional program, chiefly because it saw no reason and had no funds to do otherwise. It pumped into its pupils as much mathematics, grammar, history, and language as those average minds could hold, plus the little elementary science the school could afford. It offered no other formal instruction, and none of those connected with it saw why it should. Unity triumphed over diversity more successfully there than in any educational institution Angus ever came upon.

Nobody thought of suggesting that to organize a student mass attack on a locust grove to turn it into a playing field (the bigger boys grubbing at the roots with dull axes and sending smaller boys to the tops of the trees with a rope to sway them) was "social co-ordination," or that lifting sods from a cow pasture each spring to make the baseball diamond was "learning by doing." When the students wanted something new they had simple alternatives: create it themselves or do without it. They usually chose to do without, but that was education too. Chores were assigned at school as well as at home, not for their educational value but as necessary contributions to the general welfare. The school did not often need to urge the merits of co-operation; it was in the air as a necessity of life.

It did not occur to trustees and staff that beauty was important in all its varied forms, and that boys and girls should be helped to perceive and enjoy it. So far as the fine arts were concerned, the Academy was not only uncreative but uninterested. It did nothing to correct the ignorance of Angus or any other pupil about the graphic and plastic arts. Perhaps one out of every ten students "took" piano lessons as an "extra," but since they consisted of pounding out scales until one could learn a "piece" well enough to play it at Commencement before the bated breath of parents who hoped for no mistakes and small boys who prayed for them, and since the school possessed only two pianos, most of those who took this fling into the arts soon abandoned it. The appreciation of literature, so far as classwork was concerned, consisted of the compulsory memorizing of "selections" in the earlier and more docile years, and the expedient reiteration of phrases of simulated enthusiasm over Wordsworth, Keats, and Robert Browning in Senior English—a necessary concession regarded by the bigger boys as bordering on effeminacy. So far as the creation of beauty in any form was concerned, if it happened it happened by accident. In that respect the minds of its graduates were as blank as the catalogue of the school.

Like all Quaker institutions, the Academy was coeducational. Later Angus realized how lucky he had been to attend a school where sex was not regarded as a regrettable educational complication. Coeducation did not make sex more innocent but it made it less self-conscious and troublesome. Most of its boys and girls missed the thrills of intense romantic sentimentalism, but they also escaped the extremes of shyness and prurience. The advantages of that kind of coeducation were like those of growing up on a farm, where sex is all about one and can be absorbed without strain. Angus never heard of perversion until he was halfway through college. The school was not without its tensions, flirtations, and even private experiments in sex, but less of them would have been almost abnormal. When Angus, as an educator, compared the life of his Quaker school and college with what he later saw and learned of the false monasticism of Eton and Oxford, he was grateful for the emotional balance of his intellectually inferior schooling. It was only the healthiness of school education that overcame a background otherwise full of sex ignorance and inhibitions, and kept boys like Angus from serious emotional complications.

The teachers at Friends Academy were not superior people in talent, education, or breeding. Instructors of high cultural quality were rare in any American schools, and could not have been secured for the tiny salaries the Academy offered. But the men and women who taught Angus had patience, good will, decency, and a sense of mission—and some of them had humor. Those who were the least exacting were of course the most popular, but the more demanding ones were the more respected, for if their methods were severe they were also painfully just. They insisted on honest effort, and most students of the school honored that objective even while they tried to avoid it, for they had been brought up to accept industry as the key to success. As he later looked back from relatively prosperous academic heights at the penurious and limited lives of his first teachers, Angus could not understand why they were not all low-spirited and frustrated, but if they were they did not show it.

Angus would later sit in the classrooms of great teachers and scholars, and even claim friendship with some of them, but the finest teaching he ever knew, except his father's, came from an energetic little Quakeress whom the public school authorities of today would not even list as qualified. Fortunately for Angus, she caught him young and held him through three grades, for she taught all three simultaneously. He forgot most of the facts she taught him, but few of the values she exemplified. Thirty small desks and benches filled nearly every square foot of her crowded classroom, but even in winter she found room for flowers. While the third-graders were writing compositions under her remote but unfailing eye in one corner of the room, the fourth-graders by the windows were preparing a recitation in American history, and the fifth-grade boys were shambling to the blackboards to append answers to the arithmetic problems that the fifth-grade girls had, with malevolent glee, written there according to instructions. There was never disorder, for even the most loutish farm boy would, at one glance from her, abandon his tortures of the boy or girl at the desk in front of him. He would stop because he feared her, but his fear was not of her punishment but her disapproval.

This little widow, who supported herself and put two sons through school and college, never showed irritation, weakness, or unfairness. If she were ever ill or tired she concealed it. She could not have taught so well had she not loved young people as much as she loved teaching. But she was not soft; she practiced as well as preached the succinct old-fashioned doctrine of "Use thy gumption." She demonstrated the educational effects of gentleness, discipline, and affection combined—and the power of certainty in aims and values. She gave Angus more of the essentials of education than several universities, though she had never attended one.

Although the teachers in the Academy did not pretend they had scaled Parnassus, they managed to do something pedagogically more important. They made some of their pupils believe there was a Parnassus and that its ascent was worth attempting. "Go beyond us and above us" was the message they conveyed, though rarely by the spoken cliché. They had a high respect for learning, culture, and good manners, and imparted the desire if not the attainment. The tacit assumption was that one should get only what one had earned, and no pupil thought of education as his natural right, but as an opportunity to be made the most of.

One thing was understood by all: personal achievement depended on personal effort, and the climate was the most effortful and the least cynical of any Angus ever knew.

Most of this was good in itself, but as preparation for the America of 1950 it was anachronistic. Its flavor and values were closer to John Bright than to Franklin Roosevelt, to Lincoln than to John L. Lewis. Social Security and the Forgotten Man were meaningless phrases to its students; Americanism was whatever an American thought and no question of his right to think it. Wall Street and Washington seemed almost as remote as St. Petersburg and Peking. Such education looked backward without knowing it. That might be a good place to look, but not for the purpose of material success in the twentieth century, which was busily discarding much that the nineteenth had held precious. What was a boy trained to the values of Emerson and Horatio Alger to do in an age of state socialism and the atom?

Those questions did not trouble Angus as he stepped forward to receive his diploma from the hand of an awkward uncle, miscast as chairman of the school's trustees. Angus was as confident of his own future as of the future of America and the virtues of the Republican party. In that June of 1917, national success meant the defeat of the Kaiser and then the building of a new world in which peace and democracy would universally and permanently flourish. It lay with Americans to sweep away the rubble of a Europe that was destroying itself, and to create a new Europe that would copy American freedom and remove the last traces of its autarchies, prejudices, economic rivalries, and outworn traditions. As for the other continents, on which were living more than half the human race, they would eventually follow where America and a reformed Europe led.

That was the message the four girl and three boy graduates of Friends Academy heard from their Commencement speaker, as they might have heard it that day on hundreds of other Commencement platforms across the country. In so far as they listened to it they accepted it. They knew the time would come when they would have to play their parts in building the new, peaceful, sanitary world that President Wilson was already outlining—and they were not unwilling. But in the meantime the summer vacation was upon them, and the excitements of college would soon follow. That was enough to think about, far enough to look ahead. Sentiment about leaving the old school yielded suddenly to the desire to get out of Commencement white flannels, away from sticky seats and sentiments, and into the salty coolness of Long Island Sound. The world would have to wait a little longer for Angus and his classmates to take over.

III

The Pursuit of Praise

THE boy of sixteen who entered Swarthmore College was no longer the insecure child of his first years at school. Though still self-centered, he had grown outwardly amenable and even gregarious. His final years at the Academy had been happy and successful, and he could laugh wholeheartedly at his childish pains, when he remembered them at all. He looked forward to college with confident enthusiasm. It would, others told him, bring him knowledge, friendships, and the prestige that then came with a college degree. It might, he hoped, also bring him what he craved—admiration.

Early in his freshman year he analyzed his chances for collegiate eminence with rather surprising realism, though with the lack of humor and perspective that accompanies the ardent pursuit of limited ends. He realized that he could not become outstanding in studies or activities if he took them as casually as most of his classmates. He observed that few of them were as ambitious as he, at least for immediate college goals. Since Angus did not look beyond those goals, he determined to work for them harder and more exclusively than his rivals. He knew how to work, and was ready to eliminate some of the social pleasures that took the time and energy of his classmates.

If someone had asked Angus why he was going to college, he would have replied that he was in quest of an education, and added quite sincerely all the conventional maxims. It was only subconsciously that he viewed college as a place not to gain understanding but to gain kudos—a four-year marathon race in which the fastest runners might be beaten by one who kept himself in better condition and his eyes more firmly on the goal. Angus was fairly certain he was not an academic hare, and was ready to race like a tortoise. He accepted the general opinion that the real measure of collegiate success was the length of the list of honors, from football to Phi Beta Kappa, after one's name in the college yearbook. The "all-round man" was the most popular while in college and the most likely to be offered a good job on graduation. Even as a freshman, Angus suspected that most all-round college heroes were not first-rate in anything, but that suspicion did not deter him from wanting to be one. He liked to be different, but school days had finally convinced him of the advantages of keeping in line.

His real independence was soon tested, and on the issue that would trouble him always—his personal relations to organized society. Even before he set foot on the Swarthmore campus he met it in a seductive form. In spite of the fact that the college offered an intense social life of its own, that its smallness called for close internal social unity, and that it professed the simplicity and democracy of Quaker ideals, fraternities flourished there and three quarters of the students belonged to them. Angus' only first cousin had been graduated from Swarthmore two years before, as President of his class and a leading member of Phi Kappa Psi. He was eager that Angus join that fraternity, and saw to it that he was carefully considered. Angus was invited to a pre-college house party, where a group of promising freshmen were looked over by the upper-class brethren.

The boys he met there were the most attractive he had ever
seen, and he was flattered as only a freshman can be flattered by
the attentions of urbane and potent upperclassmen. At the first
moment the rushing regulations permitted, he, like many another, was invited to join. The youth who had suffered so long
before being accepted into schoolboy society found himself urged
to enter the arcanum of the collegiate elite. Membership in a leading fraternity would ensure him the social acceptance he had
craved so long.

There were other good reasons for joining. Not to do so would
disappoint a cousin he loved and admired. The few men who
declined fraternity membership were regarded resentfully by
men of all fraternities as socially subversive. To be a nonfraternity
man in the Swarthmore of Angus' time was to be condemned
to a limbo thinly populated by the leftovers of the social system.
Most of the attractive girls were members of sororities that had
informal "sister" affiliations with the men's fraternities, and did
not "date" with nonfraternity men. The fraternities were powerful political units in college elections, and Angus' ambitions for
college honors were almost certain to be frustrated if he lacked
fraternity backing.

Yet many of Angus' instincts opposed his joining. College fraternities seemed in principle undemocratic, and arguments to the
contrary were unquestionably specious. The basic lure of membership was to belong to something exclusive, and because he
had known the pains of being excluded he disliked the effect of
the system on those who were left out. The interfraternity rivalries of organizations based on brotherhood, the endless politick-
ing, the assumption that a fraternity man must always vote for a
"brother" in collegiate elections, regardless of merit, repelled
him. So did the barriers that fraternity membership indirectly imposed on friendships outside the pale. Being of literal mind, he
disliked the thought of having to call other boys, some of whom
he did not really like, "brother"—especially since he had already seen enough to know that the brotherhood was often a pre-

tense. And although fraternities at Swarthmore were less expensive than elsewhere, membership in Phi Kappa Psi would bring a further and indeterminate financial sacrifice upon his father. The dues were not large, but the incidental obligations might be.

Angus staggered everyone, including himself, by declining to join. Under heavy pressure he agreed to reconsider after a month, and the intervening period was a trying one. All the cards were stacked against his holding out. It became more than ever clear that fraternity membership was the first and essential step to social happiness as well as collegiate success. He saw nearly all the new classmates he liked best sporting pledge pins, and in their new mutual enthusiasms he was isolated or forgotten. Only one nonfraternity man had become "a big man on the campus" at Swarthmore. Even some of the girls he liked the best, commissioned by their friends in Phi Psi, pleaded with him to join, and implied that if he did not he could not hope to compete for their friendship on an equal basis. Important alumni brothers took him into back rooms, locked the doors, and talked to him of duty—to the cause of friendship, to his cousin, and to his own advancement. His cousin came down from Long Island and the restraint of his pleading was the most effective of all. It was not a matter in which Angus could ask his father's advice, for his father would have replied that he was not a college man, and that Angus must make his own decision.

Angus was rooming with his school friend Alfred, who had not been invited to join any fraternity, though Angus knew Alfred was a better man than many of the new pledges. To join a fraternity without him would be a kind of desertion. But the pressures were too much, and the attractions too, and before the month was up—a little ashamed of himself for giving in so quickly—Angus joined. The results were on the whole happy, and he discovered that once he had established himself as a figure of importance in college, he could be more independent in his friendships than he had thought the fraternity would allow.

Phi Kappa Psi gave him a social training he badly needed, but he was never a wholehearted "brother." The lifetime enthusiasm and participation of some graduate brothers seemed to him examples of retarded adolescence, and he could not stomach the cheap horseplay that preceded the serious initiations. On only two occasions he asserted his reservations. He conducted an abortive minority movement to have the fraternity waste less time by meeting less often, and he insisted, against the strong pleas of his fraternity, on rooming with a friend who was a Jew, and naturally a nonfraternity man, in his senior year. Apart from those mild negations, Angus let a little collegiate salesmanship and ambition seduce him from his convictions.

In spite of those local absorptions of a freshman year in 1917, Angus followed the events on the Marne and the Somme with spectator intensity, though not with any sense of personal involvement. The problems of the war were an intellectual exercise to be considered in the classroom course on War Aims; the events of the war were an emotional experience but a remote one. No one he knew had yet been killed or even badly wounded. The young men in the colleges were being urged by the authorities to remain there until they were called to service. Angus and his classmates regarded the war, at that time, as a larger and more serious football game in which they were at the moment only in the cheering section. Their time might come; they might even be killed, but that would be later, and perhaps before then the home team would have won, as it was certain ultimately to do. Keeping the home fires burning was said to be a patriotic duty, and it was not their fault if it was a pleasant one. Normal collegiate ambitions and activities therefore throve.

It was not patriotism that led Angus to renounce some of the diversions of college. He gave them up in accordance with his Plan to Succeed. He did not really like dances, bridge sessions, or endless desultory dormitory talk, and enjoyed the sense of his own virtue and its hoped-for rewards more than he would have

enjoyed the diversions he missed. Why he should think it virtuous to give up harmless pleasures for the ardent pursuit of selfish
personal aims was not a question he considered.

As the freshman year continued, the enlistment of a few acquaintances and the sight of returning wounded brought the
war closer to Angus. He underwent his own internal war between
the Quaker pacifism he had inherited and the natural instincts of
a patriotic young man. The war divided Quakers into those who
stuck to pacifism and those who joined the armed forces or did
not claim exemption on religious grounds. Angus rationalized
his urge to do what others were being admired for doing by the
belief that since this was the war to end war, he should help to
win it. He was only seventeen, and in theory too young even to
enlist. Had he been closer to military service he might not have
been so fervent, for even as he dreamed of becoming a hero he
was terribly afraid of being killed or wounded or of proving a
coward.

The college year ended early in May so that students could
start serious summer war work. Next to military service, shipbuilding had the highest priority, and Angus joined an older
Swarthmore friend as a highly paid apprentice in a Camden
shipyard. To the winning of the war he contributed only a few
badly fitting pieces of steel to a new oil tanker, but to his own
education he added much that was useful in physical and social
discipline. He carried large pieces of steel up shaky scaffolds amid
red-hot rivets for some ten hours a day in New Jersey summer
heat, and shared two attic bedrooms in Woodbury with three
older college men. He learned something of the attitudes of
labor leaders and riveters, and of the domestic and boasted con-
nubial habits of tough machinists. He discovered at first hand
how a grimy workman, searching for a spot of shade on the hard
ground in which to eat his salami and pie during the forty-minute
lunch period, reacts to the sight of top executives gliding in
chauffeur-driven Packards across the river for lunch at Philadelphia's Union League. He delighted in his shipyard name of

Polack Charlie, for it meant that his fellow workmen did not think of him as an effete or superior college man. Although these mixed Americans, Irishmen, Poles, and Italians complained vigorously about everything connected with the job—the bosses, the wages, the equipment, the working conditions, and the endless speeches and posters about working harder and longer to win the war—he noticed how hard they really worked and how firm was their determination to lick the Kaiser. If there were dangerous subversives in the plant, he did not meet or hear of any.

Hot nights and Sundays would have been unbearable in his stifling half-bedroom piled high with malodorous working clothes and made hideous by the ceaseless grinding of a cheap phonograph below, except for the physical exhaustion that made sleep inevitable. There were some spare hours after overtime work that could not be spent in sleeping, and good books and magazines were hard to come by. Angus had his first real experience with good music and made it his one modest extravagance. He spent many hot evenings in the top balcony of the old Philadelphia Academy of Music. Much of the music did not thrill him, but the "Liebestod" uplifted and disturbed him without his quite knowing why, while Tchaikovsky and Strauss's *Death and Transfiguration* left him limp and trembling. He wanted to like Wagnerian opera because he thought he should, but was finally honest enough to admit that most of it bored him. To be honest about what he liked, and then to try to find out why he liked it, was the beginning of his education in the appreciation of the arts, but it was years before he applied the test of his own reactions regularly and with courage. He found he preferred symphonies to operas, and a detectable melody to what seemed only pyrotechnical display. Sometimes he would miss the last train back to his bed and would sleep, more or less, in empty freight cars in Camden. He always made these expeditions alone, and twice after concerts went into a saloon and drank a glass of beer. He did not like the taste and wondered if he had ruined his chances of making the football team in the fall. He reveled in the personal freedom that accompanied his particular form of economic regimentation; he enjoyed the sense of being effortful to help win the war, and forgot almost entirely his defensiveness and his ego. By overtime pay and economy he was building up his first substantial bank account, and for the first time took a personal pride in the possession of money. He became more approving of capitalists.

Into this scene of sordid surroundings, strenuous industry, malodorous clothes and jokes, and spiritual elevation came a sudden interruption in mid-July. Angus got early word that Swarthmore, like other colleges, had been asked to name a few undergraduates for immediate officer training at Plattsburg. These men would return in September to become student officers in the new Student Army Training Corps of the colleges. The young men selected would be at the top of the pile in their colleges, and Angus promptly wrote impassioned letters and telegrams to the Dean at Swarthmore, followed by persistent and supplicating evening calls. At first the Dean was adamant against including an unimportant freshman in the college quota, but he finally yielded. A few hours later Polack Charlie, in a new role, was stifling in an ancient day coach of the Delaware and Hudson Railroad as it wound grimly through the foothills of the Adirondacks. Somehow the enlistment officer at Plattsburg overlooked his age, and that night he slept fitfully, with a carelessly given vaccination already paining his arm, in the barracks of Company G of the Officers' Training Camp, while older college boys from the South, inured to barracks life by military schools, played poker by flashlight in the bunk underneath.

Learning the ways of Plattsburg and the army took Angus back to his first initiations at school, except that the military bullying was less concentrated on him, and came from officially authorized sergeants and second lieutenants. Again he was the youngest, and though Camden had made his muscles strong they were not as enduring as those of the college juniors and seniors

around him. Painfully he carried his Enfield on an aching shoul-
der up and down in the hot sun of the drill ground or along dusty
miles of back roads. Since the trench shoes he had been issued
did not fit and he dared not ask for others, he was never for two
months without blisters so deep that the boardlike uppers were
softened by the blood that soaked through them. He was determined not to drop out of line unless ordered, and only once did
the top sergeant notice his limp and send him back to barracks.
He did faint twice at attention, the second time rather dramatically at the feet of an inspecting French general, but that was
due to his vaccine infection. It was serious training and should
not have been slowed up in deference to the minor pains of an
overambitious freshman, for it was apparent now that the war
would not be won by a few divisions of American volunteers,
and that all the men in training might be overseas in a few
months. Angus did not exactly enjoy the months at Plattsburg,
but he never for a moment regretted being there. The exhilara-
tion made any griefs and fears incidental.

In September a few of his company were offered commissions,
and Angus, to his surprise, was one of them. The idea frightened
him even while it pleased him, for it brought him nearer to real
danger and to officer responsibilities he was not sure he could
meet. Then it was discovered from his papers that he would not
be eighteen until the following February and the commission
was withdrawn. Angus was outwardly disappointed but secretly
relieved at being ordered back to college, with the promise that
in February he would be commissioned. The summer had not
sweated out all his conceit but it had made him at least physically
a man.

Until the war ended in November, Angus served, without being an official member of the unit, as second ranking student
officer in that serious farce of military training, the Swarthmore
SATC. The rifles of the unit did not arrive until two weeks before it was disbanded and the embryo soldiers drilled with sticks.
Angus spent many nights, as supply officer, measuring every

man, but when uniforms finally arrived they were all in a few average sizes. Tench Francis had to get his size-twelve feet and six-foot three-inch frame into shoes and clothes very little larger than those worn by Pum Koo Park, the diminutive Korean who had somehow found his way to the little Quaker college.

During this time Angus was so envious of those who had secured their commissions and gone off to bona-fide war service that he tried to enlist in the Canadian army, but this was only a gesture, for once he admitted his age he was rejected. The war was to Angus no more than excitement without danger and personal advancement without personal sacrifice. Long before it ended he had forgotten his earlier soul-searchings about pacifism, though he would return to them later. They had gone by default in his quest for collegiate admiration. As soon as the armistice was announced he reverted very happily, like other Americans, to the normalcy of personal ends.

Lines in a college yearbook are an adolescent objective, but collecting them brought Angus rewards more mature than themselves. His activities widened his horizons and strengthened his ambition and capacity to go further. The process of working for good grades made him interested in what he studied, and he developed a respect for learning for its own sake. By his junior year he had more than realized his goals as a freshman and had formulated new ones which, if more vague, were more exalted. They were still centered on self-advancement, and he did not suspect how ignorant he was of other values.

He was too enthusiastic about undergraduate life to view it critically. Swarthmore was the best of all colleges, and he was proud that its ethical atmosphere was reputed superior to its neighbor institutions. Yet he was troubled by one or two experiences, and torn between protesting them in his role of reformer and accepting them in his new role of realist. One episode proved what he had previously loyally denied: that the administration of the college, in spite of its public professions, was not above conniving with certain alumni in secret subsidies for some of its leading athletes. Angus was not only shocked at the ethical compromise but annoyed that since it existed his own athletic record had not included him among those invited to be its beneficiaries. The procedure was so common in American colleges that Swarthmore was merely more conformist than he had thought.

The second experience could be regarded as an amusing triviality of college life, or as an example of the wise flexibility of college officers. But when it happened, Angus was too offended to accept it as either. Nearly all colleges are troubled by vestiges of their more callow pasts, and Swarthmore in 1920 still harbored two undergraduate eating societies that felt obligated by the hallowed traditions of a decade to stage an annual pitched battle on the campus. Its main purpose was exhibitionist: to display to the college at large and its young women in particular the magnificent male at his most uninhibited. It was similar to the courtship dance of certain birds, or the head-on clash of two rams for priority in mating. This was harmless enough until the tradition came to require added verbal exchanges before the battle, decidedly inappropriate though obviously not uninteresting to virginal ears.

At last the college President quite properly insisted that the two clubs abandon these exhibitions of virility, and in the resultant negotiations Angus unwisely agreed to act as the sole spokesman of the Devils, to which he belonged, and to insist on certain face-saving concessions as conditions of voluntary dissolution. The President would not accept these, and arbitrarily disbanded the clubs, placing on indefinite probation all their members except one—their spokesman.

In the highly charged campus atmosphere that resulted Angus was the most emotional of all. While others resented their punishment, he resented even more his exclusion from it. It was unjust discrimination and a slight on his sincerity of opposition. He yearned to share the popular martyrdom and believed he had earned it. He went to the President and demanded to be placed on probation with the rest. The President explained that he re-

garded Angus as a valuable student leader generally on the side
of the administrative angels, and did not want to diminish his
usefulness to future college uplift by impairing his college standing. Angus insisted, and the President finally promised to put
him immediately on probation. Angus shortly received his official note to that effect. It was only after he had been graduated
that Angus found the President had made no record of his probation on the college books, and that consequently he had never
been included among the heroic martyrs.

Angus kept just enough sense of humor to see that the whole
affair was an amusing teapot tempest, but when he thought of
the President's motives and procedure he became angry all over
again. There were worse things for a young man to lose than his
sense of humor, or even than his temper, and one of them was his
faith in the ethics and pledged word of those in high places. The
episode was not trivial because it did not seem so to a few dozen
young men who never forgot it. The demolition of youthful
idols is a serious matter if not only the idols fall but with them the
habit of faith. To Angus the lesson was important for the implications went beyond the techniques of pedagogy. It was his first experience with the priority of expediency over integrity in a man
he had greatly admired, and with the fine art of concealing the
expediency behind gestures of human flexibility. The two episodes left him more badly shaken than he realized at the time.
Was idealism only a youthful illusion, and education a device to
show how it should be tempered or outgrown? Which was education, the President's platform professions or his neat but equiv-
ocal footwork? And whichever was education, why indulge in
the other?

Angus was familiar with expediency and practiced it often
enough, but finding it beneath academic robes was a disillusion.
If expediency was universal, then the sooner one got down to the
concentrated pursuit of it the better; the rest was apparently
only chapel talk. Angus wanted success; college and society were
teaching him what success was, and the practical ways of gaining

it. Success, it seemed, was the discreetly unscrupulous acquisition of power. Admiration for power was as natural to Swarthmore men as to any others, even though it was their fashion to call it success or public service. Their particular personal ambitions were in a lower key than those of more favored youths at Harvard and Yale, for most Swarthmore graduates wanted only to hold their own with others of the upper middle class in the respect of society and the pleasures of prosperity. Few of them were eager for great wealth or great power, though none of them would have declined it.

These relatively modest ambitions were not wholly selfish. All but the most hedonistic of these young people wanted to contribute, someday, to the welfare of their fellow men, but they accepted the comfortable advice of their elders that a young man could serve society best if he waited awhile. Rome was not built and South Philadelphia could not be rebuilt in a day. To move too impatiently would be to move unwisely, or even to gain the reputation of a hotheaded reformer, and there was no reputation more harmful to useful public service in the 1920s. To agree with Lincoln Steffens, even to admire Norman Thomas, while a sophomore in college, was a healthy sign of an open mind and a warm heart, but one should recognize it as a stage through which one must pass, and restrain oneself from words and actions that might later be embarrassing. It would be foolish for any young man to shout critical comments at the economic powers on which he would soon be dependent. The way to civic and social service was through apprenticeship to the existing system; it led through the gate of affluence, for affluence was influence; leadership rested on social acceptance and social acceptance on economic stability. A poor man, no matter how wise or able, could do little for society, and what was more, poverty was likely to make a man radical and therefore not to be trusted. The quest for personal standing should precede the quest for the welfare of society. Time enough to serve mankind after one had done justice to oneself, one's wife and children. That was not precisely what the professors said, or alumni or parents either, but that was the implication. It was in the atmosphere one breathed, and Angus and his classmates, with only occasional and minor gasps, accepted it. There were warm hearts and nobilities of purpose in some of those young men, like Detlev Bronk and Frank Fetter, and as for the rest, their ambitions were not so much cheap as uninspired, not so much mundane as unawakened.

They were also of a college generation whose thought and ways of life would be dominated by the spirit and applications of science. This was unfortunate for those who, like Angus, had no aptitude in science and mechanics, some doubts of their absolute priority in human values, and an instinct for avoiding their study as much as the rules allowed. It was possible, then as now, to be graduated creditably from most colleges and professional schools ignorant of all science except the bare smattering of a course or two. It was also possible (and this was worse) to emerge from college with a high degree of specialized scientific knowledge but no understanding of the meaning of history, philosophy, economics, and politics; no habits of reading or speculation, no appreciation of the fine arts, no literary style above the compositions of the eighth grade, and indeed no grasp of the implications of science itself.

Whatever talents Angus had were in the liberal arts, and in selecting them he simply followed the course of least resistance. He never knew whether his academic success was due to some natural ability or to his mastery of the techniques of getting good grades, but he became increasingly suspicious that it was chiefly the latter. He had a good memory for facts, was glib and flatteringly attentive in the classroom, and knew how to generalize impressively from very little knowledge. He discovered that most college textbooks of the time were written in such a way that if one read carefully the first and last sentence of every paragraph one could omit the rest. Since he was also interested in the subject matter and many of his classmates were not, it was easy to become a teacher's favorite. Once a reputation for intelligence and interest was established with a faculty, it could be maintained until graduation with very little effort. This too was education, and the talents for intellectual ingratiation Angus developed at college would have been very useful in almost any American enterprise had Angus made the most of them in later life.

Once he had skillfully skirted mathematics and science, the only academic problem was to choose a major subject of study. The issue was simple: no major, no degree. College students, then as now, were often pressed by impatient advisers, eager to get their records settled, into selecting fields of concentration before they knew what their real interests were. Angus' stubborn indecision led him to postpone his choice and then to change it from economics to literature to political science, and he thus gained horizons a little wider than many of his classmates. Vacillation proved in this case a greater educational asset than concentration or planning. Angus' refusal to specialize continued throughout his life, and though it diminished his capital, it widened his interest.

Another accident seemed at the time an educational advantage, though much later Angus was to wonder whether it had been a real one. As a rather solitary child he had read omnivorously, and the average quality of his reading was good, since cheap thrillers and comic books were then harder to come by, and elders even dared to forbid them. His tastes were formed on Stevenson, Dickens, Scott, Poe, and Mark Twain, for these were available and encouraged by parents who read aloud to him nearly every evening.

Reading leads naturally to writing, and Angus developed some skill in clear though unimaginative expression. The habit of expression leads in turn to the search for something to express. It was there that Angus bogged down and was finally forced to recognize his creative infertility. He tried to begin a novel but could never develop a satisfactory plot or create living characters that were not obvious imitations of people he knew. All he could do was to absorb and recast the ideas of others; he was no more than an editor and synthesizer. For a long time he refused to admit this limitation, and blamed it on his education.

If he had any doubts about his abilities, his emotions, or his relations to those around him he rarely raised them with others. His instinct told him that family, professors, and friends could not answer them to his satisfaction, and he did not want to make himself vulnerable by disclosing any Achilles' heel of sensitivity or uncertainty. He turned to books instead for answers to the few unknowns that troubled him. Books kept confidences; one could stop reading a book when one found the answer or found that one could not find it, but people told one's secrets, and one could not turn off so easily a troubled or loquacious elder. Books were better organized and less prone to irrelevancies than most of the discourse he heard about him. Thus, early in life, Angus developed the habits of depending more on the written than the spoken word, of running away from people into privacy, and of dropping with impatience any conversation when it bored him.

These habits kept him from learning from people much that he might have learned. He never developed facility in small talk or any enjoyment of it. His point of boredom was often quite apparent, for he made few attempts to conceal it, and thus gave more offense than he intended. In serious discussions he would talk like one of his books and try to convince rather than to persuade. It was only on those occasions when he met a man or woman whom he immediately accepted as his superior, or when he remembered that truth and polite conversation are not best pursued with a bludgeon, that he was able to avoid verbal belligerence when a subject really interested him. Finesse in any field he admired but could not attain.

Whatever the cause of this mental belligerency, it ran through the whole fabric of his subconscious and always asserted itself when he felt presumed upon or taken lightly. He came with delight, in his sophomore year, on the "Invictus" of Henley, with its defiance of the bludgeonings of fate and its boastful assertion of a head bloody but unbowed, for that was the way Angus liked to think of himself whenever things went wrong. After the most trivial disappointments he would dramatize himself into a stoic figure rising superior to fate and his persecutors. It was only long after his college years that he suspected that what he had admired as great poetry and profound courage might be only the compensatory bombast of a talented but sickly man, and what he had thought admirable in himself was no more than hurt egotism.

Had Angus held any deep religious conviction he might have recognized his own unimportance in the universal scheme of things. He was satisfied with a crude version of Quakerism that was moral but not spiritual. His days were too full for soul-searching: God, whatever He might be, would presumably not hold it against a young man if he postponed serious religious thought and practice until he felt the need for them—so long as in the meantime he was deferential to the Higher Things.

Indeed, he found it difficult to imagine how his own affairs could ever get so out of hand that he would need to turn help-lessly to God. He was willing to accept the opinion of his elders that this would prove to be the case, but he did not see that most of them had any very deep faith, or that their religion had sweet-ened their natures or made them wiser than others. Until he had time to find or formulate a creed more rational and generous than theirs seemed to be, he would play safe by being in favor of God and trying to observe His basic rules as interpreted by the best local authorities.

Quakerism seemed on the whole to provide the most reasona-ble basis on which he might ultimately build his personal reli-gion. He liked its simplicity and its emphasis on "faith through works." It appealed to him particularly because it let him alone. By making each man directly responsible to God it left it to the individual to decide when and how he would call upon Him. It removed the necessity of dealing through intermediaries, who might be misguided, and were likely to make trying demands on a busy young man. And best of all, if a man might follow his inner light, then he could believe as he pleased and still be a Quaker; no one could overrule him except God, and Angus felt that he had reached a mutually satisfactory arrangement with Him. Although it was rather too bad that Quakerism had abandoned the appeals of music and beauty in church, the gain in directness offset any losses from such minor aspects of spiritual development.

This religious thinking of Angus' was no more elementary or self-satisfied than that of the majority of his low-church Protestant classmates, though it was probably as primitive as that of any "educated" young people in history. They had fewer religious prejudices than their grandfathers, but that was because they had fewer religious convictions. They had only a sense of morality, derived chiefly from their mothers and somewhat broadened by a dawning concept of social welfare. They were moral from habit and lack of imagination, and because they had not been severely tested by temptation. Fear of punishment by God was a less powerful deterrent to sin than fear of disapproval by society.

Arguments over doctrine seemed to most of them as remote and useless as medieval debates on the number of angels who could be accommodated on the point of a needle. Theology had done the human race more harm than good, for it had divided men into competing sects for the most abstract and esoteric of reasons and had confused the individual. The really important principles of faith were held by Jews, Christians, Mohammedans, and Hindus alike—though Angus had never met a Hindu or a Mohammedan and could not have told them or their religions apart. After all, a man's religion should be judged by his way of life, and anyone could judge that because everyone knew the essential rights and wrongs of conduct. The idea that morality was a code adopted by a particular society for its own protection and convenience had not dawned on them. No one "took" anthropology; psychology had not entered their lives or the college curriculum; courses in philosophy had few takers, and one of the favorite academic games was to avoid the required course in Bible.

In these attitudes Swarthmore was not much different from other colleges of the time, but it did create habits of living more sensible than many of them. Its social sanity redeemed its over-emphasis on social respectability. In rather different ways than its faculty intended, the college prepared its students for the century they would live in, where one could be successful without ideas and happy without excellence if one accepted majority opinion and got on well with people of one's kind. Four years at Swarthmore developed fixed principles which were assets to its graduates, and though they were hardly adequate to the problems they would meet, few of them ever suspected it. In one respect Swarthmore was unique. Like Angus' Quaker school, its special virtue was the healthy atmosphere of its coeducation. It taught both the sexes that neither was superior or inferior, neither to be worshiped or feared. Its young men and women lived with mutual respect and flirtation, in an atmosphere more rational than the five-day separation and excessive week-end fervor at most men's and women's colleges.

The 1920s were a decade when the young of America ceased to regard higher education as a privilege and began to assume it as a right. The change was important because it removed from the students a sense of personal responsibility to repay society for the special privilege of higher education. It was also important because students began to question the offerings of college and the omniscience of their professors, who became salesmen of their subjects rather than beneficent donors of the pearls of learning. The decade was also a period when American society became most avid in its pursuit of pleasure, and challenged the merits of austerity and discipline in principle as it had previously challenged them only in fact. Those trends were not invented by undergraduates but were promptly reflected in their attitudes.

Swarthmore had, however, much less of the country club at-

mosphere than the Princeton of Scott Fitzgerald or the Yale of
the secret societies and week ends at Poughkeepsie. This was not
especially to its credit, since Swarthmore's relative sobriety was
due as much to financial limitations and natural parochialism
as to any Quaker ideals. Few of its undergraduates could afford to
sport motorcars or coonskin coats or to join the social life of
Philadelphia's Main Line. Most of them had no more access to
the elite of New York or Philadelphia than to that of London or
Paris, and their philandering needs were amply satisfied on
their own campus. Alcohol was banned, and few undergraduates
drank regularly if at all. All were so immersed in campus activities that they were remarkably isolated from the flaming youth
portrayed by John Held, as well as from much interest in the adventures of Woodrow Wilson and the misadventures of Warren
Gamaliel Harding. They were not averse to the enjoyment of
whatever pleasures and luxuries were available without great
effort or initiative.

So Angus and innumerable other Americans at hundreds of
colleges received at their 1921 Commencements diplomas that
carried the assurance that they were well prepared to cope with
life. Yet most of them stepped from their graduation platforms
with minimal understanding of the forces at work within society or themselves. Many did not even suspect that such understanding was important, or know what the forces were. They
knew much that their fathers did not know, and had covered
more miles and spent more dollars than any previous college
generation, but it is doubtful that many of them had thought as
deeply, felt as keenly, or believed as firmly as their ancestors had
done at the same age. The future would bring them closer to
reality, but at the moment they were better fitted to gain material success than personal happiness. As for understanding the
new world of social, ideological, and nuclear fission, they were
no better prepared than a foot soldier with a broadsword at
Bastogne.

The best chance for men with elementary weapons is to select ground where elementary weapons are as effective as refined ones. The way to make up for lack of quality, in culture as in weapons, is never to be caught on terrain where quality can demonstrate its superiority. This was the strategy that Angus' college generation instinctively followed. They kept to the cultural lowlands, where broadswords *en masse* can hold their own with intellectual rapiers. They helped to demonstrate that democracy can get along to its own satisfaction without high cultivation, just as a forceful man can advance without social finesse or deep understanding in a world in which they are only secondary virtues. The graduates of 1921 have been less handicapped by their cultural shortcomings than they would have been in an age of higher values.

If college had not given these young men and women the power or desire to be superior citizens, it had given them nearly everything they needed to be comfortable and respectable ones. The trouble is that democracy needed from them something more than that. They were not able to distinguish very clearly between the second-rate and the truly excellent in men and ideas. Their colleges had professed to make them leaders, but had given them almost no idea where to lead or why; it had concentrated on the elementary how. Their teachers had professed to instill humanistic ideals, but not one in ten of their graduates could have stated any distinction between the ideas of Plato and those of Aristotle, or between the opinions of John Dewey and Calvin Coolidge. Their bachelors' degrees were useful watermarks on human sheets of paper spiritually almost blank. What they had learned of their emotions had been largely in spite of their educators. At best the student's mind had been somewhat disciplined, good habits firmly established, good will encouraged, intellectual interest in some limited field developed, vocational competence increased, and the imagination slightly stirred. This was much, under the circumstances of American life and values, and the achievement is not to be underestimated. But four years of college had been, in some important ways, little more than the prolongation of competent adolescence.

Viewed from the sticky eminence of a hot June Commencement platform, the future course of life was to Angus, the Class Orator, as simple as it was promising. He had but to follow the formulae he had already practiced to win a success which would include worldly esteem, the benign use of acquired power in some field, and a respect if not a position comparable to that granted their Commencement speaker, Mr. Herbert Hoover. He did not include happiness or self-understanding among his objectives, and if someone had asked him why, he would have replied that happiness would naturally follow success, and that he understood himself well enough to have made a success of college and acquired many friends. It has been said that until a man realizes he can be a fool he has not begun to achieve wisdom. If that is true, then Angus was still a freshman.

He had at least the perception to see that the academic system he had encountered often missed its aim, and that its measurements of intellectual power and promise were often faulty. It made education a ladder of courses in which the rungs had little relation to one another—an ascent by easy grades to meaningless degrees. By docile footwork a student could attain the level assumed to indicate the cultivated man. Like the making of a motorcar, each detail of education's anatomy had to be given the formal approval of its separate tester before it could be moved on for the attachment of the next. It was an assembly job, but, unlike the motorcar, the Bachelor of Arts had no functional unity and was sent out to the market with no final test run.

The fact that this method gave the collegiate imprimatur to some whose intellectual power and discipline were dubious misled the student into believing he was abler than he really was, and thus exposed him to the pains of later disillusion. It also led society to believe that education consists of the mastery of some vocational specialty plus a confused collection of unco-ordinated facts. Though Angus suspected he might not be as good as he looked, he was encouraged by collegiate success to believe himself abler and wiser than he was, and society temporarily accepted the collegiate verdict. His piecemeal academic successes had coagulated into a reputation far more impressive than his actual performance. His mastery of the arts of grade-getting had swept him up the academic rungs by a kind of gravity in reverse. Some of his teachers must have realized that they were rewarding him not for his brains and character but for ambition and facility in adjusting himself to their system. He was approved because, like a good Western pony, he would stand without being tied and move when he felt the spurs. The encouragement they gave him might be good educational psychology, but as higher education it confused the values, and misled him.

One incident of this academic fortuity illustrated the inaccuracies of the measuring system. At the end of his junior year Angus developed academic ambitions because he found his record good enough to be capitalized into honors. The highest honor he could hope for was election to Phi Beta Kappa, but his record was well below the society's normal requirement and only some impressive demonstration could turn the trick. Drastic action was indicated, and Angus took it. He enrolled in his senior year in the beginners' course in Greek. The faculty members of Phi Beta Kappa were eager to encourage student interest in the classics, and the Professor of Greek was an influential member of the society. She welcomed into her class of serious young women the first varsity football player who had ever seemed curious—even though suddenly—about Xenophon. The rest was easy. Angus did a minimum of work with a maximum of appealing enthusiasm, and made it clear that his eyes were being opened to a whole new world. He emerged knowing only a dozen Greek nouns but with an excellent grade and was elected to Phi Beta Kappa. That hallmark was almost certainly an important asset in his record submitted for a Rhodes Scholarship.

The year Angus spent after Swarthmore further opened his eyes to the dubious mechanics of the academic formulae. The expedient scholar of the *Anabasis* was invited to teach industrial geography to five sections of undergraduates approximately his own age in a leading university school of business. He had never set foot in a business school; he had never taught anyone anything; he had studied no geography since the age of twelve, and his college courses in economics had included no study of industry. Incompetent as he seemed to himself and must have seemed to others, Angus was probably no worse qualified than any other new young instructor whom the able head of the department could have secured for the money.

The course he taught was based on mimeographed material prepared by men in the department, which Angus simply memorized a little sooner and better than his students. The standing of each student in the course was determined by sketchy recitations and occasional written tests, graded by Angus, who was nearly as ignorant of the arts of mental measurement as his students. Those who could parrot back an adequate minimum from the mimeographed sheets passed the course; only literacy, docility, and memory were tested. A college graduate twenty years old was almost alone determining whether some 140 young men would pass the course and be issued their passports to further work in the school—and he was doing so in a field of knowledge he had never studied.

To that experience of undergraduate instruction Angus added another on standards of graduate study. In spare time during his senior year at Swarthmore he had casually exposed himself to two graduate courses in English literature at the University of Pennsylvania. He had taken three graduate courses in American and general literature at a summer session of Columbia University. All of this work had been done while he was an undergraduate. Then, while teaching at the business school, he had been physically present at another graduate literature course in the university, and also a seminar in applied economics. The courses in literature were almost as unrelated to each other as they were to economics. All except the last were large lecture courses at which no attendance was recorded, and in several no examinations were required.

In the late spring of his year at the business school it occurred to Angus to investigate whether any of the credits automatically awarded for these sporadic and diverse undergraduate efforts in two universities could be assembled toward an ultimate Master's degree. His inquiry brought surprising results. After a single superficial examination of only part of the work theoretically covered, he ended the year a Master of Arts in English Literature. He had never studied Shakespeare, Milton, the Romantic poets, or any other English literature between 1400 and 1800 after his sophomore year, and his Master's thesis was an amateurish outline of the resort industry of New England, which was never seen by the English department of either university.

Angus thought the meaning of academic degrees could reach no higher confusion until, on taking his Bachelor's degree at Oxford three years later, he learned that, by payments totaling some $150 and with no further physical or mental activity, he could become a Master of Arts at Oxford. This purely commercial transaction was completed in 1928, and Angus did not even have to cross the ocean to receive the degree. A handful of the initiated knew that Oxford did not pretend that the Master's degree represented any intellectual achievement beyond its Bachelor's degree, but the public did not know it, and Oxford did not go out of its way to explain. In 1932 Angus was told that he had been made a Master of Arts at Yale. It was explained to him that this was neither an earned nor an honorary degree, but awarded "privatim" to non-Yale men appointed to major posts at Yale. Angus thus became the possessor of three Master's degrees from three leading universities, which added substantially to his advancement in academic circles.

Meanwhile Angus had successfully offered his academic record in application for a Rhodes Scholarship. As he sailed that

September on the *Rochambeau* to begin his Oxford career, he gave little thought to what Oxford might do to his mind or his spirit; the fact that his years there were an envied prize and a step up the ladder of admiration was enough for him. On his election to the scholarship he had been too pleased with himself to take seriously the questions of the only two friends who had their reservations. A professor of English asked him what career he intended after Oxford and how he expected Oxford to help him toward it. Angus thought the first half of the question irrelevant and the second half absurd, for surely the prestige of Oxford would be an asset anywhere. Professor J. Russell Smith of Pennsylvania inquired whether he realized that Oxford would probably ruin him for later success in America. Angus did no more than wonder casually what personal limitation or unfortunate personal experience could have jaundiced the judgment of so good a man. Oxford was obviously the next step; the future might be vague, but it was rosy and would take care of itself.

IV

Puritan's Progress

AS Angus set out for Oxford he took with him new visions behind old blinders. He was still under the impression that education is chiefly the acquisition of facts. He conceded that good taste, imagination, and human sympathy are important to the cultivated man, but assumed they would come as by-products of his effortful devotion to factual knowledge. They were still only words to him; he had not felt them or the lack of them. He did not apprehend what wiser men really meant by human understanding, or how cultivation could be cultivated except through books and lectures. Friendships and the gentler arts were valuable and pleasant, but they were diversions and not education.

A summer of European travel during college years had done only a little to open his eyes to the spiritual sources of beauty and aspiration. Glimpses of Paris and Venice, of the Jungfrau and the English Lakes, had been extravagant pleasure and stimuli to the imagination, and Angus thought he appreciated them as much as anyone. They had indeed widened his horizons, but he still thought the solid values of travel lay in the facts, not the emotions, one accumulated. From facts—whether about Italian painting, Westminster Abbey, or the morals of Montmartre—deductions could be made, and the greater the number of items in one's mind or notebook the more numerous and valid the deductions. Most mistakes in conclusions were due to inadequate or inaccurate facts, and hence precision and thoroughness were the roots of wisdom. The accumulation of knowledge would by some mysterious alchemy be transmuted into imagination and humane culture. Angus laughed fashionably at Americans who went through the Louvre or the British Museum with their noses in Baedeker, but he was embarking on a rare opportunity with his own nose in a personal encyclopedia. Others elected to the promised land of Oxford study and Continental travel were not very different. Angus would later cross Europe in company with an extremely able Rhodes Scholar from Australia (later a distinguished jurist there) who at every stop from Boulogne to Biarritz would first of all work out the exact distance in linear miles from Sydney, Australia.

Whatever education Oxford would give him Angus expected would come principally through organized study; the rest would have some value as well as charm, but it would be window-dressing. He resolved, as he had resolved on entering Swarthmore, not to be seduced by peripheral interests or social activities, merely because they were said to bring general cultivation. He was not a rich young English lordling of the eighteenth century, making the grand tour of the Continent with valet, postchaise, and letters of introduction to European courts. He was a twentieth-century American with a career to make in America, and that called for competence, not *savoir-faire* and Continental friends in high places. From various sources he had been provided with letters to people in England and France who could have opened doors on new interests and self-development, but he dropped them into New York Harbor as the *Rochambeau* sailed. To give his time, beyond the minimum desirable for recreation, to anything except the pursuit of knowledge, prestige, and future "success" would be just as much dissipation as overindulgence in drink or women. He envied those with time and money for casual pleasures and intellectual embroidery, but his task was defined by the Oxford Final Examinations and the Oxford conception of the "all-round man," whatever it might prove to be.

Angus had been conscious of values, but chiefly in morals and motorcars. His ethics recognized only black and white. A thing was good or bad, and no question about either. Most issues had moral implications, and life was a constant series of moral judgments. He recognized few problems that simple honesty and justice, combined of course with mastery of the facts, could not untangle. Even political questions were usually a struggle between freedom and slavery, virtue and vice, and the events of history were as clearly definable in moral terms as those of Rome were to Gibbon. The American Revolution and Civil War might have had their economic and political causes, but they were essentially moral issues in which freedom and unity eventually won over tyranny and disintegration, as they always would if men were well-informed, intelligent, and moral.

There were a few issues not quite so clear, but further education along established lines would no doubt clarify them, at least enough to get through life without personal confusions. The principles that applied to personal conduct would also work if intelligently applied to world problems. International peace depended on the adjustment of the German war debt, the elimination of economic rivalries, and the observance and strengthening of international law, and these were no more than matters of judgment plus character. Like any personal question, they were problems of measuring the desirability of the end against its risks and costs, for some consideration of expediency could not be eliminated from this human world. It was a mistake to pay more than necessary for any article, whether it was a pair of shoes or a prosperous German Republic, but it was also bad judgment to buy shoes or democracy too cheap or too fragile. The trouble

was that Europeans seemed to lack simple morality in such matters as loving their neighbors and paying their debts. They had,
for example, borrowed large sums from America and should
meet the agreed terms of repayment instead of asking for reduc-
tion or postponement. A private debtor who welshed was something very close to a thief; how could European countries see
themselves in any other light? President Coolidge had not yet
remarked: "They hired the money, didn't they?" but to Angus
and many other Americans in 1922 that question covered the
subject.

Thus Angus took his own personally limited America to Europe with him, unaware how greatly it would be challenged by
disturbing spirits he would find there, waiting to disabuse and
deflate him. They would show him qualitative values in men
and ideas far above his own; they would put originality of
thought above a laborious synthesis of existing authorities; they
would try to make him see books and paintings not as finished
relics in libraries and galleries but as related examples of men
reaching upward, trying to say more than men can express. Oxford would stagger him by its emphasis on perspective, urbanity,
and wit, and Oxford undergraduates by their freedom from intellectual docility.

There would be men like Gilbert Murray who would try to
inspire him to see and enlarge the unity in men's thought over
the ages; men like Robert Bridges and John Masefield to lift his
eyes above the drudgery of mundane facts. There would be R. W.
Chapman, the Secretary of the Clarendon Press, of all the Brah-
min dons of Oxford the most openly intolerant of the second-
rate, who in interviewing Angus for a job at the end of his Oxford
years would, after a silent inspection of several minutes, bark at
him only one question: "Can you suffer fools gladly?" Angus
did not know what the right answer was, so he told the truth.

There would be other, more saturnine, spirits, casting doubts
on all Angus' most cherished assumptions: on the progressive
perfection of man, the values of popular democracy, the virtues

of conventional morality, and even the superiority of the twentieth century and the American way of life. By no flight of prescience did he suspect that in the quadrangles and byways of Oxford would lurk the spirits of Karl Marx as well as Adam Smith, of Schopenhauer as well as Shakespeare, of James Joyce as well as Thomas Hardy. He would discover the power of Mussolini and the Big Lie as well as of Stanley Baldwin and the cautious tradition, of Beaverbrook and popular taste as well as A. E. Housman and eremitic classicism, of Astarte as well as Minerva. Had the raw young Quaker rationalist foreseen what revelations and confusions were in store for him he would not have stepped so blithely from the *Rochambeau* into the ubiquitous clatter of the Plymouth docks.

There were minds in America equally disrupting to Angus' complacency, but Angus had met very few of them, and they did not set the note in the society he knew. Oxford proved to be full of such minds. Angus' ideas started immediately to undergo a sea-change of demolition and reconstruction that Oxford would always mean to him. By innumerable little lessons it revealed that there was more than one way of looking at things, and that even Angus could not be sure his way was the best.

Having previously seen a little of Europe, Angus approached it less tensely and naïvely than he would have otherwise, but still with his guard up. It would be full of opportunities and pleasures but also of dangerous old-world doctrines and temptations. He did not fear intellectual corruption but was not sure he could resist the more obviously wicked attractions of Soho and the Place Pigalle. More from fear than virtue he had scouted only the peripheries of sex but had found them incitingly attractive. He had resisted temptation partly from the knowledge that his mother would have been deeply disappointed in him, and partly from superstition that the fates had been kind to him because he was virginal. In Europe it would be all too easy to yield to this strong but evil urge. On the *Rochambeau,* in intervals between nice flirtations with nice American girls, he wrestled with Original Sin and concluded it would defeat him unless he fortified his resistance with a Vow. This time it must be a negative Vow: instead of forcing himself to jump to the ground he must force himself to remain on the heights. He resolved that during his years at Oxford he would resist the Ultimate Sin. All that can be said for him in this extraordinary attitude is that he saw a little of the humor of it, and in fact that he carefully excluded any denial of the preliminary pleasures of sex. Tennyson's Galahad had never been his favorite hero, and it had always troubled him a little that he much preferred Lancelot.

Angus was eager to make a head start in this new and exalted competition that was Oxford, and arrived at Balliol College two days before term officially opened. He was not as warmly welcomed by its Master and Fellows as he had expected; they were not even in evidence. Rooms and food were grudgingly allotted him by porters and scouts, who made it clear that he had violated all local decencies by arriving early. After a rather uncomfortable first night with cold dinner, cold rooms, and cold water (not running), he set off the following morning to consult his tutor and begin the three-year race for honors. Five days later he found him, and very charming he was, but the interview was limited to seven minutes in the quadrangle, for the tutor was in tennis flannels and hurrying to a men's foursome. Angus derived the impression that he was displaying a naïve eagerness for the process of "reading." There was plenty of time, said the Reverend Mr. Ridley in an accent so Oxonian that for the first three months Angus could hardly understand him. The list of term lectures would not be available for several days; he himself was just back from the French Alps and hardly settled in—why not spend a week or two looking round Oxford or getting acquainted with the men of the college? Did Angus play a fair game of tennis? If so he might be useful later on to make a fourth, unless of course he intended to give his first term to rowing or rugger. That would be the most important matter to decide immediately. It was two weeks before Angus saw him again.

As for his advice, Angus did not say that he had looked pretty thoroughly about Oxford two summers earlier, and had done nothing else for the past week. And Angus did not know quite how to go about advancing his acquaintance with his interesting-looking and apparently completely oriented English and Scottish college mates. He had secretly hoped that his tutor, or someone, would make the formal introductions apparently necessary before one even asked one's neighbor in hall to pass the salt. He had sat across from these mutually chattering youths at three meals a day; he had shared with them the nudity of the college baths; he had met them constantly in quadrangle and common room, but not one of them had offered more than a startled "Oh" to his advances. Only one had taken the conversational initiative in hall one day with a sudden "Do you row?" When Angus pleaded not guilty the exchange ended and was not renewed for the term, although they shared the same staircase in the college.

Angus searched for the Dean's office, the Registrar's office, the gymnasium, and the multicolored paper forms he had been conditioned to believe essential to educational progress. None of these, he found, had ever existed in Balliol, and it was implied that they never would. In the end he decided there was no alternative to the postponement of educational activity and took himself, alone, to the playing fields and local tea houses. There his collegiate acquaintance began; several men spoke to him and proved far more shy and eager than he. In three months he was wholly at his ease, and two years later had friendships at least as close as any he had ever had at home.

After the highly organized life and studies in America, the Oxford customs, at first so baffling, came to seem refreshing. The ingenious structure of paradoxes that was the Oxford educational system was a challenge to an American's intelligence and adaptability. The Oxford youth studied more in vacations than in terms; he learned more over tea, beer, and port wine than in the lecture hall; he was expected to master not precisely what he was taught but something a little different and more his own; he played games not for admiration but for fun; he knew not the term "extracurricular activities" yet engaged in them as continuously as the American youth; he deplored organized work or play yet was continually forming new clubs and "rags"; he would have denied that they were connected with his education but made them a great part of it. With a psychology the reverse of American, he pretended to be less ambitious and less studious than he really was.

Oxford education was based on tradition and guided by instinct, but it took Angus a long time to pry off the cover of its apparent irrationality and recognize the unspoken logic beneath. American educators had taught him to fear the irrational and suspect the clever, yet here was a great university where professors and students gloried in their paradoxes, put ideas before facts and wit before logic. When they did casually descend to the rational, no minds were more keen. The effect on Oxford undergraduates seemed to be qualitatively far more successful than the American system, though one could not be sure that the results were not due to their superior schooling in Rugby, Winchester, and the rest. Certainly the product of Oxford was outwardly more uniform but inwardly more diverse and mentally independent than our own. Truth was pursued as ardently as at Columbia and Chicago but less effortfully and impatiently. To Oxford dons many questions were ones not of morality but of judgment, and therefore much more complicated to understand and evaluate. Men on either side of intellectual controversies could be partly right and partly wrong, and since generations had argued them Oxford felt no need for haste in supplying the ultimate verdict. It was more important to look all round a question than to force an answer. Meanwhile there were excellent bypaths to be explored in the Bodleian and the Cotswolds, and the ale at the Trout Inn was worth the pleasant walk along the Isis to Godstow.

Angus wondered how far he should go along the road of Oxford's open-mindedness. If there was much to be said for both

Charles and Cromwell, for both Inquisition and Reformation, then the same catholicity must apply to all history and human effort. Deferred judgments might have to be applied to emotions, art, and even sex. If the French Revolution was neither a glorious victory of human freedom nor a barbaric orgy of sans-culottism, if Napoleon was neither pure hero nor pure ogre, then even the events of our own 1776 might have to be evaluated in a new light. If the first cultivated audiences that had heard Wagner's music had condemned it as unbearably discordant, then perhaps the dissonances of the moderns might survive their present critics. Even chastity might not be so indispensable to virtue as Angus had been led to believe—an interesting possibility.

It was as shocking and invigorating as stepping out into cold, fresh night air to discover that there were whole areas of life and thought in which one could escape the moral conscience and enjoy the intellectual chase. Education became infinitely more complicated but infinitely more interesting. The naïve young moralist in Angus was a little frightened; the opening mind in Angus was exhilarated. He was being set loose in a new land where there were few roads and signposts and where Oxford tutors seemed reluctant to provide firm guidance, even if they could. Angus had never expected to find professors, and with international reputations too, who constantly talked about how much they did not know. Oxford was leading him to intellectual freedom and moral confusion. He wanted to throw away his mental and ethical crutches but was nervous about discarding them altogether. He wanted to explore but feared he was no pioneer.

In contrast to his expectations, what Angus got from Oxford that later seemed to him most valuable came not from books but from people, not from work but from play. The fringes and by-products of the scholastic regimen; the constant curiosity and talk about everything; the pursuit of an idea from one book to another and from books to men; the new quality of living revealed by visits to English country houses; the occasional concerts or appearances of poets and statesmen in college halls, common rooms, and clubs—these were education by apparent accident, but the accident was planned. They were worth far more than the lectures one heard and the essays one labored over writing. Part of the genius of Oxford lay in its simulated inefficiency, in its insistence on lying receptively open to all the blessings of coincidence. Its system placed so little stress upon time and the mechanics of education that one felt no irresponsibility in spending an evening listening to Ramsay MacDonald debate with undergraduates at the Oxford Union, or in accepting a chance to have tea on Boar's Hill with John Buchan. Angus once talked with Rudyard Kipling, and it was like Oxford that the conversation took place in Biarritz on a tour of the Oxford Rugby team.

The capacity never to be hurried irritated Americans eager for action, but it brought events into perspective and ideas into discussion. It turned minds into intellects, schoolboy conformists into individuals, work into play, and play into knowledge. The process was advanced less by didactic instruction than by social osmosis. Oxford knew how to make the mouths of young men water for wisdom long before Pavlov learned to stimulate the salivary glands of dogs, and did it with an air of casual amateurism that concealed its professional skill. It forced even young Americans in a hurry to relax and learn through enjoyment.

Whatever Oxford failed to do for Angus, it made him temporarily very human. It showed him how narrow and absurd were some of the dogmas he had cherished. Much of his intellectual pride dropped from him as he discovered finer minds than his, and observed that even they discounted the perfection of their intellectual processes. He also realized that his mental capacities were handicapped by his method of using them. By concentrating on the accumulation of facts he was not developing the ability to draw meaning from them; by accepting authority with what he had thought was shrewd docility he was losing the capacity to have ideas of his own; by emphasizing thoroughness he was becoming pedantic; by wallowing in what he thought was the heart of the matter he was developing a congested mind, dogmatic opinions, and a heavy style. A tactful tutor urged him to forget what the best critics said he should think of Milton's Satan or Keats's "Lamia"; to search honestly for his own unalloyed reactions and then write them down persuasively.

When he tried to do this he slowly perceived his lack of intellectual independence, imagination, and verbal felicity. His attempts to catch all three were at first pathetic and then desperate. Painfully he struggled for originality and lightness of touch, but the product always betrayed the midnight oil or the mental flagellation. Oxford could not give him imagination or urbanity; it could only develop what puny talents he had, and convince him of the value of what he lacked.

When Angus first arrived at Oxford he set his cap for a degree with highest honors, and was sure that with enough industry and concentration he could secure it. As Oxford began to teach him, he saw that application and devotion were not enough, and that excess of them alone was not virtue but myopia by Oxford standards. Had he been less effortful and more relaxed, had he known less and understood more, had he given less time to reading and more to savoring, his final papers might have seemed better to his examiners. Even when he sensed his faults he worked too hard to repair them. In the final weeks before his examinations his tutor told him to forget them and read anything irrelevant. When the Master of Balliol then asked him whether he liked Conrad and Barrie, Angus replied rather smugly that since neither was important to his examiners he had not looked at them during his three years at Oxford. The Master directed him to take two weeks off and read nothing else. Angus read all of Conrad and most of Barrie over the following two weeks, but he did it in the small hours after he had completed his self-assigned review of *Beowulf* and Milton.

When the final results were bruited, the examiners had rated all Angus' papers as high seconds, but had found no originality or brilliance worth a first. In spite of recent self-illuminations,

Angus had expected top honors, and the verdict shook his self-confidence and pride as they had never been shaken before. He recognized that the examiners had correctly assessed his abilities, but that made the blow hurt even more. It was Oxford's last and best contribution to his education.

In human wisdom Oxford gave Angus a lesson still more valuable, for it taught him the merits of flexibility. He developed, though lamely, the capacity to relax with people, to enjoy friendships, to taste the trivial amenities of life. In time he broke almost all his own earlier rules of conduct, at first defiantly and later with spontaneous ease. He learned the delights of long inconsequential afternoons as one drifted in a punt down the Isis between osiered banks, of ardent arguments on everything and nothing over a coal fire and mulled claret in the paneled fastness of some friend's lodgings. He learned the prideful joys of escorting a pretty American girl (so neat, so helpless, so overdressed) among the barges, quadrangles, and envious glances of Eights Week. He wallowed with enthusiasm in the muddy exhilarations of Rugby football and the acclaim of being the second American ever to win a Rugby Blue, and secretly gloried in his captaincy of lacrosse and membership in the all-England team. He took very kindly to sherry, whiskey, and champagne at college binges or as a guest of the Claret Club of Trinity, the Archery Club of St. John's (where Charles I was always toasted "for having graciously sent his son Prince Rupert to dwell among us"), and the Shakespeare Club of University College (where the exuberant dinners were always begun by a statement from the white-tied President that he would "entertain a motion to dispense with a reading of the Immortal Bard"). No one prized more than he the select dinners of his own Annandale Society in Balliol, which began with impeccable dignity, progressed through exchanges of what seemed rare wit over pheasant and Burgundy, and ended in a friendly wrestling match, in evening clothes, with Prince Olaf of Norway or the future Duke of Hamilton or the son of a sheep farmer from New Zealand. Oxford, for the time at least, freed

Angus from social defensiveness and the austerities of his origin, and there as never elsewhere his spirits throve and mellowed.

That was the genius of Oxford, but even Oxford genius had its limitations. In the conservation of culture it had no peer, but for creative growth it was more stimulating than fertile. It gave the minds of its dons and students a highly critical bent; some of the ablest could see so clearly the flaws in Shakespeare and Shelley that it seemed egotistic to attempt serious creative writing themselves. Others less cautious diverted their creative impulse into wit or fantasy or semantics, or were anemic from emotional malnutrition. Oxford's famous spate of undergraduate verse and novels was deceptive: they far outnumbered those in an American university of the time, but their authors were more given to conceits of fancy and sophistications of style than to deeply perceptive development of character or the honest presentation of profound emotion. Many wrote only as undergraduates because it was the fashion, and the brilliant young poetasters seemed to lack strength or staying power or much to say. In the twenties, at least, its creative minds seemed to be self-conscious and precious; they wrote as if they needed more Fielding and less Proust, more solid roast beef from the fields of their native land and less bubbly champagne or fancies from Fiesole. As for the Americans at Oxford, what most of them needed more than anything else—whether for artistic creation or productive lives—was something Oxford did not give them: understanding of their own emotions and of the changing America to which they would return.

It did not occur to Angus, or so far as he could see to most of his contemporaries in England or America, that men's emotions were as great a source of potential power as their minds, and as much in need of cultivation. Instead of being developed as an asset, the emotional force was generally treated as a liability, and the case of Angus was only somewhat more extreme than most. The desiccated puritanism that had conditioned his boyhood had opposed emotion on principle, except when it was clearly identified with personal obligations like filial affection, marital devotion, and disapproval of Roman Catholics and Democrats. As for the public display of feeling, that was regarded as appropriate only in conventional forms on certain occasions. A wedding was sweet, and the mother of the bride was expected to weep, whether from happiness, bereavement, or relief. A funeral was sad, and close relatives sobbed or dropped a manly tear while an atmosphere of unrelieved gloom was carefully maintained until normal conversation was regained with relief on the way back from the cemetery. A baseball game was a permissible excitement, approved for partisan passion and vernacular release. Apart from events like these, any display of deep feeling was in bad taste. Emotions were messy and those who gave way to them led lives lacking in order and self-control. They were personal indulgences and hence questionable, and they disturbed the smooth surface of civilized life. The idea that they should be understood and on occasion encouraged was absent from the minds of any relatives or educators Angus knew.

The English tradition of repressing emotion was even more strict than the American. It was cherished by the upper classes partly to distinguish them from the more vulgarly spontaneous lower classes. The properly schooled Oxford youth was supposed to frown on any display of love, anger, pain, or jubilation. The only exceptions were when exuberance was in the tradition, like getting tight and smashing hats in Piccadilly on Boat Race night. Admiration was particularly taboo; the Oxford youth of twenty felt called upon to conceal it even for his greatest heroes by phrases like "poor dear Winnie" or "sweet bumbling Baldwin." One should not display more than casual pleasure at meeting a friend or relative, or show serious regret at his departure, but reduce all degrees of feeling on both occasions to the common norm of "cheerio." Only women, Latins, and the lower classes let themselves go emotionally or verbally, and thus revealed their inferiority to the well-bred Anglo-Saxon. Exalted expression was suitable only to poetry and even there was a little

démodé. One expressed the greatest satisfactions by the most restrained understatements.

Angus concluded that British understatement is really a more
effective way of expressing strong feelings by indirection than
the flamboyant exaggerations of the American press and "smart
set," who use superlatives so constantly that they become meaningless. When an Englishman did offer a compliment it meant
something. The contrast was most striking in the way sports
events were reported. If a Notre Dame halfback had performed
well the local press would put his name in two-inch headlines,
with adjectives like "devastating" and "stellar" profusely scattered through the text. When the Captain of the Oxford Rugby
team played really brilliantly in the big game of the year against
Cambridge, the *London Times* impressively applauded his skill
by the tiny subcaption "Macpherson plays useful game."

Understatement had its merits, but British repression went
deeper than the cautious use of language, and vitiated emotion
itself. Oxford carried self-control to the point of starving sentiment, and disapproval of spontaneity to the discouragement of
feeling anything too deeply. The process destroyed exaltation
and distorted sentiment into mockery. Emotion about girls—that
most natural reaction of young men—was under the code the
most objectionable of all. In confessing the love of his life or an-
nouncing his engagement the nice young English gentleman was
so casual that most American girls would have felt insulted at
his lack of enthusiasm. Restraint of expression and sentiment
about women was only part of the code of sex repression. Oxford
set up every barrier to normal friendships between the sexes, and
when it did not make sex sterile it made it cheap.

Disapproval of the emotions leads to neglect of the senses as
media for expressing or appreciating beauty. The Oxford or
Harvard graduate was likely to be almost as unfamiliar with the
beautifully sensuous as with the beautifully emotional, whether
in art or in people. The senses were vaguely allied to sex and
primitive life, and therefore to be repressed or only secretly grati-

fied. In Angus' case these denials had left him ignorant of the beauty in personal relations as well as in the arts. Enthusiastic appreciation either of a flower or of a Haydn string quartet was a little effeminate. The code of Oxford was better, but not much. It approved the sensuous if it was enjoyed through the safe medium of the fine arts—through odes to intellectual beauty and Greek vases—or in the more normal and virile forms of horseflesh, the pony ballet at the Palace, or the colder beauty of the Matterhorn. Oxford allowed these exceptions because it was so intellectually tolerant that it could tolerate even the senses, provided they were enjoyed in forms at least one generation of Oxonians had found permissible. If Oxford had anything to give Angus to develop his stunted perceptions of beauty through emotional understanding, or to cultivate his wise use of his sensory perceptions, or to deepen his knowledge of his instincts, he did not find it, and neither, I think, did his classmates. Whatever growth he made in such matters came in the warmer soil and more natural climate of the Continent.

Though Oxford had little to offer the heart, it laid infinite wealth before the mind. American Rhodes Scholars had been mentally well fed at home, but there the diet was not always well chosen, well cooked, and well served. In America they had simply assimilated, and digested as best they could, everything that had been set before them—a heterogeneous mass of facts and opinions with not much apparent relation between them. Their burdened minds had been so busy accumulating that they had had no time to mature or mellow. They arrived at Oxford with a limited sense of unity in knowledge, or of continuity in history and their identification with it; they were ignorant in the arts even if they had taken courses and studied guide books; they were uniform in their mental reactions, and they were dubious of originality in others and fearful of being original themselves. They had learned by routines that did not encourage mental independence, and were mentally docile. The American college graduate was better informed but intellectually and philosophi-

cally more adolescent than many an English boy fresh from public school.

The young American had one notable advantage for the current century: he was more competent in adapting himself to
whatever environment he fell into. He had had far more varied
experience than his English contemporary, and though he might
complain about foreign ways he adjusted himself to them rather
quickly. He could talk with equal ease to Oxford dons and Oxford scouts, to tradesmen and to lordlings, to Indian students
and fourth-generation Etonians, and in much the same terms. He
was incapable of varying from his instinctive democratic approach, and that made his conversation more pertinent and less
impertinent. His approach was more universal, for he assumed, as
many a young European did not, a basic equality and mutuality
of interest among all human beings.

Angus used to predict that if two boys of eighteen, one English
and one American, were dropped penniless by parachute into
Siberia or the Argentine pampas, the English youth might
emerge with a publishable travel diary or might never be heard
of again. The American would almost certainly turn up, eventually, with some money, a collection of souvenirs, and a book
of telephone numbers. This might be a primitive skill but it was
a useful one for young men whom the twentieth century would
strip of all impedimenta and send into unknown places and situations. To confident young Americans of the twenties the world
was a personal oyster; to many an English youth more international in attitude, with finer sensibilities or better mental training, it was a baffling and alien place outside his own familiar circle, and he had less ability to make it his own.

Oxford was in that respect the worst possible place for a young
Englishman to be educated for the twentieth century, for it was
the most class-conscious spot in the British Isles. It made no
provision for its students to meet anyone except those classified
as gentlemen, and encouraged their remoteness from nine tenths
of their fellow citizens. Most of them took their degrees with no

understanding of the workingmen and shopkeepers who would rule England in their time. They were experts in dealing, in the traditional manner of the British upper class, with servants and tailors, but the barrier of class distinction thus erected made any real rapport all the more difficult. The average Oxonian did not even know how to develop interclass understanding except through books, games, and horses, for he never worked, even in war, on equal terms with the cockney or Midlands pottery maker. Oxford dons could not have told him, for Oxford dons did not know. Oxford servants could not have helped him, for they were themselves social anachronisms. The scouts who valeted in Oxford colleges were often sons or nephews of earlier scouts who had spent their lives bringing meals and hot water to Victorian scions of the upper class. As conservators of Oxford traditions they were superb, but that fact made them inverted snobs and proud of it. Whatever were their innermost attitudes, they acted like spiritual successors to ancient peasants who touched their forelocks in the presence of the squire's son. Oxford men were being educated for a social system that was ceasing to exist.

To Americans at Oxford, who had little if any class consciousness, the system was less harmful because they never took it seriously. Its cultivated vestigialisms yielded educational values as well as minor irritations and old-world charm. It was a better lesson in social history than any Oxford lectures could provide, and it gave Americans a useful experience in the amenities and priorities of an English gentleman. It was pleasant for a Rhodes Scholar brought up to do the chores on a Minnesota farm and work with transient laborers to find himself waited upon, called "Sir," and regarded as almost a member of England's elite. The experience had the same harmless uniqueness as drinking a toast in port to the King and then hurling the glass into the fireplace, or joining a society to restore the Stuart dynasty, or finding that an Oxford shopkeeper was shocked if one insisted on carrying home some small purchase instead of having it sent two blocks "by hand." Angus lost so much caste with his Hanover Square tailor when he walked in to collect and pay cash for a new suit that he was taken into the back room for a glass of sherry with the staff—a social libation that would never have been offered a true gentleman. Along with Oxford scouts, Bond Street and Mayfair shopkeepers were England's strongest exponents of class distinctions. Nearly every American at Oxford disapproved a system that made a man a gentleman by purely conventional criteria, but few of them objected to being temporary beneficiaries of its privileges. The trouble was that young Americans could not help making friends with their scouts, and this broke the code.

Cecil Rhodes had believed in the system which had made the English gentleman the sahib of the world. He had financed young men from America and the Dominions through Oxford so that they might be molded to the traditions that he thought had built the empire. As a place to educate them in traditional English culture Rhodes could not have picked a better, and the experience was no small benefice to any American. But as a preview of the new Britain, Oxford was medieval. The men who would set the tone of Britain in Angus' lifetime were not at Oxford, or Cambridge either. They were working in coal mines in Wales or dockyards in East London, or building ships at Clydeside, or studying economics in Manchester and London night schools, or sitting on high bookkeepers' stools in Eastcheap. Americans did not meet them, or those millions who would elect them to Parliament. Neither did their Oxford classmates, and that was still more unfortunate.

While immersed in Milton in the Balliol library or spending a luxurious vacation at a country house in Kent, Angus half sensed the unreality of his English education. Once he wondered if he would not be spending his time far more profitably by talking with steelworkers in Sheffield or spending a few nights with a cockney family near the Elephant and Castle. He did nothing about it and neither did other American Oxonians, so far as he knew. Life was too full and too pleasant. If Oxford tutors ever thought of that kind of social experience as education they gave no sign of it. If it occurred to Lord Lothian and the other distinguished Britons who administered the Rhodes Trust that it would be good insurance for future Anglo-American relations to put their American beneficiaries in touch with the other four fifths of the British people, Angus and his friends never heard of it.

Rhodes Scholars were the beneficiaries of the most exalted plan for international education the Western world had produced. What they got from Oxford was invaluable, but what Oxford failed to give them made the scholarships a little unreal, except as preparation for a professorship or a diplomatic post. Some of America's ablest young men were following a path laid out in the nineteenth century which might prove to lead nowhere in the twentieth. That so many of them made it lead to careers of distinction and public trust is a tribute to their own ability and perspective.

After years of diplomatic and social life in England, Henry Adams had concluded that "the young American who should adopt English thought was lost." He had developed a poor opinion of British logic and eccentricity of thought. It took Angus a long time to reach the same conclusion, though for quite different reasons. Adams believed that in logic and character the American was superior to the Englishman. Perhaps that was true in 1865, but Angus concluded that in his own time American cultural standards were inferior to those of England. To Adams the danger was that the American would adopt an English intellectual standard inferior to his own. To Angus the danger was that the American who brought back home the cultural ideals of England could not maintain them in America or be happy if he did not. Adams' young American would be handicapped because he could no longer think like an American; Angus' young American would be handicapped because he would not want to.

So far as the mind as an instrument of pure rationality was concerned, the English mind and the American mind seemed to Angus equal in efficiency but different in their values. To draw distinctions between the best minds of different nations, as thinking machines, seems impossible. The trained mind is the trained mind regardless of its national origins; the disciplines and processes of reasoning are identical whether learned at Oxford or Harvard, whether achieved by reading Plato on an Iowa farm or in a Yorkshire parsonage, whether acquired by the study of John Locke or of nuclear physics. A Fermi from Italy and an Oppenheimer from California talk the same language; so do Sir Richard Livingston at Oxford and Professor Northrop at Yale. Measured by its finest examples, or its most inferior ones, the mind as an instrument knows no race or boundary. Apparent differences in national qualities of mind are no more than differences in modes of expression or variants in values. Angus was convinced of this until he later encountered the vagaries of the Oriental mind, and then he was less sure.

As the years wore on he became more certain that the young American who accepts the cultural values of Oxford in the 1920s finds it difficult to return to American values wholeheartedly. The qualities he had learned to esteem in the Balliol common room or the London Athenaeum were not those of the American public with which he wanted to live happily. The cultural ideals of Matthew Arnold or Richard Livingston do not merge comfortably with those of Hollywood, the *Daily Mirror,* or *Time* Magazine. Since the success of all but a very exceptional man depends on his happy identification with the values of the society around him, the more thoroughly any qualitative standards, British or American, work themselves into his system, the less his chance for public acceptance in the America that admires Walter Winchell, Mickey Spillane, and Senator McCarthy.

In 1925 this difference in cultural values seemed to Angus to be represented primarily by Europe on the one hand and America on the other. Time proved him wrong. The contrast is not between continents but between the traditions and values of an elite and a materialist mass. The common man now rules the culture of England almost as firmly as he determines the values of America, and there is little difference between the two. That change during a quarter century may prove, in the very long run, a political and even a cultural gain, but in Angus' lifetime the cultural sacrifices were more apparent.

The young American is also likely to find himself commercially handicapped by his Oxfordization. To the Englishmen, an Oxford or Cambridge education is a vocational asset. Those universities were in 1925, as they had been for generations, seedbeds for high-level government service, for the church and the professions. A British youth could study nothing but the classics or history at Oxford without impairing his chances of employment in several important fields. First honors at Oxford still mark a man as a potential cabinet secretary or ambassador. But two or three years at Oxford or Cambridge are as likely to diminish as enhance an American's employment value in America. Commercial doors, especially, are less welcoming to the young American fresh from Oxford honors than before he left America to secure them. American industry has managed quite comfortably without him, and employers do not see that a few years of travel and highbrow study abroad have increased his immediate usefulness. Europe may even have given him highfalutin or radical ideas. A recent President of the United States expressed a fairly common American resentment against the intellectual with overseas education when, according to reports, he called a Rhodes Scholar Senator of his own party "that overeducated Oxford son-of-a-bitch." The Oxford experience may ultimately yield dollar dividends, but at the start it has negative commercial value, except sometimes in the educational profession.

Angus had no desire to be a professor and some reason to doubt his fitness for an educational career. Yet by American standards he lacked qualifications for any other. Three years spent in efforts to master Middle English vowel changes, an urbane literary style, Rugby football, and the art of traveling far with little money were not convincing assets to most American employers. They were right: Angus on his return from Oxford was better prepared to be a contemporary of Swift than of Hemingway, of John Quincy Adams than of Harry Truman. He felt more at home in the atmosphere of the eighteenth and nineteenth centuries than in the twentieth. He was ill equipped to maintain himself on the scale to which Cecil Rhodes' fortune and his father's savings had accustomed him.

His social experience and attitudes proved equally undependable as tools to success, American style. Whatever social currency he brought back from Oxford underwent prompt deflation in America, except in very limited circles of which he was not, and did not want to be, a member. He had a wide acquaintance, from garage mechanics to the Prince of Wales, but that had small mundane value in Quaker circles or the Piping Rock Club. The pound sterling of British social standing might have theoretical prestige in America but it lacked economic convertibility. And though his social experience was broad it was also shallow. He had no roots in any society except the one into which he had been born, and that now seemed to him too limited for lifetime nourishment. He might be emotionally devoted to his family, but their ways were no longer his.

Angus had gone to Oxford to master English culture, but English culture had nearly mastered him. It forced upon him new evaluations that half destroyed the old; it turned into conundrums what he had thought were truths; it made human problems more complicated without making them more soluble. Oxford had demonstrated that social mores dwarf both the teacher and the taught, yet to achieve success in America a man should never admit himself dwarfed by anything. Angus was an American and had no desire to be anything else, but inwardly he was shaken. The task of merging two incompatible cultures was beyond a young man with so little imagination and flexibility. He could find no standard to measure human values that both cultures would accept. He had acquired a cultural indigestion that troubled him the rest of his life.

Whatever of this he suspected on leaving Oxford did not disturb his confidence in his personal future, but it did encourage him to live wholly in the present, since to look beyond it was too confusing. He had not stopped to wonder whether Professor J. Russell Smith had been right, and Europe had spoiled him for America. Travel was supposed to broaden, but although it had widened the ground on which Angus stood it had not added to his stability; it had only increased his reluctance to narrow down again. Oxford had made him more speculative, but this is not a speculative age; more tolerant of ideas, but this is not an intellectually tolerant half century; more critical of mediocrity in a period which glories in it under the misapprehension that it is democracy.

Oxford had shown him diversity where he had thought to find unity. It had trained him to be a scholar and then convinced him he would never be a good one. Yet he knew no other trade or mode of thought. His interests inclined him toward a more active life and vaguely toward public affairs, yet he knew that his acquired distaste for the predatory life and the goldfish bowl would make him ill at ease in the market place or in politics. And he remembered the advice of Sir Alan Anderson, Deputy Governor of the Bank of England, just after he had returned from sessions on the gold standard in Wall Street and Washington: "If you want a successful political career in America, forget all about it until you have made money or a success at law; then make the transfer."

In the first years after Oxford, Angus found that exponents of the academic and business worlds each regarded him as belonging a little too much to the other, and in time he found they were right. He bore the brand of the intellectual profession, and in America that brand is as permanent as an Indian caste mark and almost as limiting. Neither he nor society could be unconscious of it, and Angus was often mystified as well as annoyed when, by some eerie insight, men he met casually and who knew nothing of him called him "Doctor"—which, even more ironically, he was not.

All that was yet to come when the confident young cosmopolite, holding a promising job with the Oxford University Press, embarked for home. He saw no grounds for anything but satisfaction with Oxford and himself. He did not realize how completely he was to be caught between an old world and a new, and how little Oxford and all his education would help him to reconcile the human and the mechanical, the quantitative and the qualitative, the social animal and the eager ego. He had completed with honors and popularity one of the finest schoolings the world had to offer, and he had made England a second home. As the *Aquitania* bore the brave prodigal back to his native land, he heard no sardonic notes in the voices of the sea gulls. Angus was educated, and the gods of irony were getting ready to have their laugh out.

V

Exploration

ONE'S impressions of any country are partly reflections of one's own emotions there. England would always represent to Angus the happiness of purposeful endeavor. That is real happiness, perhaps the most dependable men ever find, but to Angus it was a familiar one raised to new peaks of challenge and satisfaction. England also gave him masculine friendships, permanent because based on common values, and it gave him a sense of security in the solid and unequivocal permanence of the English spirit. Endeavor, friendship, and security are good emotions but elementary ones, and though Angus did not know it, maturity demanded something more.

The Continent offered him expansion of spirit, and Angus got there all of it his personal limitations would allow. The process gave him happiness of a more illuminating kind: like a blind man whose eyes by some miracle discern suddenly a new world of color and variety under dazzling sunlight, Angus discovered beauty and the freedom of emotional release.

Some of this was not due to the Continent as it was, but to the Continent as mirrored in Angus' eyes. While Oxford and England meant strenuous effort, the Continent offered relaxed and wandering irresponsibility. In England Angus worked contentedly; in France or Italy he savored enthusiastically. He never knew whether this distinction was valid to others, or would have been valid to him if he had studied at Rome or the Sorbonne and made England his holiday playground. But even then, England would have been like the virtues of its durable tweeds and cockneys, and the gray permanence of its buildings and its judgments. France, Italy, and Spain would still have stood for silk, sun, and sensation. Angus loved England with the comfortable confidence of marriage, but for thirty years he carried on an exciting amour with the Continent.

Part of its charm lay in the sense of anonymity it always gave him as he steered his free and impecunious course from Bruges to Taormina like a slightly straightened demigod. He could play whatever role he pleased in the tolerant and incurious atmospheres of Paris and Venice and Vienna, and in his various impersonations he began to discover his own variety. In the same week he could be the serious scholar, the American playboy, or the dusty hiker, and each part was, for the moment, sincerely himself. There was a romantic flavor in emerging on rare occasions from the cocoon of shapeless flannels into his one sartorial splendor from Hanover Square, carefully packed under climbing boots and Skeat's Anglo-Saxon grammar. It was like the Arabian Nights to spend an unexpected month in Corsica financed by a successful fling in the Monte Carlo casino.

American students welcomed the Oxford holidays of six weeks at Christmas and Easter and four months in the summer as chances to see the Continent and the sun. But Oxford required evidence of study on one's return, and the enormous leather bag Angus dragged across Europe bulged with heavy books from the Balliol library. The pleasures of the Café de la Paix, the fiesta at Seville, or the ascent of Mont Blanc were tempered but also spiced by the guilty awareness of unopened texts of *Piers Plowman* and John Locke.

The system led to unique mental associations. Vienna would always be linked with the *Canterbury Tales,* sickeningly sweetened with liquor chocolates and eased by Strauss waltzes in the Prater; Taormina would forever remind him of sunlit pages of Sisam's *Fourteenth Century Verse and Prose* on the Castelmola parapet, and Montparnasse recalled the blending of streethawkers' cries with the poems of the seventeenth-century metaphysicians. Often in Ajaccio or Andalucía Angus would feel that he ought to be hard at work in some shabby Ebury Street lodging or in a bright but horrid cottage for paying guests in Devon. Later he concluded that the pictures in the Pitti Palace or the early-morning black coffee and hard-boiled egg with the peasants at Les Halles were better education than Chaucer on the astrolabe, and that Chaucer would have agreed.

On most of his Continental safaris from Oxford Angus traveled alone, not from preference but from economic complications. He usually knew where he wanted to go, and had to travel very cheaply to get so far; most of his friends preferred to see less in order to study more, or live a little more comfortably. They were not willing, as Angus was, to cut themselves off from letters from home and from everyone they knew, or to stagger with heavy bags the mile from station to hotel, to save the taxi fare for a trip to Fiesole. They lacked Angus' inherited capacity to eat the cheapest food without depression, or forgo an occasional cocktail at the Ritz Bar or the comforts of second-class travel overnight. Angus rather enjoyed two weeks on bread and soup in Bâle to recoup finances exhausted by one glorious evening with American girls at Maxim's, in Paris. A few Rhodes Scholars were like him, but each had fixed his eyes on a different goal for the holidays, from Stockholm to Lisbon, and in the urgencies of exploration there are few happy compromises.

So Angus would join friends for a week or two in Paris or Florence and then be off again on his picaresque own. He saw more than most others and made more casual acquaintances along the way, but those contacts were temporary because they were peripatetic. In all his semisolitary travels he was not once lonely enough to think of changing his plans. It was only thirty years later that he realized, with a sense of shock, that all his travels across Europe in his Oxford days did not bring him a single permanent close friend. His treks to Gibraltar or Girgenti were like his later expedition through life, and for the same reason. In both he preferred to travel light. He would not merge very long with any social group whose ways of spending time and money were not precisely his own. The cost was high in friendships but it seldom seemed to him too high.

Looking back, however, at his first years of Continental exploration, Angus realized that though he claimed to have traveled alone he was almost always temporarily attached to others. What he lost in continuity of personal associations he gained in variety. He shot grouse over the former preserve of Franz Josef with Viennese sportsmen imposing in their effortful tradition of Bernard Shaw knickerbockers, Mercedes Benzes, and bristling mustaches. Three weeks with an Austrian family at a country house near Graz gave him an impression of what pre-Sarajevo life in the upper classes of Germany and Austria must have been like, and it was warmly disarming. Back of his host's *pro forma* domestic fierceness lay a pattern of family felicity new to Angus. But there was sadness beneath the cheerful and affectionate surface: in the brilliant son who had taken the university's highest degree, but for five years had found no employment and was eating his heart out in frustrated ambition; in the blonde daughter who yearned to see—just once—an American rodeo before she gave her life to the distasteful rounds of a Viennese society struggling to maintain the grandeurs of a vanished past; and in the old General himself, torn between admiration of the Germany of his youth and fear of its economic hegemony over his beloved Vienna.

On other holidays Angus lived intimately with other new friends. He tramped through the steep mountains of Corsica with a staff member of the Geographic Society, who fired his ambitions for more remote and arduous exploration. There were the weeks in a chalet under Mont Blanc with Angus' Oxford tutor and his family—days of climbing and study and nights of elevated arguments or samplings of the Anglo-Catholic volumes of its owner, the famous "Sligger" Urquhart of Balliol.

Then there was the brief idyl with two English sisters, begun in the mutual airless suffering of a third-class night train from Paris to Rome. The older, a dancer in the London ballet, presided with spritely camaraderie over a mild sirocco of tender passion that must have amused more than it troubled her. For the younger sister, dewy with shyness, beauty, and the romance of a first trip to Italy, turned Angus overnight into a perspiring pulp of restrained sentiment as the trio explored the Villa d'Este, the seven hills, and the Colosseum by moonlight. All three knew the devotion would not survive the chilly realities of London, but that did not make it less warm while it lasted. And, everywhere, there were American girls, calling for letters at American Express offices, atop the Gornergrat and the Eiffel Tower, popping their vivacious heads out of first- and second-class compartments from Inverness to Reggio. Almost invariably eager, friendly, energetic, and comely, almost invariably accompanied by harassed aunts from Lake Forest or Santa Barbara, they were not above whispered connivance to escape from chaperonage for an hour at the Lido or in the local casino. Some of those gay intervals initiated lifelong acquaintance.

All such interludes were in contrast to Angus' British friendships, and the comparison threw light on the ways of England and the Continent. In The Weald of Kent Angus acquired a second home. It would have been miracle enough for an unacquainted young American to find an English country house full of unvarying welcome of the undemonstrative British kind, where he could stay for days or months. Merely to walk the green lawns under broad oaks and chattering rooks ("no respecters of persons," as the Master of Balliol had remarked to relieve the embarrassment of an untoward descent); merely to be given the daily routine of family life and good food; merely to be able to succumb at squash to a septuagenarian colonel who fought the Boer War, the Labor government, and his squash opponent with equally vigorous invective; merely to have the chance to bat out "fours" off the bowling of the local curate and village postman, or to receive and obey the secret instructions of his hostess at her tennis parties ("now win"; "now lose")—these would have been more than good enough. But to be treated like a favorite nephew; put to bed and read out loud to when judged to be ill; to bring the soiled linen of an Oxford term and take it away freshly laundered; to become the godfather of a family grandchild, were more than one could hope for or deserve.

Angus fell comfortably into an established routine very different from that of his Long Island home or Continental pensions. One's days were one's own except for a few inviolate conformities. Angus must drink (or otherwise dispose of) his early morning tea, be on time for meals, pass the watercress sandwiches and make polite conversation with the forbidding rector's wife at exactly five o'clock, dress for dinner and always circulate the port decanter clockwise. It was over the port that Angus received the most well-intended but unacceptable compliment of his life. His host, normally the most impeccably courteous of Englishmen, embarrassed the company by indulging his vestigial but emphatic disapproval of all Americans. A New Zealand friend of Angus' finally summoned up his courage to interrupt the barrage:

"But, sir, you forget that Angus here is an American."

The Colonel stopped, stared at Angus as though he had never seen him before, and then remarked with finality:

"Nonsense! Angus is not an American. He is a gentleman."

The Colonel might not have thought so had he seen Angus in his more plebeian moments on the Continent. But not all his associations were plebeian in the economic sense, for several fortunate chances gave him a wide range of social acquaintance. One of them made him the vacation tutor for a tour of Europe by a likable big son of Texas oil. Angus saw from a Daimler the

Italy he had discovered in charabancs and on foot. He viewed the Riviera this time from the windows of the Negresco Hotel and the rose gardens of villas at Cannes. Angus' efforts to inject in his pupil the minimum of ancient history that Princeton then required further widened his acquaintance. As they sat in the Garden of the Alhambra, Angus, in a desperate attempt to make Themistocles more than a name to his amiable Texan, compared him to Sam Houston. At this point a Dundrearied figure in weather-beaten tweeds sitting alone within hearing approached, and with shy apologies in a very English accent said, "My name is Dawkins," professed his interest in this unusual pedagogy, and inquired whether that was the standard method of teaching in America. He then delivered a brilliant little lecture on Themistocles that left Angus and his pupil with open mouths. At its close he hesitated and then said: "As you see, I am vaguely acquainted with Themistocles, but do relieve my ignorance; who is Samuel Houston?" He became a charming friend who accompanied and enriched their Spanish travels, but Angus never quite overcame the shock when he discovered, on returning to Oxford, that Mr. Dawkins was the Regius Professor of Byzantine and Modern Greek.

Traveling in France with the Oxford Rugby team brought the broadest social range of all. With the son of a leading public school headmaster and an Australian medical student, Angus lunched with one of the great French generals of World War I and spent several hours that night in a Lyons gendarmerie. There the officers of the law who had brought them in for driving a borrowed Citroën without a license genially cooked them a magnificent omelet and took them home in a police wagon, all singing, at three in the morning. On another occasion Angus and the son of an Anglican bishop drank champagne with former Premier Herriot and later the same night dodged bottles of much inferior champagne hurled at them from the windows of a more notorious mansion by young women less exalted. Angus was the chief target of their ire and their surprisingly accurate aim because he had rescued, at the penultimate moment, a younger English team-mate from their dangerous embraces. On the Continent the sordid and the beautiful were sometimes inextricably entangled, and Angus made no attempt to separate them. He was still a Quaker but his puritanism was growing frayed at the edges.

Angus had no facility at languages. The ten Greek words that had helped him to membership in Phi Beta Kappa, and the few phrases of French, German, Spanish, and Latin gained in many years of language courses, helped him almost not at all. When he found that out, it was his first disillusion about education. He could have learned more French in three months with a French family than by three years with Fraser and Squair's *French Grammar,* and learned it far more pleasantly. If American schools and colleges did not teach modern languages for purposes of speaking and understanding speech, what was the purpose of offering them? Were they taught primarily to train the mind? Angus believed he could have acquired better mental discipline from the study of logic or physics or elementary jurisprudence, which might have been useful as well. If the purpose of language courses was to introduce the student to foreign literature, the method was inefficient and the end could have been far better achieved by reading French and German books in English translations.

English youths were taught by the same grammatical method as Americans, and fared little better on the Continent. But in the countries of Europe he came on boys and girls no better educated in other respects than their English and American contemporaries, who had effective speaking mastery of several foreign languages. They had, of course, the advantages of greater motivation, for to them foreign languages were not dead things in books and grammars but living tongues spoken by people almost next door, and essential to general communication. Angus spent many hours in maturity painfully working on phrase books and newspapers to learn the languages school and college had failed to give him.

So he traveled back and forth across western Europe with only a few phrases in any tongue except his own, and found most Americans doing likewise. In his case it was less of a handicap than he had feared, for even in remote spots in Sicily, Spain, and Scandinavia he got on comfortably. But his inability to converse at any length with the people he was so curious about seemed to him a tragedy of education. His loss was greatest in communication with the educated classes of Continental countries; with peasants, tradesmen, and children he was able to gain more rapid understanding.

Angus consoled himself by discovering that his handicap had compensations, and thought that someone should write an essay in defense of verbal illiteracy. Ignorance of languages throws the traveler on his ingenuity, and on the more primitive resources of human exchange, and sometimes they go deeper than facile words. Nothing arouses more easily the sympathy of others, at least in the less sophisticated areas of Europe, than an obviously well-meaning young man struggling to convey some need; Sicilian villagers and Bavarian artisans did not give up until they had made out what Angus was trying to say. The episodes almost always ended in smiles, good nature, and general friendliness all round. Distress and good humor combined are more universally appealing than any words, as Angus learned when he sat (obviously trying to be sporting about it) with a peasant woman's constantly damper baby in his lap on a crowded bus from Rome. By the time he was relieved of his burden at Tivoli, every one of the passengers was his amused and cordial comrade, though no intelligible words had passed between them.

This was good training for Angus, who found that to travel without languages he must drop his self-consciousness. It was easier to do that when he was without companions, where no one knew him, and where the stammering tourist was a frequent experience for the natives. When, in desperation, he once conveyed his need to buy new garters at the Grands Magasins du Louvre by planting his foot on the counter and exhibiting his worn-out pair, the method brought him not only a startlingly exotic purchase but a lesson in the effectiveness of sign language. Thereafter he made the most of it. He doubted that a European without English would have been as generously received in America; that was a form of internationalism in which the Continentals came off best. The most friendly Europeans, with a few exceptions, were in the lower classes, and Angus came to know and like them better than their "superiors." Though Europe was historically the parade ground of kings and aristocrats, it became to Angus the proving ground of the democratic spirit. It was only in the Grand Hotels patronized by the prosperous that he found porters and waiters infected by the snobbery of their clientele. Among the more cultivated Continentals Angus met were some whose fine sensitivities and humanity it would be hard to duplicate in America, but he came on rather more who put class or economic boundaries around their emotions of sympathy and justice.

In breadth of sympathy the middle and upper classes of America seemed to Angus superior to comparable Europeans. If an American was generous at all, he was universally generous, less from tutelage or *noblesse oblige* than from instinct. If he were angered at the mistreatment of a child, he would be equally angry whoever the child. If he saw an animal mistreated, his reactions would be identical whether the persecutor was in polo jodhpurs or a coal-dealer's burlap apron. If a rich young man seduced the decent daughter of a workman, such an American would think it just as reprehensible as if the girl were a country club debutante—in fact more so, since the young man had used his wealth to unfair advantage.

Angus had thought those undiscriminating reactions common to all decent mankind until in Europe he came on other points of view. A young Oxford man was expected to behave with the greatest propriety toward girls of the upper classes, but if he seduced the daughter of his landlady it was a somewhat amusing though hushed peccadillo, pardonable if he did "the right thing" with a few pounds a month for a year or so. And some European gentlemen who were charming to the children of their friends would automatically push or even knock aside less attractive and well-born urchins who got in their way in crowded streets.

When English youths described the canings administered in the name of discipline by schoolmasters, or the fagging imposed by top-formers in the best English schools; when French or German young men recounted somewhat similar experiences, Angus was not convinced of the merits of the systems. His own minor hazings and bullyings had not been organized or maintained by his teachers as self-government or a fine old tradition. When he saw cart-horses whipped until they shuddered in the streets of Naples, Manchester, and Marseilles, without protest or even apparent interest from well-dressed passers-by, Angus' hackles rose almost as much against the indifferent spectators as against the perpetrators.

During Easter week in Seville he sat at a bullfight beside his redheaded friend from Texas—a state most Europeans of 1923 regarded as semicivilized—and watched defenseless, half-starved horses disemboweled for the edification of *aficionados*. The big Texan was so shocked that he suddenly went berserk and began to flail with his fists every Spaniard within reach, crying tears of pure anger. Angus finally got a half nelson on his friend and forced him from the stadium, but he secretly gloried in the devastation American humanitarianism had wrought on Spanish cruelty, and was a little ashamed that New York had not joined Texas in the fray.

That episode suggested that culture meant one thing to most Europeans and quite another to Americans. The American may have a lower standard in manners and the arts than the European of equivalent class, but he has a stronger sense of the relation of culture to daily action. America is dominated by a Protestant emphasis on "faith through works" and is in the habit of judging men by how they act. No matter how primitive may be the philosophy and emotions of the American, he stands more instinctively for kindness to all living things and equal justice to all humanity.

Even in the matter of sportsmanship Angus found no overwhelming distinction in favor of England. As a former player of American football he was familiar with foul play behind the back of the referee, and was delighted with the normal English tradition of clean sportsmanship. It was pleasant after American collegiate semiprofessionalism to see English Rugby played hard but played for fun. But as the only American to play Rugby three years for the Oxford varsity, he had experiences that forced him to qualify his admiration of British sporting habits. In his first game against Cambridge—the only game each side was as eager to win as Yale is to beat Harvard—and just after he had shaken hands with King George V, Angus went on the field expecting an exceptionally clean contest. He was determined, as the first American on the field since 1907, not to risk the slightest infraction of the rules and thus bring discredit on America. Within ten minutes he found himself on the receiving end of more deliberate foul play than he had met in four years of American varsity football. He was not a special target because he was an American, but he was specially vulnerable because he did not feel able to fight back. By the second year he was better prepared and less noble, and evened the score. On Rugby tours he found that each nationality had its own special definitions of fair play. The roughest opponents were the Scotch and Irish, but Angus never received from them an injury that was deliberate. The nations that talked the most about the ethics of sport, and the nations that entertained the visiting team most royally after the game, were more likely to kick a man when he was down, and in the most vulnerable areas—if it was a game that must be won. The only difference from America was that there were fewer games Europeans really wanted to win.

This was education, and for once it revealed some unity, at least in human nature. Given similar incentives, men act much the same; the variations are matters of local custom. The English sports tradition was in many ways superior to the American; it was on the whole higher education, but it was not above its compromises in the pinches. Angus could not have learned so much about the general uniformity, and the national variations, of human nature if he had spent all of his three years in the Bodleian library.

In a few matters like these, the Europe Angus saw in the 1920s increased his respect for America. Europe professed democracy, and in some respects its version seemed more elevated than our own, but not in the basic relations between all men. The European divisions between economic classes seemed to Angus too rigid; they established barriers almost impossible for the individual to surmount, unless he were exceptionally able or exceptionally lucky. The peasant or domestic servant must reconcile himself to being a peasant or a domestic servant all his life. That fact robbed most Europeans of incentives and mental liberties Americans take for granted. It also robbed their nations of the full use of the talents of their citizens, for manpower means something more than a total of the employable. Even communication between the social classes of Europe was difficult, and inadequate to democratic exchange. The flexibility of American life, with its free and easy access and communications, might lead to brashness and bad manners, but at least it was more effective democracy of the spirit.

The people of the Continent also suffered from a confusion between pride in their cultural inheritance, which was justified, and devotion to the ways and limitations of the past, which was not. The results went deeper than English lack of plumbing and the primitive plows and machinery of the Continent. Habitual dependence on the ways of one's ancestors had also led Europeans to a lack of confidence in the present and the future. If the somewhat pessimistic attitudes of most European intellectuals were only a fashionable pose, it was a silly one. If they represented the wisdom of a mature culture, then cynicism about men's motives and upward progress might be justified—but there could be no progress unless people believed progress possible. Were not Americans, with all their excessive emphasis on material achievement, wiser in assuming that human improvement was possible, and acting accordingly?

The American faith in the perfectibility of man had brought Americans many good things, including standards of living that most Europeans envied. It also gave them an inner optimism that was on the side of personal happiness. Granted that high wages, high productivity, and domestic comforts do not assure higher culture, they were nevertheless bringing to Nebraska farm wives freedoms and opportunities that German *Hausfrauen* and well-born Spanish señoras yearned for. American optimism might be merely emotional adolescence, but adolescence meant a youthful spirit, and the great ages like the Renaissance and Elizabethan England had possessed it.

Angus never could reconcile the beauty and wisdom of Europe with its sordid commonplaces; the magnificence of its survivals of the past with the poverty and defeatism of its present. He was aware that the Europe from which he was skimming the cream was far from creamy underneath. He was not exploring the Europe painfully familiar to the unemployed German intellectual, to the Calabrian peasant toiling on rocky hillside acres for a landlord at ease on the Riviera, to the inhabitants of the long rows of dark hovels in England's Black Country, or to the superannuated Paris mechanic barely existing on a pitiful pension. But Angus had walked too many hours through the depressing squalor of European cities not to know that that Europe existed too. America had its slums, but Americans thought of them as temporary excrescences and they were slowly vanishing. The Europe of the 1920s seemed to accept its own economic inequities as unhappily inevitable forever.

In Europe one saw, as one could not see in America, the finest of man's creations through the ages, but the generations that had built them were also generations of war, filth, disease, and starvation; cathedrals and art masterpieces had not made these evils less prevalent in modern times. Even worse, perhaps, was the narrowness of life and prospects for those very peasants and petty tradesmen Angus had found so outwardly cheerful. American tourists would not conceive of living in the ancient cottages they found so picturesque, yet they were the primitive and insanitary homes of a large part of Europe's millions. In the decencies and securities of living it was America, with all its cultural poverty, that seemed superior. Where was modern Europe moving, Angus wondered in the 1920s: toward a recrudescence of the spirit and ideals that built the Cologne cathedral, or toward future starving and bitter Germans like those Angus saw in 1923; toward the sunlit spaciousness of the Paris of the slum-clearing Boulevard Haussmann or toward an expansion of the rapacities and defeatisms so evident in the Paris of 1925?

To attempt to estimate the over-all assets and liabilities of any culture posed problems of judgment for which neither travel nor education seemed to provide an answer. In evaluating total Italian culture in 1925, did the Sistine Chapel offset the ignorance and poverty within a mile of it? Did Westminster Abbey and the quality of Parliament make up for the drabness and vulgarity of most of London? Did the endurance and integrity of the French peasant—not to mention Sainte Chapelle—redeem his provinciality and the political chaos that was the Chamber of Deputies? What is the real level of the current civilization of Naples, and how can that level be measured against the over-all culture of Amsterdam or Chicago? It seemed to Angus essential to measure such values if one were to know where society was going, and yet how to measure them seemed insoluble. Angus, brought up to believe that cleanliness was almost godliness, that private morality outlawed tax evasion and sexual promiscuity, that government should insist on equal justice for all its citizens, realized he was too prejudiced to judge. Travel was making him more, not less, confused about values.

Such thoughts were of course only occasional amid the pleasures of exploration and the excitements of discovering varieties of beauty he had never known. Of all that the Continent gave Angus, its most valuable gift, because he had lacked it so completely, was the revelation of the importance of creative art. Long before he went to Oxford, Angus had recognized without dismay that he had no creative talent in the arts and only a Philistine's appreciation of them. This did not prevent him from enjoying what he liked and from trying, perhaps with too much docility, to understand what he did not. At first the challenge of galleries and concert halls was primarily intellectual, though many times they gave him a pleasure he had not anticipated. Whether his reactions were mental or emotional, they were sometimes overwhelming. In spite of cursory visits to the Metropolitan Museum, he had not really believed the treasures of beauty could be so abundant that there would be a Louvre and also a Prado, a Vatican gallery, an Uffizi, and all the collections of Dresden, Vienna, Amsterdam, and the rest. And their abundance was matched by the architecture of the Continent. No previous reading or reproductions had prepared him for the first impact of the perfection of Sainte Chapelle, the twilight magnificence of Milan cathedral and its colored glass, or the bright gaiety of the Duomo at Florence. When he first stood in the square before Notre Dame de Paris he would not have been in the least surprised to see Quasimodo clambering among its gargoyles.

Many other interests had priority over galleries and monuments during Angus' first excursions to the Continent. He always went to the markets, for he liked to see what produce was brought there, and to watch it bargained for, bought and sold. But he was conscientious about seeing the local masterpieces, and as he saw more of them his pleasure in man-made art increased. What had begun as an intellectual endeavor necessary to a well-rounded young man, with Baedeker as textbook, became a pilgrimage for its own sake. When he finally gained the courage to look at painting and sculpture and cathedrals with his own eyes and emotions he was surprised and delighted at how much more he saw and enjoyed. After a while he used his guide-book only for convenient facts, and leaned less on the exalted critics; if he did not understand or agree with Ruskin or Pater he was not ashamed. In reaction to his previous artistic insecu-rity he then became too confident in his judgments and too in-tolerant of what he did not like, but these were at least better faults than his previous sycophancy. When in Florence in his Oxford days Angus declined a chance to meet Bernard Berenson from the conviction that Berenson would be unintelligible to him and that he would look a fool to Berenson. Later when he did visit the famous man at his villa, he found he had been a fool for neglecting earlier opportunities. But that illumination came much later, at about the time he found that some paintings that had previously meant nothing to him were now messengers of revelation. He had lost much understanding by being too much concerned with the subject matter of art; it was many years be-fore he could appreciate any painting of St. Sebastian because he did not like to see a naked man stuck with arrows.

Angus' first unalloyed vision of Greek beauty came not from the Venus de Milo or the Winged Victory, but in an unexpected moment so thrilling that he never forgot it. On a slow and dismal night train from Sicily to Naples he read in the dim light of a crowded third-class compartment that the "rapido" stopped south of Naples at a place called Paestum. The name was vaguely familiar; he thought there was something Greek there. In the blackness of pre-dawn January he shoved his kit bag off the train and followed it. No one else descended and the train pulled away, leaving him alone on a dark and deserted platform. Even the omnipresent Italian dog was missing. Angus half hid his bag in some vague shrubbery and started to walk toward what he hoped was the west. He had gone perhaps a mile when the sky behind him began to lighten. He turned round, and at the first gleam of the sun found himself standing squarely in front of the most beautiful building he had ever seen. Against the orange disk just appearing above the rugged line of black mountains to the east, the tops of even temple columns showed, first dark and then rosy pink as the sky turned from black to deep violet to mauve to blue. Some aromatic plant gave flavor to the still cold air, and he could hear cowbells in the distance and the first calls of birds near by. The rest was silence; the temple rose from the flat pasture as the sun moved down its columns. Over it to the north a pale wisp trailed from the cone of Vesuvius. If Angus had known a Greek invocation he would probably have repeated it.

The temples of Girgenti gave him something of the same sensations, but when he first saw them they were cluttered with sightseers like himself. It was many years later that Angus caught a comparable moment of that completely impersonal exaltation, this time in the best of company. He stood with her on the high plateau before Segesta and saw its temple stand out against the green mountains of Sicilian spring like the most enduring of all classic dreams. Dark clouds hurrying from Africa hurled themselves across a late afternoon sky and filtered light and shadow upon the rolling, wide valley beneath. A solitary goat, that most Greek of all animals, munched indifferently in the shelter of the temple steps; otherwise they were alone. . . . To gaze over the Bernese Oberland from the hard-won ridge of the Wetterhorn was exaltation too, but there one's sense of infinite majesty was too remote from all mankind except oneself. It was confused by the sense of personal conquest in reaching the top, and by the nervous fear of getting safely down. Before Paestum and Segesta the elevation was enhanced by earlier men but unalloyed by self.

Yet of all the pleasures of European exploration the greatest to Angus was the sight of new mountains and valleys, plains and villages. Natural scenery gave him more effortless delight than any of the works of man. Even Paestum and Segesta had brought their revelation of the Greeks because they had been set perfectly in the frame of nature. The curve of the mountainous coastline where Italy meets France, the immaculate white of the Matterhorn, the turbulent rush of the Isère near Grenoble, the watery

chasm of Sogne Fiord, the blue sea mirroring the Dantesque red
rocks of Piana, the lush fertile meadows of Denmark—each of
these brought an elation purer and more spontaneous than even
El Greco's St. Ignatius or Hadrian's Arch or Chartres. Natural
beauty asked nothing of the intellect, for it was beyond understanding; Angus' pleasure in it was wholly unself-conscious.

And yet, again, the finest beauties of nature were not quite
perfect to Angus without some unobtrusive evidence of man.
Meadows were the better for being neat and loved; the rocks
of Piana were enhanced by the stone steps the Genoese had cut
from the mountain to the sea. An upland Swiss valley, friendly
and flower-strewn in the June sun, was incomplete without the
tinkling of cowbells and a distant group of steep-roofed houses
around a solid little church. The rocky pinnacles of inland Sicily
were merely grimly spectacular unless the eye could detect,
emerging from their rough rocks, the storybook cluster of ancient
walls and habitations. The green flatness of Dutch polders under
their shifting purple light gained meaning from the brown cir-
cling fans of the windmills. Pompeii was disappointing because it
was a dead relic, made the more lifeless by voluble guides and
chattering tourists. Better no one at all, or the solitary goat of
Segesta. Later Angus would find the grand sweep of the Rockies
an overpowering but empty boast of nature, less pleasing than
the peopled foothills of the Pyrenees and the sudden shepherd in
the Apennines. Mountains and sea were majesty, but majesty
needs humanity to warm its heart. Nature alone diminished man
more than Angus liked.

He was far from mystical, but something he could not understand touched him on his first view of the Scottish Lowlands. As
the train wound through the open hills of Dumfries and the
shaded vales of Lanark, Angus had the sensation he was coming
home. Everything seemed familiar; surely he had been there before. He must have waded in that quiet pool and sat over oat
cakes and tea in that upland cottage. He crossed the Border

many times after that, but never without a sensation of native belonging. Yet no member of his family had been in Scotland since
a great-grandfather left the lowland farm a century earlier, and
Angus knew Scotland chiefly from Stevenson and Scott. Was
this unsought and unexpected emotion only romantic imagination or was it something deeper?

Whether in Scotland or Andalucía, it was line more than color
that gave Angus pleasure. The outline of an Etruscan village, the
bare swelling curves of Westmorland hills, or the spread of a
white oak in a Cotswold meadow gave him more delight than
even the Tyrian purple of Ravello sunsets or the shafts of lumi-
nous light on Vermeer's checkered tiles and rounded figures.
Angus' first purchases of "art" were etchings, where line was un-
complicated by color: a Brangwyn tree storm-lashed against a
threatening sky, the bare bones of a roofless little church in Old
Aldgate, and Dürer's clean outlines of human hands and figures
pregnant with action. Many years later Holland would win him
to the perfection of colors in its skies and interiors, and in the
artists who could re-create them. When Dutch skies led him to
the discovery of the Dutch painters' fidelity to their light, and
then on to Van Gogh, nature began to illuminate art as color,
and set Angus off on a reappraisal of all his values in painting
and scenery.

Appreciation of color should have been the beginning rather
than the end of education, but it was still in Angus' future when
Oxford and his *Wanderjahre* came to an end. It was not the Continent's fault that he had stayed half blind, for like Oxford it had
offered him its best. He could accept only what he could see, and
even that much left him dazzled. He ended as confused about
beauty and mankind as Oxford left him confused about wisdom
and ethics. The confusions were only temporarily forgotten as
Angus stood on the afterdeck of the westbound *Aquitania* for his
last glimpse of the Scilly Isles. America would add its new uncertainties to the educated young gentleman's mental potpourri,

and it would not resolve the older ones. But it would never duplicate the elations he had known in the lands he was reluctant to be leaving.

Back home after nearly four years, Angus was asked by family and friends to tell them "all about Oxford." This was a rhetorical request born of good will, for often, like Herod, the questioner did not pause for a reply. But Angus could at least begin to tell something of what Oxford meant to him, for Oxford's significance to his education was largely tangible. When someone inquired what had meant most to him on the Continent, Angus knew he could not even embark on an answer. What words or pictures could he offer that could convey the stone-damp smell of Rome after a spring rain, or the mixed sensations of one's first view of Ronda or Rothenburg or Taormina? How can one describe, even if one could bring oneself to expose such personal emotions, the feeling that within one something unknown has been stirred and something new has begun to grow? Angus could not even clarify his emotions about the Continent to himself. All he knew was that the moments that had lifted him highest above himself were in lands whose languages he could not speak. Cecil Rhodes had conceived a great vision and had let Angus share it, but the Continent had given him glimpses of still greater visions he could never wholly share.

America was Angus' native land and had his first devotion. But Europe would always be a symbol of the highest moments of his youth and of his first intimations of a beauty beyond the power of a mechanistic America or an inadequate Angus to recreate. Europa was after all a woman, with a woman's infinite variety and power to stir men not by words but by nuances and half-promises. Reputedly old and cynical, she could always recall to Angus the excitements of youth and the sensation of indestructible *élan*.

VI

The Academic Mind

A MAN who makes a career of education *faute de mieux* does not merit its best rewards. It treated Angus better than he deserved. At twenty-eight he was a Dean at Swarthmore and an American officer of the Rhodes Trustees. Four years later he was Master of Pierson College and Director of Admissions at Yale. At thirty-four he became President of the University of Rochester and served happily there until his resignation fifteen years later.

In these posts his associates were congenial and the atmosphere was stimulating. Since each of the three institutions was an exponent of quality in education and had funds adequate for its essential purposes, Angus could not have been more fortunate in his academic circumstances.

He was aware that his promotions came not because he was a good scholar or teacher but because he was thought to have sound training and some executive ability. When a young man in the collegiate world develops a reputation for administration he is likely to be lifted to power and emoluments greater than those of the most distinguished professors. Angus profited from this, but at the time did not suspect how much he owed to good fortune and good friends.

Comforts and *kudos* are as pleasant in the university world as elsewhere, but university presidents pay a considerable price for them. They have little or no time to teach or do research, or even to think or read, unhurried. Gradually they lose their intellectual habits of mind amid the activities of being the top sergeant of an academic platoon. They acquire a maverick status—a little of a businessman, an educator, a public citizen, a police officer, and a traveling salesman—but into none of those professions are they fully accepted by its regular members. The realities of budgets and buildings keep them on their economic toes, and the mental maneuvers of professors on the tactical alert. They cope in the same day with scientific research, educational theory, public relations, plant maintenance, faculty dissensions, and deans of women. The scope of their outside activities rests partly with themselves, but even the most eremitic of college presidents spends much of his life in airplanes and lower berths; at alumni and directors' meetings, luncheons and conventions. Words are his weapon, omniscience his guise, and indigestion his occupational disease.

Angus never regretted his twenty-two years of academic life. Higher education should be the most distinguished and rewarding of vocations, and at times it seemed so. At other times Angus felt as though he were merely shadowboxing in an artificial contest, or housekeeping for a varied and critical lot of boarders, or trying to keep his finger in the dike of excellence against beating waves of mediocrity. The efforts were strenuous but they were so much concerned with logistics and maintenance that while some of his mental muscles were being stretched others were growing soft. He was like a man enjoying small talk or arguing about drainpipes while the walls of the academic citadel were crumbling about him. He realized that he was losing enthusiasm over the organization and direction of the academic parade. But at the beginning of his university presidency he had no such malaise. He was too busy coping with the immediate problems of his own orientation.

Angus had gone to Oxford determined not to be lured from his main objectives, and he went to Rochester with the same resolution. As a university primate he found many insidious and honorable temptations to dissipate. There was the constant danger of spreading one's mind and words too thinly over endless meetings of educators and uplifters, or becoming known as a willing and omniscient speaker for every kind of occasion. He accepted dutifully the required regimen of platform oratory, and adhered to the proven formula for a presidential address: a judicious mixture of idealism, exhibitionism, and mendicancy. The course of events gave him, in spite of his earlier resolutions, a wide acquaintance in nonacademic circles, and he took a rather juvenile pride in his business and financial directorates. He sometimes amused himself by wondering what would happen if he assembled in one room all his disparate friends, from steel magnates to academic rebels, from football coaches to museum directors.

Gregariousness without intimacy is the professional fate of college presidents. All twentieth-century Americans are more or less victims of the busy bustle and split-second conversations that extend human relations but also make them shallow, and the university president is particularly so. He finds close friendships especially difficult. He is never on quite equal terms with professors who are also his employees, or alumni who are both his products and his patrons. Angus was always annoyed by the silly bit of protocol that made him go first through every local door, for this was a symbol of the formal deference professors feel they should pay to the official priority of the administrator, and citizens to intellectual leadership—even as they privately question the merits of those priorities. They put the relationship of scholar, citizen, and executive on a false basis. President Angell warned Angus as a President-Elect that he would become a man without close friends in the profession, and added: "They treat me as if I were a delicate invalid or a mental case, or with the polite tolerance they would use toward the Dalai Lama or a Harvard man."

College presidents are therefore completely relaxed only when they are well away from their home grounds, but even that is no sure escape, for alumni and undergraduates are everywhere. It is only in the sole company of other college presidents that they can take down their professional hair. Then they delight in comparing their troubles and their stratagems, but enjoy even more the chance to escape from all pretense except the pretense of being unpretentious. Even those friendships are based on mutual sympathy and trade secrets, and rarely go very deep. Contacts are peripatetic, and a sense of rivalry is almost inescapable.

When a professor becomes a president the attitude of his old colleagues subtly changes from easy familiarity to mild discomfort. They seem convinced that academic power corrupts more efficiently than any other kind. As to an imported new president, faculties do not regard that form of free trade with enthusiasm; they are academically protectionist, and view an administrator from without their ranks with the forlorn hope that the trustees have shown better judgment than could be expected. No matter how much a faculty may like its president as a person, professorial confidences about him are woven with vague apprehensions and embroidered with pessimistic conjectures. These negative reactions are tempered by natural good will, by hope that the new president will prove more amenable to promotions than the last, and by a desire to grind a departmental ax with the neophyte before his financial defenses go up.

Any alteration proposed by a president is as dubiously regarded by his faculties as legislation suggested by the White House is viewed by the Senate, and for the same reason: it comes from outside the club. One college president told Angus that his best device for recovering unity in a warring faculty was to urge his own proposals upon it, and thus unify its members against himself. The greatest power in faculties, and sometimes their greatest satisfaction, lie in their capacity to negate. Academic legislation can be applied only by those who teach, and a faculty can easily nullify any university rule by passive resistance in its operation. Successful leadership in a university therefore becomes a test of tact and patience, and for Angus to maintain either for a long period was a major effort.

The first job of a university president is to understand the academic mind; the second is to win its confidence. The third is to support it; the final job is to guide it. Few men achieve all four, but the good administrator must never stop trying. To the outer world the university president is himself a professor and therefore a prejudiced witness, but to the professors themselves he is a possible academic subversive likely to betray them to the misguided policies of trustees, alumni, or large benefactors. Caught between the economic and the scholarly worlds, he is a fully accepted member of neither. The businessman and the teacher each suspects him of catering to the other, and each is sometimes right.

Most college and university administrators sense the suspicion that lies deep in the subconscious of their faculty friends, and are distressed by it. They cannot fully understand it, for most of them are on the side of the academic angels, and Angus was clearly so, for whatever may have been the quality of his mind, its attitudes had been formed by a lifetime of academic conditioning. It is true that a president must wear his academic rue with a difference, for his duty makes him more conscious of budgets, plant maintenance, and public relations than most of his professors. In spite of this, he and his fellow executives are less corrupted by outer materialism than their faculties fear, and are often as clear and firm in their academic ideals as their professorial colleagues. They are in the last analysis sincere champions of what is called the academic mind.

After years of observation Angus concluded that there is really no such standard product as the academic mind. The points of view of professors are no more uniform than their intellectual ability. To assign them a mental unity distinct from the rest of society is to do both a disservice. The academic mind at its best is the nation's keenest intellectual tool; at its worst it is as dull or bent as any other. Professors are even losing the outward marks of their common profession, for their training is no longer similar; the education of a chemist and that of an historian have little in common. Yet the world beyond the campus insists on lumping all academicians together and assigning them common traits. For instance, they are impractical. Angus denied this generalized impeachment though he sometimes found individual educators, like some other people, impractical. It is true that most professors have "never met a payroll," but many businessmen who mouth this cliché have also never met one personally. Few men in large firms are directly concerned with payrolls or even, as the cliché experts really mean, in the balancing of an over-all business budget. Most men in commerce and industry are responsible only for balancing department or personal budgets and keeping themselves or their immediate staffs within them. Every professor who heads an academic department, conducts research on a grant or allocation, or is allowed a secretary or an expense account does likewise. He must cope with his family finances as much as businessmen and Congressmen, and under more difficult circumstances. The instructor who manages to support a wife and child on a three-thousand-dollar salary and still dress decently and keep out of debt could give lessons to many a businessman whose income is considerably larger. Angus knew a few academicians who were notoriously improvident, but the percent of their total is probably no higher than that of other citizens. He was familiar, as the public is not, with the variety of devices invented by academic minds to augment their incomes, and doubted whether most businessmen were more ingenious in that highly practical aspect of life.

Critics of the academic mind are aiming at the wrong target when they call it impractical. They really mean two other things:

that the professor is not worldly and that he is habitually theoretical. When put thus, the impeachments are valid but hardly surprising. If a professor esteemed worldly values as much as the average man he would not be long content to remain a professor, for academic salaries permit few mundane pleasures. He adheres, with varying fidelity, to a somewhat different set of values, rating knowledge for its own sake more highly. To call this impractical is to call all higher learning impractical, which is what some of the critics mean but do not want to say. They cannot understand why men reputed so intelligent care so little about some of the things they value so much.

And yet the academician is slowly winning social and economic acceptance in the atomic age. Men of industry are beginning to appreciate the professor who can master the particular abstractions that trouble them in policy or research. Laymen are more inclined to listen to professors. Even military men have found out that theoretical scientists can be very helpful in developing highly practical gadgets like hydrogen bombs and guided missiles. Businessmen are buying professors in certain fields away from the colleges. Thus far the public has valued academic thinking chiefly when it has paid off in products or profits. The time may come when professorial opinions in humane fields will be equally appreciated and followed by society, but that happy marriage of precept and practice seems very remote. It might come more quickly if humanists did not flaunt their charms too compromisingly, or disguise their culture with too much of the lipstick of the market place. The danger is that when the market place does ultimately turn with appreciation to the humanist ivory tower, it will find that the ivory tower has been converted into a factory for research or a salesroom of applied training, and has nothing more to give.

Since the academic mind should be an open mind, receptive to all new ideas, it tends to be politically a liberal mind. But "liberalism" in our times covers a variety of attitudes and theories, not all of which are free from their own dogma and intolerance. The liberalism of the New and Fair Deals had a very different political and social philosophy, and sometimes very different origins and motivations, from the liberalism of John Stuart Mill, William Ewart Gladstone, or Woodrow Wilson. Many professors, misled by the shibboleths and emotions of liberalism, supported causes they later found were not truly liberal. They failed to distinguish between the liberalism that has as its ultimate goal the independence and self-responsibility of the individual and the liberalism that sacrificed these to the social patronage of the welfare state. Truly liberal intellectuals might have rendered a great national service in the 1930s by formulating a consistent political policy somewhere between reaction and distorted liberalism—a middle ground on which those who favored both social justice and the primacy of the individual could happily stand. In such an effort professors might have led. They did not do so.

Another failure in leadership by the academic mind is its compromise with excessive specialization. Education is undergoing an inflation of its activities that depreciates its moral and intellectual currency. Vocationalism is turning the quest for understanding into the pursuit of what are no more than trade techniques, even when they are glorified by highbrow titles in graduate school catalogues. Specialization is destroying whatever homogeneity the minds of academicians once possessed. By dividing the corpus of knowledge into fragments small enough to master in detail, professors are losing the humanistic unity and spirit for which the learned world has traditionally stood. Though specialization has made a few professors better able to communicate with men in the same specialty in the outside world, it has impaired their ability to communicate with one another. The average physicist and philosopher no longer talk the same language or base their opinions on the same assumptions; intellectually they do not worship the same gods. Either can convey thought more confidently to a foreigner in his own field than to a faculty colleague in another division of study. A national economy that demands specialists, and a national society that admires experts, have led universities to vitiate their aims in order to please popular opinion. A few leaders of education have opposed this fragmentation of knowledge and corruption of humanistic unity; a greater number have deplored it but climbed on the bandwagon.

Democracy is especially vulnerable to loss of unity through educational disintegration, and this is the fundamental social case against excessive specialization. But within a great university it also means dissipation of its energies and resources. Every specialist demands recognition in the curriculum and remembrance in the budget. The academic mind is several minds: the scientific, the humanist, the vocational, the engineering, and the sociological. Each group has its own values and objectives, and the larger the institution the more its cliques consort chiefly within themselves. Each seeks a maximum of administrative independence. Departments clamor to be divisions and divisions to become separate schools. University administration of the mid-century reflects the feudal nature of its educational concepts and the increasing disunity of learning. Expertism has created a solar system in which countless little worlds break off from the central university sun, and each then enlarges as its academic gases expand. The original sun divides into a universe of almost independent bodies, in which its central gravitation is overwhelmed by centrifugal force, until the diminished core can no longer warm or feed its satellites. Diversity overwhelms unity in higher education.

Angus, troubled, wondered whether it was this loss of unity that resulted in another lapse of academic principle. If the American undergraduate college has any purpose beyond the purely intellectual it is to promote ethical principles. At least, thus read the catalogues of most of the colleges and thus speak their leaders. The basis of ethics is honesty, and an institution that fails to pursue the principles it professes deserves neither society's respect nor its own. Angus could condone collegiate tolerance of

weak intellectual standards, frequent deflections toward vocationalism and specialization, and glorifications of physical plant
that impoverish and unbalance educational values. They were all
compromises of circumstance, degree, and judgment, and they
were not wholly within the control of faculties. But on almost
every campus there have been two compromises of expressed
ideals that most professors have accepted and even defended for
decades. One is racial discrimination, and the other is special concessions to athletes.

On both issues Angus knew what he was talking about, for he
had been intimate with them as a student and very closely in
touch with them as Dean and President. He had seen discreet
discrimination against Jews and Negroes in more than one
American college. For many years this discrimination operated,
so far as official action was concerned, in the acceptances and re-
jections of students by admissions committees. For the last two
decades this official kind of discrimination has been distinctly on
the wane, though more as a result of public opinion and legislation than through collegiate leadership. Even the flare of opposition to the admission of Negroes to white schools in the South
after the Supreme Court decision of 1954, though regrettable, was
a negative sign of progress, for it was last-gasp reaction to an advancing public opinion that the Supreme Court at long last recognized and cautiously supported.

With the permission of the colleges, fraternities flourish on
their campuses. Sometimes the local chapters, sometimes their
national organizations, refuse to admit Jews or Negroes. College
officers excuse this discrimination in the social life their colleges
sponsor, on the grounds that fraternities are on the whole valuable contributors to the social welfare of the campus. This
seemed to Angus like praising a man because he is useful or attractive even if he occasionally joins in a lynching.

By 1950 this situation had improved over earlier years, and a
number of fraternities had opened their sacred doors to Jews and
Negroes—but many had not. A few courageous chapters defied

THE ACADEMIC MIND   131

their national organizations in order to admit whom they pleased, but in most cases this defiance was by undergraduates without the inspiration of college authorities and sometimes against the wishes of their graduate brothers. Yet what college president or professor failed to castigate Hitler's mistreatment of the Jews? When undergraduates took the lead against social discrimination, many college and university officers cheered—from the sidelines.

Equally disillusioning as to academic ethics is the athletic situation. It has grown beyond the bounds of healthy exercise to develop physical skills, and even beyond truly amateur competition. Athletes receive a wide variety of indirect compensations and academic favors they would not be granted if they were not athletes. There were many academic occasions that demanded of Angus a sustained minor hypocrisy, at which he became practiced. But none of these occasions so tested his self-control as those on which reputable educators blandly boasted the simon-purity of their own athletics, when they knew some of their auditors knew it was not true.

Angus used to wonder how an intelligent college student could fail to notice the discrepancy between what his college preached and what it did, and how much respect he could then retain for the President and faculty. The student heard overemphasis on athletics deplored but saw stadia built before more-needed library and laboratory equipment was purchased; he saw his fellow students subsidized for their athletic prowess; he watched professionalism infuse and absorb the spirit of his college teams; he learned that the football coach was paid more than the best professor. The average undergraduate found the best athletic facilities preempted for varsity practice, and he saw his college president preside, apparently without embarrassment and from the best stadium seat, over scenes of hysteria, vulgarity, and drunkenness among student and "guest" spectators at big games.

Only a few university leaders, like Hutchins of Chicago, did anything to end the situation, and his drastic action was deplored by most of his presidential associates; if what he said was true, then the rest of them were derelict in their educational responsibilities. No college president should have to be a policeman of his own constituents, and Angus became increasingly bored and irritated by having to walk his athletic beat. He was also constantly disillusioned that so many otherwise mature and honest men could revert to adolescence and chicanery on the subject of collegiate athletics.

The fact that most undergraduates take these athletic hypocrisies for granted shows how effectively their own colleges are conditioning them toward ethical compromise. American youth is, all things considered, remarkable for its honesty, but no one can expect it to develop that virtue without examples. When presidents, professors, and all society assure undergraduates that hypocrisies are not hypocrisies when indulged in by their own college, most young men naturally accept the wisdom of their elders. What American young man does not want his team to win and his fraternity to rank socially at the top? Undergraduates have moments of great prescience, but the merciless perspicacity of the young is only legend. They are often fooled into mistaking demagoguery for idealism, volubility or oft-rehearsed witticisms for intellectual brilliance, a sympathetic manner for warmth of heart, and grave pomposity for profound wisdom. There are few things more persuasive than elevated cant, particularly if it advocates the end one desires. Why should undergraduates take a higher ethical line than their presidents and faculties?

On only one aspect of education is there full academic unity, and that is in defense of academic privileges. Unfortunately, professors as a whole have not been as ardent to meet the responsibilities inherent in their academic freedoms as they have been to claim its privileges. Angus sometimes felt handicapped in defending the academic freedom of some individual on his staff by the fact that the man had made himself vulnerable by his own academic irresponsibility. If, in attacking McCarthyism on a public platform, a professor adopts McCarthy's own methods by making loose charges and misstating facts, how defensible is he? If a professor devotes his classroom periods to urging his students to be for or against a specific political candidate, is his right to do so a question of academic freedom or is his failure to teach the material he contracted to teach a neglect of duty? If an assistant professor running for Congress uses for his campaign, without university authorization, its official stationery, its stamps, and the services of his salaried secretary, is he then justified in claiming that a protest from the President is an attack on his academic freedom? These may be only occasional errors by the academic individual, but other professors often rally round to defend them as academic freedom. They are frequent enough to confuse the issue and damage the real cause of academic freedom.

The local flurries caused by these occasional episodes create an impression in the public mind that professors are radical. Yet what the atmosphere of many American colleges needs is more radicalism of opinion in areas outside politics and headline controversies. Angus wanted more professors who were independent in their nonpolitical ideas, but he found his leftward professors to be just as conventional in their radical opinions as reactionaries are in theirs. He longed for teachers who wear no intellectual uniforms of right or left, who subscribe automatically to no organized clique of opinion, but are loyal only to the challenging independence of their own minds. The colleges need more professors who openly and cheerfully question all values, especially in educational ends and procedures, in social routines and in acceptance of the commonplace.

Higher education would gain by substituting a few leavening intellectual eccentrics for some of the conformists and expansionists and go-getters in its faculties. Every intellectual assemblage needs its devil's advocates, and needs them more in the fields of ideas than in political partisanships. Universities are suffering from a shortage of theoretical iconoclasm and an excess of applied caution. Although radical exhibitionists are a glut on the

academic market, men with brilliant minds who quietly ask
questions that no one has thought of asking; who look at accepted idols with humorous and good-tempered unbelief; who
challenge accepted thought not from frustration or party line but
from Socratean curiosity—men like those are hard to find and
still harder to retain. Modern America does not breed many of
them, and there are faculties, which ought to think them precious, that do not welcome them. And although a president like
Angus may in theory desire a little more professorial eccentricity,
in practice the only individual thinkers he can get are likely to
prove less original in ideas than indiscreet in conduct, and become more trouble than they are worth.

Probably every educator in America has tried to define the
aims of education, but definitions that are clever are never adequate, and those that are adequate are certainly not succinct.
After forty years of exposure to education Angus could not even
define it to his own satisfaction. An imperfect definition has,
however, some value, and Angus found the one offered by
Henry Adams to be the most provocative: "The young man himself, the subject of education, is a certain form of energy; the object to be gained is the economy of his force."

The definition unfortunately lends itself to various interpreta-
tions by educators of all breeds to justify their own activities—a
fact which would have annoyed Adams. The vocationalist, the
engineer, and the scientist each could claim that he was teaching youth to use his force economically. Force can be whatever
one defines it to be, from ions to ideals, and few men have read
Adams' definition or taken the trouble to find out just what he
meant by it.

Angus thought he knew what Adams meant, but was not sure
that education should aim primarily at economy of force however defined, any more than nature does. The natural world is a
spendthrift of force of every kind, from seeds to waterfalls. The
secret of nature's power lies not in its conservation of energy
but in its tremendous productivity. Would not men, even in their

education, be wise to concentrate on creating intellectual and moral energy rather than on efficiently directing the uses of what exists? This is what America is doing in the field of physical force and material production, with impressive effects. Nature, by its free expenditure of force, ends up with no waste at all; natural energy is never destroyed but only transmuted from heat to motion and back again. Could education achieve that same creative and indestructible profusion? Angus sometimes thought that the men who dispense the greatest personal energy seem to have the most left. Perhaps the exuberance of spending is the key to mental and spiritual creativity, and profusion of creation is the secret of intellectual progress.

Yet of course Adams was quite right in what he presumably meant, which is something quite different. The eighteenth century he had spiritually inherited had told him that man is or can be a moral force. Then Adams had gone back to the thirteenth century and extracted its message that unless force, even moral force, is wisely used it will ultimately explode in the faces of its expenders. The twentieth century is in danger of illustrating the conclusion of the thirteenth by forgetting that of the eighteenth. Its education is neglecting the lessons of both centuries in its concentration on teaching its young men how to create physical force, which is amoral, *ad infinitum,* and very little else. Of any other forms of force the young scientist, engineer, and economist are almost unaware.

There are many causes of education's neglect of all but physical power and physical economy, and the chief one is scientific materialism. Angus came reluctantly to the conclusion that there is a second cause in the absence of effective religious education in the public schools. Even some private schools virtually ignore it, and although that is less excusable it is less harmful, since most Americans are public school products. American democracy has always thought itself wise to have insisted on the separation of church and state, and to have forbidden any teaching of sectarian religion in the public schools. Any other decision would have created still greater immediate problems. Nevertheless the separation of church and state has taken from democratic government the slightest trace of any spiritual leadership of the nation, and the elimination of sectarian religious teaching from the public schools has left them with no effective vehicle for religious instruction or spiritual elevation. Neither state nor education has been able to develop any religious impulse that is both nondenominational and fervent. The nonsectarian state tends to become the agnostic state, and nonsectarian religious education to become no religious education. On one occasion after he had left Rochester, Angus listened at a distinguished dinner table in Washington to a deploring of the lack of religious instruction and understanding among American youth. When he gently inserted the suggestion that one of the reasons was the ban on denominational religious instruction in the public schools, his words created a shocked silence followed by a hurried change of subject. That possible remedy was too un-American to be even conversationally considered.

Any state is primarily concerned with its own perpetuation and advancement, and the pressures it brings on its educational system are directly or indirectly to that end. If a state does not realize that the impulse and guidance of religious faith is essential to its own perpetuation, then there is no reason for it to bother about religious instruction in its schools. The all-wise state, on the other hand, would see that its long-term security and quality lay in the development of the highest powers—spiritual as well as temporal—in each of its citizens.

The reason America does not really attack the problem of its citizens' spiritual development is that it has not clearly recognized its need. The goal of contemporary America, apart from security, is the efficient mass production of things for people to buy and of people able to buy the things, and this is called raising the standard of living. The state seeks to turn out human power and satisfactions by the same mass methods that produce its impressive output of mechanical energy and material goods. This is

America's concept of the economy of its power. The spiritual and cultural advancement of its individuals is of course desired, but only if it does not disturb the delicate balance of material productivity and consumption in democratic society. Culture must not complicate the main production line.

Despite America's special admiration for scientists, even they must stay in line. Government can find no place for the brilliant physicist whose rare talents have led him into detours from the beaten track of political and social thinking. It was sincerely troubled by what to do with an Oppenheimer, without stopping to realize that if there were flaws in Oppenheimer's judgment the fault was its own. Its system capitalized so heavily on his scientific talent that it left him uninformed and perhaps undisciplined in the social ways of man. Had Oppenheimer been a poet, a sculptor, or a modern Socrates of equal talent, the issue would not have arisen, for modern America would not have specialized him, called him to high service, and then been concerned about the outcome. The public does not take poetry, the fine arts, and philosophy seriously enough to regret the loss of their highest talents to the nation. They are less useful than atomic physicists and therefore less important. The state would either ignore the vagaries of poets and painters or jail them. Had it considered their case at all, it would have reached sooner than in the case of Oppenheimer its verdict that the securities of conformity must come before the deflections of genius.

The case of Oppenheimer was actually decided by American society many years before he went through his inquisition. About the beginning of the century the state was faced with a choice between two mutually exclusive first objectives in its public education. It could decide to make the first objective the full development of all the talents and potentialities of all youth in all directions, no matter where they might lead. That would have emulated the profusion of nature, and like nature many of its products would have fallen by the wayside. Society would deliberately have created trouble for itself if it had adopted that educational policy and really operated under it, for it would be encouraging young men and women to develop ideas and ideals at variance with existing society.

Or public education, directed by the state, could have made its primary purpose a quite different one. It could devote itself to adjusting the individual to accept things as he finds them, and to convincing him that he is already in the best, or almost the best, of all possible worlds. It would direct the talents of its young men and women into the channels thought to fit best the existing aims and mores of society, and would discourage those who tried to stay outside the main currents of thought and activity. This is the method attempted, with some temporary success, by totalitarian states. The first alternative would lead to a profusion of nonconformist talent and fully realized individuals; the second to an economy of directed talent and docile co-operators.

To that choice the democratic state has given a confused answer: it favors in theory the development of the individual to his highest talents and widest freedom, but it favors in practice a stable society to a questing one—for to any government social stability is the highest virtue. The national confusion between these two objectives is painfully reflected in the mixed ideals and practice of public education. Most professional educators, university trustees, and local school boards act as though the first purpose of democratic public education is to guide the young toward happy immersion in the current values and mores of American society. They limit acceptable changes in education to greater numerical coverage of the increasing population, and the further advance of education to improve health, sanitation, literacy, mechanical efficiency, and civic co-operation. Vocational training assists these ends. It also aids economic productivity, and pleases mass educators because its problems of instruction are relatively simple and make no heavy demands on the spiritual, philosophical, or cultural quality of its teachers.

At the same time, some academicians and elements of the

American public urge the other alternative: the free development of the talents of the individual even if they do not seem to be of the kind immediately useful to the state, and the continuance and deepening of the atmosphere and values derived from the humane studies. This school of thought is now in the minority, and education is drifting away from its goals, though still giving them lip service. As a result, education is suffering from a dichotomy of aim and a conflict in practice. So far as the academic mind is concerned, it is as divided as the public mind. Faced with the increasingly conformist attitudes of general society, schoolteachers and professors fumble with the issue and watch it go by default.

It could hardly have been otherwise. In a society already largely standardized and bereft of spiritual influence, education to encourage uniqueness in the individual and humanistic values in society is faced with almost insuperable difficulties. How could education justify to popular society the teaching of humanism to a boy or girl who would then find humanistic ideals out of step with the spirit of the times? If education made the world of Plato and St. Paul, of Whitehead and Schweitzer, seem really desirable to its graduates, it would only make them unhappy and inefficient in a world so full of soap operas, tabloids, and the ubiquitous sales talk. The disciples of Schweitzer would either have to accept modern vulgarity or revolt against it. If they accepted, democratic society would augment its frustrated humanists; if they revolted they would make a happily settled society less stable. Would any sensible society support the teaching of a philosophy likely to upset its own values? One might as well ask the Catholic schools to teach Quakerism, or vice versa. For the efficient operation of machines, happily over a lifetime, a man is better off to have no dreams beyond them, to feel no limitations in his life and thought of the kind that might be pointed out by a Matthew Arnold or a Sir Thomas More. Throughout history the greatest waste has been the waste of the human mind and spirit. How much waste of spirit is involved in our current education and mechanistic civilization? Angus believed it great, and increasing.

He tried to find in education some middle ground, but no compromise proved workable in practice. To turn out graduates who are neither good mechanics nor good humanists, neither wholly happy with present popular values nor capable of promoting an alternative, would do both the individual and society a disservice. He could only reach the conclusion that the trouble is not with the ideals of humanistic culture, no matter how outdated some might think them, but with the ideals and life of current society.

When Angus talked about humanism he meant much more than collegiate acquaintance with the classics, or four cluttered years of scattered courses in what are called the liberal arts. Humanism was both more and less than these. He certainly did not mean, either, humanism as the word has sometimes been used, as a negation of religious faith—quite the contrary. The cause of real humanism has suffered from being identified with agnosticism on the one hand and with college courses, often desiccated and pedantic, on the other. Humanism meant to Angus a point of view, however derived, a lifetime search for an understanding of men's minds and emotions, a perspective on their long struggle upward, and some acquaintance with their ideals and dreams as voiced by their best spokesmen. That seemed to him the only kind of education consistent with the ideals of democracy or the concept of man as more than a clever animal. Angus hoped he saw, though he was not sure, beneath the surface of prevalent scientific materialism an increasing dissatisfaction with the dominance of the mechanical and the meretricious—a recognition that their rule is sapping the spirit of the individual and diminishing his stature. On that hope he had some optimism for the future, but believed that unless the American people could see the need more clearly, and act on it more courageously, the forces that are flattening out human elevation would go rolling on.

Even if Americans perceive the danger of their spiritual emptiness, the cures for that kind of self-ignorance are not as easy as for other kinds of ignorance. Self-understanding must be achieved largely by the individual, in solitude and concentration of mind and spirit; humility is essential to soul-searching. American society does not develop humility, and it abhors and destroys solitude as nature abhors a vacuum. The average American is a little like a spider busily spinning the single thread of gregarious expansion about the periphery of its own little world. Yet the place for a sensible spider is in the center of a closely woven web. The American mind ignores the nucleus and spins out its strand of scientific materialism without knowing where it will lead or how it will provide inner sustenance along the way. Angus' own mind was typically American in that respect. It tried to move ever outward toward the only objects it could see, which were tangible objects; it looked neither sideways nor upward but only downward at its own spinning process; it sought only facts it could categorically accept or reject from its limited pattern; it was capable of only one kind of conventional analysis and conventional conclusion, at the same time believing in its range and flexibility. It was not aware that it was only two-dimensional.

While contemporary minds try to hammer their way to understanding, the century challenges them to find how to consolidate emotion with thought and faith with reason. It cannot be done by neglecting any of the four. American society needs to see the ineffable universe as more than a medium for conquest by chemistry and spaceships, or as separate narrow vistas of nuclear power, psychological revelation, and freedom through any form of government, even democracy, alone. It needs to see that the elevation of man is something more than raising his standard of living.

We are absorbing the separate new facts of the modern age without weaving them into a pattern of unity and relative significance, because our education has taught us to absorb but not to co-ordinate. In the new world of communism, atom, and conditioned reflex we are tourists as naïvely accumulative as we once were in the old world of cathedrals, castles, and cafés. We hurry through the galleries of an infinite universe without knowing what we are looking for or how to get meaning from what we see, for in that new universe there is no Baedeker to tell us. We carry with us scientific tools Bacon never dreamed of, but lack Bacon's grasp of the meaning and boundaries of science. We know facts of history that were to Gibbon the unknown future, but are without Gibbon's power to draw principles from events. We walk daily through the universal laboratory with only piece-meal hypotheses and isolated conclusions. We have only the skill of that expert in art who can determine the authenticity of a great picture by chemical analysis of its paint and canvas, but who has no sure sense of identification by the quality and meaning its creator put into it. The only sequence we can find in the world is in its tangibles. In this myopic parade of the twentieth century Angus stumbled along with the rest. He and most of his fellow academicians were as unimaginative as pragmatic education and secular society had made them.

All this depressed Angus when he finally took time to think about it. He felt he was vending a form of education he could not wholly approve, and wanted to vend another kind that was not widely desired, and that he himself could not teach. He was not sure that he knew any longer what the ideal education is, though he knew what it was not. He felt crowded into a negative position when he wanted to be in an affirmative and constructive one.

When he consulted his faculties about an educational ideal and how it could be translated into teaching, they seemed at least as confused and uncertain as he. All they could agree upon was to do better what they were already doing. Angus was heartily in favor of improved quality, but quality in what, and to what end? To reach agreement on what quality is, or how to produce it, or toward what goals it should be directed, seemed beyond the power of the collective academic mind. Here were some of the best-trained and best-intentioned intellects in America, in bafflement and disagreement about the fundamental aspect of their lifework, and some of them even reluctant to think about it. Angus decided that he would do well to hand his presiding reins over to someone more confident of the virtues of current higher education, and of his own wisdom.

VII

Men of Science

DURING and after World War II Angus' university work brought him into contact with some of the nation's leading scientists. It was a stimulating experience, and as education more rewarding than any books or courses. He could not understand their work but approached it with the humility of conscious ignorance and sometimes grasped its larger significance; he could sense the high personal quality and character of leaders in physics, chemistry, and medicine, and he was impressed with their attitudes and values. There were some fine examples of the scientific mind in his own faculties at Rochester, and friendship with them enhanced his respect for the potential excellence of human society, if men of such quality and motivations could be produced in far larger numbers and with broader education.

Like a civilian who can brashly talk with a general as a colonel or a sergeant cannot, Angus was able to put elementary questions to the experts, and get better answers than he deserved. Since he had no personal responsibility for the research itself, he was in the happy position of sharing its successes while escaping its labors and disappointments along the way.

Angus was brought early into a layman's acquaintance with the exciting developments in nuclear physics. The atomic bomb had few amusing aspects and he was lucky to have encountered one or two of them, though their implications sobered any light-heartedness involved. Long before the Normandy invasion, Angus received at his university office a telephone call from Albert W. Chapman, then Vice President of the Eastman Kodak Company. In characteristic clipped phrases Chapman conveyed that an army general engaged in work of importance wished to fly immediately to Rochester to talk with Angus, but was reticent as to the topic to be discussed.

Like nearly all civilians, Angus was secretly pleased that any general would go to such trouble to see him, but masked his satisfaction with the indifference that self-respecting academicians normally show toward the military. What was more, visitors from Washington had not been infrequent since the war began, and usually came to kidnap some university professor for war work. Rochester had already given teachers until it hurt, and Angus' reaction to further raids was to lower the portcullis. He told his friend Chapman, rather brusquely, that he would see the General if he had to, but was not likely to be acquiescent to whatever it was he wanted.

At the appointed time Chapman appeared with two men in uniform whom he introduced as General Groves and Colonel Nichols. The names meant nothing to Angus, who was not more than coolly polite. General Groves said he had immediate need for the services of Dr. Stafford L. Warren in an extremely important war project. Warren was a key man in the medical school, which had already lent so many men to the government and armed forces that further losses would impair its teaching and medical care. Angus rejected the request in words more emphatic than those officially current in academic circles. He added that every bureau and agency in Washington was demanding men

from the university, each with the claim that its particular project
was the one most crucial to the winning of the war. He asked
what project General Groves claimed so important that it would
justify crippling the medical school.

At this point Colonel Nichols rose and silently laid on the
desk before Angus a copy of one of the more flamboyant periodi-
cals of popular science. The magazine was open to a certain page,
which Angus gathered he was expected to read. He glanced
through an extremely unscientific prediction that someday scientists would split the atom and be able to produce power which
could destroy whole cities in one explosion. Slightly irritated that
army officers read that kind of stuff and expected him to take it
seriously, Angus bluntly said so, and inquired what this hack
writer's fantasy had to do with their visit. Chapman, who had
been even more silent than usual, put on a curious expression
that might have been either embarrassment or amusement. General Groves then conveyed, without quite saying so, that the
article, though indeed unscientific, indicated what his project
proposed to do, but underestimated the probable power of the
results. He also implied to Angus that this was a business so
secret that he must take it largely on faith, but that take it he
must.

Nothing was more calculated to bring out the stubbornness in
Angus than the suggestion that he must accept anything blindly,
and with some asperity he repeated that he did not propose to
release any man, and especially one as valuable as Warren, for
such an extraordinary flight of military fancy, or merely because
some army officer said he must. Groves replied calmly that the
United States and Germany were racing to develop this weapon;
that Germany had a long head start, and that whichever nation
secured it first would win the war and control the postwar
world. He said this with such simple conviction that Angus was
impressed in spite of himself, but, secure in his presidential omniscience, he snorted that it all sounded too Jules Verne to impress

him. Unless, he added, he could get definite verification from top scientists he knew and trusted, he could only assume that his visitors were chasing a comic-strip dream. He was exerting his civilian privilege to be rude to generals.

Groves placidly inquired what scientist's word would be convincing. Angus replied that on second thought the matter, if reasonable at all, went beyond science: if Groves were seriously pursuing an atomic bomb President Roosevelt himself should know about it, and perhaps it was the duty of a civilian who had come upon such a fantastic military idea to inform him. Groves quietly stated that if an official request for the loan of Warren for the purpose, signed by President Roosevelt, was required by Angus, one would be in his hands in twenty-four hours.

Angus was so staggered that he climbed down a little, and said that if the project had any scientific importance his friends Vannevar Bush and James B. Conant would know about it, and that his first thought would be to call one of them by long-distance telephone and inquire. Groves said nothing would suit him better. Within five minutes Angus, now uncertain whether he was calling a bluff or entering a dream world, was talking with President Conant's office in the National Defense Research Council in Washington. The answering voice was familiar, for it was that of Fred Hovde, Angus' own personal assistant at Rochester, on leave as special aide to Conant. Hovde said that Conant was in the building but at a conference so important that he could not come to the telephone. Angus had heard that one before but, knowing Hovde, for the first time believed it, and simply asked Hovde to hand a note immediately to Conant saying that "a certain general" wanted Warren for a project he stated to be of such importance that whatever country succeeded in it first would win the war. Angus had agreed with Groves that if Conant wrote: "I concur without qualification" at the bottom of the note, Warren would be released. Conant's reply came almost immediately. Hovde's voice said:

"Mr. Conant's answer is as I expected. He has written: 'Entirely correct, assuming the war does not end before either nation is successful.' "

Feeling like a very small boy alone in a very dark wood, Angus hung up, conceded Warren, and pledged every possible support from the university. The first outcome was a large secret participation in the medical aspects of the atomic bomb by the university under Warren's direction. A part in the founding of the Brookhaven nuclear laboratories was a second, and there were others. Two by-products were the loss, after the war, of Warren to be Dean of the new medical school at Los Angeles, and of Hovde to be President of Purdue.

The sequel does credit to the memory as well as the humor of General Groves under trying conditions. The announcement that an atomic bomb had been dropped on Hiroshima came suddenly from President Truman in mid-Atlantic. Since Mr. Truman referred to the research agency involved as the "Manhattan Contract," and since the local public knew that a major project by that name existed at the University of Rochester, Angus was immediately inundated by demands for information from press and public. He and the others involved had been sworn to top secrecy and did not know whether the President's statement released them from that pledge. Yet the story had come directly from the President and its implications regarding the work done at Rochester were clear. Angus had no alternative to an immediate call to General Groves for advice and authorization. As he put in the call, he could imagine what the reporters, Congressmen, and others were doing to the telephones in Groves' headquarters, and had no expectation of talking to him personally. But he assumed that Groves' office must have been privy to the President's release, and that his staff would be ready with full instructions. To Angus' surprise, he almost immediately heard Groves' voice over the wire. "This is Angus," he began, and was interrupted by a chuckle and then Groves' inquiry: "Now what price Jules Verne?"

That chastening riposte did little to relieve the deep sense of the awful import of their work that Groves and all his fellow workers felt. But the telephone talk brought further education to Angus. Groves told him that the President's announcement had come to him completely unexpectedly, without any guidance as to what Groves should or should not say. He and his staff, like Angus and many others, were still under oath not to confirm, deny, or comment. Groves could only say to Angus that he could offer no authorization or advice; Angus would have to remember his oath and use his own judgment. He did both, and confirmed in guarded terms the fact that the university had been a participant in the Manhattan Project. He was not shot at dawn and no comment was ever offered from government circles. Participants in other universities and industrial companies made similar statements under similar conditions. Angus' own problem was relatively insignificant, but he wondered how men like General Groves reacted to the way the President had handled the matter. Here was a lesson in Mr. Truman's methods which Angus might have weighed more heavily before enlisting under him five years later.

Of the distinguished group of scientists directing national research during the war, Angus found Alfred Loomis unique. Loomis had retired early from Wall Street and taken up scientific research with such energy and imagination that he had become the only nonprofessional member of the scientific inner circle. On the occasion of the inauguration of Lee DuBridge as President of the California Institute of Technology shortly after the war, Loomis invited a group of his scientific colleagues to be his guests for a week in California, and since DuBridge had been Angus' Dean and close friend, Loomis included him in the party of scientists. For over a week they enjoyed the luxuries of Pasadena, Santa Barbara, and Del Monte, and the excitement of the unveiling of Ernest Lawrence's new cyclotron at Berkeley, in company with David Lilienthal and the new Atomic Energy Commission.

Academic life has its oases, and sometimes they bring greater understanding than the institutional pursuit of knowledge. No busman's holiday could have been more refreshing than this one. As specimens of American education these men did honor to the system. Any perceptive person wholly unaware of their scientific pre-eminence would nevertheless have recognized them to be men of unusual intellectual power and discipline, good will and social conscience. Vannevar Bush could bring his humorous Yankee wisdom into everything from native bridgebuilding on Cape Cod to the prima-donna attitudes of research biologists or the art of wangling war research funds from reluctant and mystified Senators. The mind of Alfred Loomis found challenge and stimulus in everything he saw and heard, and ranged over the peaks of human ideas from modern architecture to enzyme research. Carl Compton, reserved but cordial, reflected in his talk the humane values and ethical stamp of his family background at a small Ohio college, as well as the wisdom of a scientific elder statesman. Conant, always direct, incisive, and disarmingly simple in manners and tastes, with a questing imagination held in close curb by scientific discipline, and with a puritan fervor sweetened by humor, threw his own original light on topics from education for democracy to the private habits of eminent Bostonians. DuBridge, whose warm personality was reflected in the quality of his voice, was as always a reassurance to Angus that science and humanity, mind and emotion, can be brought into almost perfect balance in one man. Isidor Rabi, switching suddenly from sensitive reserve to self-forgetfulness and enthusiasm as his mind was caught by some challenging idea, transmuted conventional liberal opinions into a philosophy wholly his own. Oppenheimer was then and later the personality most challenging to Angus because it was never wholly revealed. His talk reflected varied lights from the infinite facets of his mind—flashing from sober melancholy to witty gaiety. Here was a man gentle and perhaps a little mystical; profoundly thrilled by the success and promise of his work yet equally disturbed by its threat to mankind, and a little overwhelmed by the social and ethical responsibility he had incurred in the making of the bomb. Confident as a scientist but baffled as a human being, at once impressively wise and disarmingly naïve, with personal humility and professional pride, so adored by younger physicists that they even imitated his mannerisms, he was then as later an enigma, but one compounded of qualities so rare that no society could afford not to cherish him. Conscious cruelty, deceit, or disloyalty to any person or cause to which he had once given his allegiance would be remote from such a man; his problem might lie in the conflict of his intense loyalties.

Yet (although who was Angus to say it?) these men were not without their common limitations. Each bore the intellectual stigmata and emotional scars of his profession. One of these was dismay at the moral responsibility with which their own atomic creation had brought them, for the first time, face to face. One could read it in the eyes of Oppenheimer, in the democratic passion and liberal fervor of Conant, in the sober moralisms of the Compton brothers, in the enhanced speculative turn of Bush's mind, in the defensive cynical pretenses of a basically ethical Rabi. It was not a thing they liked to talk about or even to reveal when outsiders were present, but one felt that it always hung like a shadow over their spirits. Their limitation did not lie in their moral concern, which did them credit, but in the fact that their new responsibility found them so spiritually unprepared. Personal responsibility for the effects upon society of scientific research was a new emotion for many men trained to the traditional impersonality of the scientific creed. Before this new problem of morality the scientific mind faltered, and faltered all the more from inexperience with human social problems. The indiscretions of Oppenheimer are explicable as a scientist's search for the highest ethic in an area where his scientific specialization had not previously led him. These men were forced to think in new fields and were fumbling to reorient their minds and emotions. Conflicts of loyalties—between human life and national security, between scientific impersonality and humane ideals, between the principle that scientific truth should be open to all men and the secrecies of security—these arose daily in their atomic work.

Only a few years before, Angus had heard men like these state their scientific credo of detachment from mundane considerations and popular reactions. Some of them had insisted that the scientist should pursue truth through research without regard to the uses to which that truth might be put; that he could allow no place for social or ethical concern in his professional scientific mentality; that his mind must be as cold and impersonal as a surgeon's knife. The scientist's only good and evil must be the good and evil of truth and error in his methods and conclusions. Even at that time most scientists belied in their actions the ethical impersonality and emotional detachment of their own creed, for they were devoted to the personal development and nonscientific welfare of their disciples, and sometimes warmly prejudiced in their reactions to the work of other scientists. A decade later, after the bomb had shattered their comfortable theoretical amorality, many of the same scientists were agreeing with Leonard Carmichael, Angus' former Dean and now head of the Smithsonian Institution, that "if we are to try to glimpse even some aspect of an elusive cosmos . . . above all . . . it would be well to recognize more fully than we have, the importance of vital instruction in the studies that record the most sensitive and subtle solutions of human problems as recorded in all fields of study we call the humanities."

Physical scientists shared another defect of their scientific virtue. The specialization of their training had split more than the atom; it had split them from most of the rest of mankind. Just as men who have been through the worst horrors of war, or who have stood on the top of Everest, can never be quite the same again, can never convey the whole essence of their experience to those who stayed at home, so the scientists who had scaled their own painful nuclear Everest or gone through their own atomic purgatory were not precisely what they had been. They could never again communicate with full freedom except to one another. The irradiated dust of Hiroshima hung like a veil between them and those who had not shared their specialization and the new world of their fission. To others they could be affectionate, interesting, devoted, even intimate, but there was always something of themselves they could not share.

Their isolation was not due to the private idiom that specialists in many fields can share only with the initiated. Angus was familiar with that kind of limitation in other professions. Physicians, for example, have difficulty in communicating their diagnoses to laymen, but their limitation is not the special spiritual isolation of the atomic physicist of 1945. Circumstances frequently made Angus the only nonmedical man amid doctors; they sometimes talked a trade language beyond his comprehension, but this was a purely technical separation. He did not feel with them, as he could not help feeling with the men who made the bomb, a further remoteness of the spirit.

Exposure to the medical profession was another example of how education by plan led to education by accident. The presidents of universities with medical schools are in a special position to explore the medical mind, but most of them serve institutions so large and complicated that they have little time for more than a purely administrative relationship to their medical faculties. Physicians do not turn to lay educators for advice; they are supremely confident of their ability to conduct medical education, and ask of their university presidents only that they be generously financed and their hands left free. Angus' university was relatively small and its finances were relatively adequate, and he was able to spend more time at its medical school than most university presidents. Its Dean and professors were willing to add the education of their President to their other charity services, and he found their problems of instruction, patient care, and public relations absorbing. They were so different from the rest of higher education, and yet so much the same.

Few men not themselves physicians have more than a superficial understanding of the education of medical men. As an innocent bystander Angus thought he could serve a useful purpose as a lay interpreter. That was the excuse he gave himself; actually, he admired the profession, took pleasure in the quality of mind and performance he found in it, and was flattered by its appreciation of his interest.

The physician's position in society, his responsibility to it as an educated citizen as well as a doctor, and his need to win more public understanding and support were the aspects of medical education Angus felt least unqualified to discuss. It was probably more from lack of lay material than for any other reason that the medical profession selected this raw recruit from the liberal arts to serve as chairman of a national survey of medical education. During four years he spent many long days working with the committee and its staff, and even joined in intensive surveys of two widely separated medical schools. As his knowledge and friendships in medical circles widened, he found the effort more and more rewarding. When at last two volumes of considerable weight appeared as the survey report, Angus felt relief that the job was done, but regret that his close association with men like Whipple of Rochester, Berry of Harvard, Weiskotten of New York State, Hinsey of Cornell, and Johnson of the Mayo Clinic would presumably come to an end. He was delighted to find that they did not, and later saw some of them at medical meetings in London and Chicago.

Education by medical men proved unqualified personal gain to Angus, and reassured him regarding society's capacity to produce a profession of elevated standards, social responsibility, and integrity—even if society had achieved it largely by leaving it alone. Though the medical world is not without its limitations and its weak members, it develops traits especially attractive because elsewhere so rare: capacity for impersonal judgment, absolute devotion to human welfare, willingness to confess ignorance, and reluctance to talk unless one has something to say.

To a greater extent than most other minds the medical mind

is independent in attitude and individualist in operation. Though
the man of business shouts more loudly in advocacy of free enterprise, the physician is more devotedly its exponent in practice,
and is even hesitant to form working partnerships and group
clinics. In consulting a colleague the doctor follows rules of
protocol as rigid as those of diplomacy.

This professional independence of physicians is significant because it is a striking example of the social attitude of most scientists. Self-reliance is a valuable contribution to a society which is
moving toward organized dependence, but splendid isolation
brings serious losses to educational unity, to medical care, and to
public understanding. Many medical leaders are aware of this
and are urging that medical students be given an education that
will make them more conscious of their unity with the rest of
society, and of their personal as well as their medical responsibilities to it. They want young doctors to develop a stronger sense
of humanistic values to balance their specialist knowledge and
skills, though, as in academic circles, they agree only in abstract
terms on how to humanize. Some of them believe that mounting
specialization in medical education and practice is crowding out
other values, and making the younger medical men even more remote than their predecessors from the social and civic interests
of their local environments. They are wrestling, not very ex-
pertly, with the problem of the doctor as citizen.

Their problem is familiar to anyone who has met specialization in other sciences, but it is even more difficult of solution.
The training essential to professional excellence also creates personal limitations. The program of the young medical student is so
concentrated that it has narrowed the general cultivation of
many a doctor beyond his highest effectiveness as practitioner
and as citizen. Yet this is the time, and local civic duty is the
place, that America most needs the special qualities the medical
man could contribute. The average doctor is just beginning to
realize that he must make co-operation with his neighbors in

community affairs, and public understanding of his profession, his personal active concern, and nothing in his training has taught him how to do so.

It is highly important to physicians and public that they understand one another rather better, for the physician has qualities of great value to contribute to society, and he also has increasing need of society's support of his objectives in research and patient care. The American public places a low valuation on careful accuracy of statement in public affairs, on restraint of judgment, stern intellectual discipline, and distaste for the spotlight, and these are qualities the medical profession inculcates and practices. In contrast to the tone and methods of the political meeting, the sales convention, the newspaper office, and even some sessions of big business, the intellectual atmosphere of most medical conferences is open-minded and mature. The average doctor makes a sincere effort to arrive at the truth, whether or not it is convenient or profitable. Few physicians use or are impressed by the emotional appeals, the eloquent sophistries, and the considerations of personal advantage that sway so many men in other gatherings. Doctors are by no means saints or solons, and they have not always been alert in sweeping the dust and dirt from their own stables. One can find in the profession some prejudice, pedantry, and self-seeking without having to look very hard for them, but these flourish less in the measured murmurs of medical minds than in most other places.

Society could profit by speculating on why the medical mind is less vulnerable than others to the infections of self-seeking and mediocrity. The reasons must lie somewhere in the three processes that distinguish the conditioning of doctors from that of the rest of society: their selection, their training, and their practice. The selection of young men and women for the medical schools includes first of all a rather drastic process of self-elimination. Most students who apply for medical education do so aware of what acceptance will mean in hard training, exacting work, disrupted home life, and renunciation of large earnings. Intending doctors are more clear and elevated in their vocational motivations than most other young people. Then comes the careful selection by medical school faculties, sometimes of only one from every fifteen or twenty technically qualified applicants, and for the country as a whole of one from every two or three serious applicants. The young people admitted to our better medical schools are, in intellectual quality, character, and motivation, the best group of its size in the country.

The training of the medical student, including his internship and residency, is probably unparalleled in its emphasis on learning-through-doing the qualities essential to thorough diagnosis, clinical caution, and acceptance of responsibility for the health and lives of others. Accumulate all available facts; check and double check them; evaluate them with impersonal logic; consider the opinions of others, and then and only then formulate with imagination as well as reason an hypothesis or a diagnosis; finally, proceed with a firm but flexible mind. That is the code of medicine both in patient care and research. Those who once learn it will probably follow it throughout their medical careers, so that the third process of medical education, experience, deepens the standards and skills developed by the first two.

The qualities such training develops are greatly needed by American society outside the medical world. They engender intellectual honesty, personal responsibility, and acceptance of hard work. Angus wondered what would have happened to American democracy if, over recent decades, the decisions of the electorate and the actions of statesmen and politicians had been formed after a thorough application of the medical code for diagnosis. Then he wondered how long an exponent of that system would last in the upper councils of political bureaucracy.

The great disappointment lies in the fact that the education which gave the doctor those desirable qualities also disinclines him from using them in his capacity as a citizen. His strong professionalism has somewhat atrophied his civic interest and participation. Like the professional soldier and the research scholar, he has a distaste for the loose and undisciplined stridencies of the caucus and the market place. He has a special way of looking at things, even a special language, and does not communicate unreservedly with men outside the profession. His code of concentrated specialist service, like that of priest, professor, and military man, gives him a sense of apartness from the rest of the community, and this increases as the physician's specialization of training and practice increases; in social life doctors gravitate toward each other. If the young doctor thinks at all seriously of himself as a citizen of the local community, he is likely to conclude that if he does his medical job well he is making his full contribution to the welfare of society, and can leave the rest to his fellow citizens, who seem to enjoy participation rather more than he.

That is a natural point of view, but it is turning many medical classrooms and offices into aseptic fastnesses more socially and spiritually isolated than any academic ivory tower. The fault lies less with the individual doctor than with the extreme professional demands upon him, the training that has narrowed his horizons, and the popular blatancies and unreason that confuse or irritate him when he watches civic undertakings. His experience has not inured him to the wear and tear of the democratic process. The physician, whether talking to the patient or the intern, must be somewhat authoritarian in his statements of what should be done —he cannot risk the lives of patients as democracy risks the welfare of citizens while finding its way by trial and error. The organization of medical departments is also often authoritarian; they function with feudal independence, recognizing the suzerainty of the overlord dean only in external affairs. The departmental baron may administer his fief as he sees fit, and sometimes presides over it with a tyranny doubtfully benevolent. The entire medical center is usually dominated by an oligarchy of department heads. Democracy has its important place in medical teaching and procedures, but it also has its boundaries. As a consequence medical men are less used than the average citizen to the compromises, vacillations, and petty insubordinations of a self-governing community. In civic participation they suffer from the malaise of any educated and independent specialist used to an ordered and efficient little world of his own. Thrown into the caldron of crowd culture, the doctor escapes with relief.

The scientific mind, whether exemplified by atomic physicist or physician, is at its best one of the finest minds civilization has ever developed. Its ablest exponents capitalize its virtues and rise above its limitations. But not all scientific minds can match the breadth and understanding of the Oslers of medicine, the Conants of chemistry, and the DuBridges of physics. Smaller minds among the scientists, as elsewhere, tend to fall happily into the narrower ruts of thought which the limitations of specialist education make so available and convenient.

To Angus the limitations of excessive expertism in the sciences seemed one of the saddest wastes perpetrated by society and education. Good fortune had given him a wider range of training and a broader glimpse of humanity, and if he had failed to make the most of them he had no one but himself to blame. Whatever the resultant losses to himself and society, whatever the frustrations breadth of education had brought, he had had his chance. But America contains thousands of men abler than he, with infinite potentialities for human understanding, imaginative creation, and mature leadership, who have not had their chance. They have missed it because when society discovered their scientific talent it tried to make the most of it, but in doing so pressed them too soon and too exclusively into laboratories which offered no high horizons except those of their own expertism. Society utilized the genius of an Oppenheimer and then condemned him for limitations engendered by the straitjacket of scientific education. That case alone reveals the waste and injustice of the system. There will be many more such cases unless society and education insist that expertism be tempered by the visions, the understandings, the humilities, and even the temporal inefficiencies of humane culture. It would be better for science, as well as for humanity, if young scientists walked more slowly, more widely, and more humbly over the fields of human experience before they immured themselves in the laboratories and cubicles of specialist science.

PART 2

EDUCATION BY

Accident

VIII

Dollar Diplomacy

AFTER some forty years Angus was about to end his aca-demic training and move into the realism of unplanned education, where the teachers would be less forbearing and events less kindly. Life and his own weaknesses were catch-ing up with him. His new education by accident would make this clear, and would give him some painful instruction. It would also give him some high moments, and instruction by circum-stance was never so warmly rewarding to Angus as during his year as Chief of the Marshall Plan in the Netherlands. He emerged from that experience with new knowledge, new friends, and new confidence in the capacity of a free people to achieve and apply collective wisdom and character. When later lessons some-what shook his faith in the qualities of American democratic society, he could remember the people of Holland and be reas-sured.

Angus had become a director of the Committee for Economic Development and a friend of Paul Hoffman, its President. When Hoffman was appointed Administrator of the new Economic Cooperation Administration in the late spring of 1948, Angus' enthusiasm for the Marshall Plan redoubled. Late one hot night in June, he returned to his Philadelphia hotel room from the final session of the Republican Convention that nominated Dewey for the Presidency. The telephone bell rang and the voice was that of Hoffman, still at midnight in his new offices in Washington. With characteristic vigor he said Angus was needed to head one of the ECA missions to Europe, beginning immediately. Few men can refuse Hoffman when he applies his full powers of persuasion, and Angus was not one of them. Instead of returning the next morning to his summer work at Rochester, he set out for Washington.

In an interview of not more than ten minutes, with Bernard Baruch and others coming and going, Hoffman arranged that Angus would head the economic mission to the Netherlands, which was just where Angus wanted to go. His university trustees generously granted him a year's leave of absence, and he started work on the new job the same day. As the educator of the day before began to see what would be required of him as an economist tomorrow, he wondered whether Hoffman's faith in him was justified. Since no one knew exactly what would be needed, Hoffman's policy was to pick men he thought had good ability and judgment and turn them loose. No other policy would have been possible when the passage of each day made Europe's economic position even more crucial. After a few weeks of Washington summer heat spent in attempts to recruit a staff, organize a mission, and learn all that must be known, in an atmosphere even more hectic than in most new government agencies, the embryo economic diplomat took off by air for Europe and reached Amsterdam early in August. For a month, until the first members of his new staff joined him, he was a one-man mission, generously helped by Ambassador Baruch.

To create a new government agency is to substitute chaos for a vacuum and then bureaucracy for chaos. It is difficult to say which of the two stages is most painful, but the latter is certainly the most trying to the amateur in government who brings with him certain standards of independence and simplicity of operations. Both stages are baffling to men used to the order and comparative efficiency of a private business or a private university. But bureaucrats delight in them, for a new agency is a challenge to their capacity to regiment it with all the rules and habits of the older ones. Hoffman could not avoid the chaos or the bureaucrats, but he managed somehow to humanize both, and to infuse his multiplying and milling ECA organization with his own enthusiastic sense of mission—the greatest single asset of the agency. Men who were used to commanding their own quietly efficient staffs from soundproofed offices were sharing desks and telephones in cubicles where conversation was made almost impossible by the activities of movers and electricians. To go out to lunch was to risk losing one's desk and chair to a newer arrival; to ask a question was to invite twenty questions in return. Yet through it all an organization was being almost literally hammered out while carpenters hammered around it, and it would prove to be one of the most talented and effective Washington had ever produced. Its success lay in the quality of leader and staff, and in a working camaraderie free from some of the obfuscations and pettinesses of normal bureaucracy. Later the camaraderie weakened as bureaucracy took over, but the sense of serving a unique enterprise endured.

What happened to the Netherlands and the Economic Cooperation Administration is history, and Angus' small part in it is not worth recording. The year as education for that ingenuous economist-diplomat is all that is relevant here. As a program for training economists the Marshall Plan has no parallel in history. The professor of theoretical economics and the high-powered executive from an Illinois factory or a New York bank were equally inexperienced in helping to direct the complicated economic life of an entire European nation, and under emergency conditions at that. The specialist was compelled to adjust his theories to drastic realities and the businessman to adapt his experience to disrupted and impoverished industries quite unlike his own prosperous plants in Decatur or San Francisco. Western Europe became a laboratory for economic education as well as economic integration, and on a scale no university or single nation could ever provide. Though Americans contributed much to Europe's economic recovery besides taxpayers' dollars, they got in return an unprecedented opportunity for economic understanding. The businessmen learned fastest, the academicians learned most, and the professional bureaucrats continued to believe they had nothing to learn.

In this unique chance for education Angus was the most fortunate of all. He had less than most of his associates to unlearn about conventional economic practices that did not apply to emergency operations. As chief of a mission, he had what the economic specialists had not—a chance to survey the economy of a nation and observe how the pieces did or did not fit together. In a small country such a general survey is easier and more valid than in a large one, and in the Netherlands Angus worked with a nation of high economic literacy, a wide variety of economic activity, and habits of thinking strikingly akin to his own. He did not pretend to be an economist when he arrived at The Hague, but a year later he could claim a more realistic understanding of economic operations than many professionals and professors. Angus was not an exceptional pupil but Holland was an exceptional school—an ideal laboratory for applied economics.

That educational system is, alas, too expensive to be made available to all graduate students. Angus' one-year course in the Netherlands laboratory cost the American taxpayer five hundred million dollars, though fortunately that sum accomplished much besides the education of an educator. Angus doubted that he could have been made into a good economist for much less, and some of his government associates doubted whether even that sum had done the job.

In spite of differences in customs and tongue, the Dutch spoke the ideological language of the Long Island Quaker better than any other nation. They cherished the same ideals as those he had been taught in his childhood, and they preserved the old-fashioned virtues of hard work, strict literal honesty, and private initiative better than most Americans. Their social conservatism and economic liberalism, their economic caution and industrial initiative, made attractive mixtures. When Angus told them he could best understand them by thinking of Queen Victoria and John Maynard Keynes at the same time, they were amused and not displeased. As they saw how sincerely the Americans in the mission liked and respected them, they gave back real trust and friendship in return. Angus learned that it is similarity in thought patterns and human values that makes for congeniality, even if language and customs are very different. He felt more at ease in the social and mental atmosphere of the Netherlands than in many circles in his own country.

It soon became apparent to Angus and his American staff that in their efforts toward economic recovery the Dutch knew very well what they were doing. Their experts understood the economy of the Netherlands better than the American specialists understood it, or could be expected to. Not all Americans who thought themselves authorities conceded this; some of the government economists in Washington remained convinced that they could direct Dutch recovery better from Foggy Bottom and Lafayette Square than either the Dutch government or the Americans at The Hague. They recognized that Dr. Hans Hirschfeld of the Netherlands Economic Ministry was one of the ablest economists in Europe and that the Dutch government staff contained many men of international reputation, but they seemed to doubt either the perspectives or the intentions of these men. Angus assumed that the Dutch were just as sincere as anyone in Washington in their desire to use American aid efficiently in their own interest, and to forward general integration of the economy of western Europe. A few of them had been advancing those policies before some of their most critical American vis-à-vis had been born. Angus did not abdicate his authority or defer automatically to Dutch thinking or Dutch plans, or accept Dutch figures without having them carefully checked, but he approached the Dutch affirmatively, with the assumption that their proposals would prove judicious. It was better to support them as plans of the Dutch than to mess them about, delay them, and then present them back to the Dutch as American revisions. This policy of Angus made the relations of his mission with the Dutch very pleasant and successful but its cable exchanges with junior economists in Washington increasingly strained.

The expert behind his Lafayette Square desk three thousand miles from Holland's war-stricken cities and flooded polders could not or would not distinguish between the economic competence and integrity of a people and government like the Netherlands and the more dubious qualities of certain other western Europeans. Washington preferred the easy way of judging without seeing, or of reaching a conclusion after a flying "inspection" of a day or two. It tried to apply one rule or policy to all the variant European nations involved in the Marshall Plan. An economic mission that supported most of the recommendations of its European associations was suspected of being too easily led. The Washington theory seemed to be that the western European nations should be prodded, corrected, and kept a little on the defensive as junior partners. Part of this attitude was the result of pressures from members of Congress and other administrative agencies and departments whose understanding of Europe was erratic and whose interests were sometimes not wholly detached. Paul Hoffman was too busy to direct all his subordinates or to realize how far at times they were departing from his own intentions.

The Washington policy may have been a sound one for some countries but it was not for the Dutch, for when they believed they were right they lived up to their reputation for pride and stubbornness. Angus and his staff tried to explain them to their ECA associates back home, and to cite the occasions when the Dutch had been demonstrated right, and others when the mission had firmly disagreed with the Dutch and supported Washington, but Angus came to be known in some Washington circles as opinionated, sarcastic, and "too good a friend of the Dutch." On occasion he was probably all three of these, but the proof of the pudding was in the eating, and the Dutch were soon recognized to be making as effective use of American dollars as any country in Europe. During the years after his return from Holland Angus followed with satisfaction the economic advances of the Netherlands and of Benelux, the one even moderately successful effort at over-all international integration.

From watching the policies of the Netherlands after the war Angus learned that it was a mistake to be doctrinaire about economics. The rapid increase of government regulation of the American economy after 1932 had brought results in regimentation and loss of initiative that seemed to Angus as harmful as the excesses of the 1920s, bad as they were. He had gone to the Netherlands with the conviction that tight government supervision or control of a national economy is always a mistake except under the direct necessities of war. He did not believe that the best government was necessarily that which governed least, but he was convinced that the lightest possible hand on economic forces and the greatest possible measure of responsibility and freedom for the private citizen is the best economic policy for a democratic government. He granted that the increasingly complex economy caused by the industrial revolution made laisser faire impossible, and that government must act to prevent starvation, economic stagnation, instability, or excessive economic greed. He recognized that only by government leadership could the war-devastated economy of the Netherlands be rebuilt. But it seemed to him that the New Deal had overcentralized and overregulated in America, and that any nation that went equally far in peacetime would in the long run impair both its economy and its democracy.

When he arrived in the Netherlands in 1948 he found its economy regulated by government with a completeness that made the New Deal economy seem almost laissez-faire. The Dutch government controlled what was produced, bought, and sold; by whom and to what extent and at what price. The free movement of currency and even of persons within the Netherlands was subject to strict regulation. This was the kind of political economy that seemed to Angus fatal to free government and private incentive. Yet as he came to understand the postwar state of the Netherlands he could not see how its government could properly have taken any other course. The nation in 1945 was like a ship after a hurricane, with broken masts, damaged engines, a shattered hull, and little fuel or food. There was no alternative to temporary dictatorship by the officers and willing obedience by passengers and crew. Fortunately, the officers were restrained and the crew disciplined; they enacted and accepted the emergency measures, but did not regard them as wise except for this most drastic emergency. Though the Dutch people created in 1946 a regimented state, they liked free enterprise as much as Americans do, and were determined to return to it as rapidly and completely as possible. Meanwhile they were realists, as the crew and passengers of a damaged ship must be.

The contrast between postwar Netherlands and postwar Belgium was striking. The Belgians, though perhaps more socialistic in inclination than the Dutch, elected to renounce regimentation and in 1948 had the most free economy in Europe—and they were thriving. Should not the Dutch have done likewise? Angus was forced to admit that the conditions in Holland made that impossible. Belgium had suffered relatively little war damage compared to Holland; the Netherlands was fighting for economic survival, while Belgium's steel plants were producing at maximum and selling all they could produce. Belgian labor was largely employed, at high wages; Belgian consumer goods were plentiful, and Belgian currency was strong.

The Netherlands government was committed to the policy of removing economic controls as rapidly as possible, but it was not ready to lift them until production had become high, trade was

re-established, food and consumer goods were in reasonable supply, and the guilder was more firm in the international market.
There were times when Angus thought the Netherlands government should have removed this or that control a little sooner, but
Dutch caution produced such excellent final results that he was
compelled to admit he had been wrong. The Netherlands people
were prepared to endure controls and low wages until they could
be fairly sure of a sound economy for the long run. The Belgians
were riding high while prosperity would let them, and riding
with very considerable skill. It was not a question of a Dutch ant
and a Belgian grasshopper, for no one could call the Belgians
lacking in energy or foresight. Different postwar conditions called
for different treatments, and the contrast between the two ad-
jacent countries seemed to Angus to support his argument with
Washington that Marshall Plan policies or regulations should
not be applied with rigid uniformity to the nations of Europe.

As Angus watched Dutch economists and businessmen develop
their policy, his admiration of their timing as well as their judgment mounted constantly. What they lost by being on occasion
somewhat deliberate they gained by fewer mistakes and less confusion. They demonstrated to the student of economic diplomacy
what he had thought unlikely if not impossible: that a nation
could plunge deeply into economic regimentation and finally
emerge safe on the shore of free enterprise. The demonstration
did not alter his conviction of the dangers of government controls at any time, but it made him revise his opinion as to how
great that danger could be. But the Netherlands and its people
were quite different from America. It did not follow that the
American government and people could embrace regimentation
so closely and then have the restraint and judgment to escape
from it so cleanly.

The American economy has never been equally tested, for
even in 1932 it was by no means in the prostration and physical
ruin in which the Dutch found their whole agricultural, industrial, and commercial machine when the Germans fled in 1945.

American New Deal regimentation, begun with a sense of emergency, had been expanded into an economic doctrine and (in spite of political disclaimers) a policy of the Democratic party. It had come to be accepted as in itself a permanent virtue by many Americans. The New Deal also found that its welfare state program had the political virtue of attracting votes, and re-election is more on the minds of most public officers than economic theory. When faced with inflation or depression, the American people had not displayed the spirit of unity and personal sacrifice that the people of Holland maintained from 1945 until after 1950. The American government has not demonstrated the combined courage and restraint of men like Prime Minister Drees, Finance Minister Lieftinck, Economic Ministers Van der Brink and Hirschfeld, and Netherlands Bank President Holtrop. The Phillips and Ingen Heuzes of Dutch private industry set a pattern of industry statesmanship that not all American business leaders would emulate.

Angus noticed too the contrast between the leadership of the Dutch trade unions and that of American organized labor in times of emergency. He would appreciate the contrast even more after he had tried to work with American trade union leaders to hold down inflation in 1950-51. Dutch labor leaders were statesmen and called out the national patriotism in their constituents; most American leaders seemed more concerned with augmenting the power of their unions and themselves than in the general welfare and balanced stability of all American society. In the Dutch crisis of 1948, labor and management joined (not merely in the words of a public press statement but in consistent action) to organize for national recovery; they meant real co-operation and they maintained it. In spite of low wages and standards of living that no American union member would have accepted, the Dutch labor unions pledged themselves not to strike or agitate for wage increases until the general economy had notably improved, and they kept that pledge for years. Angus did not see, then or later, Philip Murray, John L. Lewis, Walter Reuther, or William Green lead their unions to a similar attitude or performance.

Could the United States have achieved what Holland did? Not unless the entire American people could summon up, in peacetime, as the Dutch nation did, the unselfishness, patience, vision, and unity essential to so drastic a need—and of that ability, in peacetime, the American people have offered no convincing demonstration. The Dutch success in accepting regimentation and then discarding it provides no assurance that America could conduct a similar liaison with the economic temptress and then extricate itself with equal skill. The lesson left its mark on the thinking of Angus, the amateur economist who would later become an economic stabilizer. It played its part in his refusal to lead America rapidly into universal price controls two years later. He believed he had many reasons, and some facts, to indicate that Americans lacked the character, the understanding, and the unity of the Dutch. It was no longer a question of the sacredness of a doctrinaire principle of free enterprise—Holland had taught him better than that—but a problem of need and judgment, and of the economic wisdom and self-control of a somewhat undisciplined nation.

Angus' position in the Netherlands gave him a unique view of developments in Indonesia's drive for independence. His interest was more than academic, for he had been commissioned to help direct the spending of taxpayers' dollars to bring about the economic recovery of the Netherlands. Since the prewar prosperity and balance of trade of the Dutch had depended very largely upon Indonesian plantations, tin mines, oil wells, and commerce, the continuance of close relations with Indonesia, at least in economic matters, was crucial to the Dutch economy and hence to Angus' work.

In early 1948 ECA had allotted to the Netherlands some ninety million dollars "earmarked" for Indonesia as a "dependent colony," and on inquiry Angus was told in Washington that he would be responsible for oversight of the expenditure of this sum. He immediately tried to discuss what staff he would need in Indonesia to act for him there, or how often he should visit Indonesia, and was told that no provision would be made for that purpose. The State Department had the matter in hand, and he would be informed in due course. That was all he could learn in Washington and in Paris before he arrived in Holland.

Throughout his year at The Hague, Angus made frequent inquiries by cable. Although it was reiterated that he was nominally responsible, it was also made clear that he would be nonparticipating and noninformed. The Netherlands government officially invited him to visit Indonesia as its guest, to go where he liked and see whatever he wished untrammeled so far as Dutch-controlled Indonesia was concerned. Paul Hoffman approved the plan, but the State Department intervened and postponed it, indefinitely. Angus was never given a reason for their action. The only information about ECA expenditures he ever got from his own government were figures on mimeographed and printed sheets which he lifted from someone else's desk in Washington, and they were reports on allocations already made, apparently by the State Department. He learned the rest from the Netherlands government, which gave him its own full reports. The Economic Minister of the United States was receiving from a foreign government facts of American operations for which his own government held him responsible but which it declined to supply him.

Angus had no wish to play the part of a political diplomat, but if, as it appeared, the policy of the United States was to set the Indonesians immediately and completely free through pressure on the Dutch in the United Nations, then the American government might well be wasting the hundreds of millions of dollars it was spending to bring permanent Dutch recovery. If the Netherlands fell into economic disaster, the whole economy of western Europe would be jeopardized and a climate favorable to communism created. Angus made these points to Harriman and Hoffman, and the State Department as well. From the nature of the infrequent replies, he got the impression that a group in the State Department was controlling the issue.

Meanwhile Angus was able to follow closely the diplomacy of the Indonesian question, even if as an economic minister he could not follow its economic developments. Ambassador Baruch made available to him every communication that reached him from Washington or elsewhere, including the recabled secret reports from Merle Cochran in Indonesia. It was almost as easy to get the Dutch point of view—indeed, it was impossible to avoid it. Angus' personal relations with several members of the Netherlands government enabled him to hear their private estimates of the situation in confidences he never broke, as when he was once a fourth in an informal and downright discussion of the subject between Prince Bernhard, the Prime Minister, and the Foreign Minister.

Seldom in history has the United States exerted such powerful pressures on a friendly nation as it directed upon the Netherlands to acquiesce immediately to full self-government by the Indonesians—if to grant full power to those who claimed to be the new government but could control only segments of its territory and had never risked a popular election could be called self-government. Seldom if ever, except in the case of Russia, has the United States been so insistent that the United Nations implement American policy. Without such vigorous American leadership it is very doubtful that the United Nations would virtually have forced the Netherlands to concede immediately to a *de facto* native government full authority to govern some seventy million people, without any effective guarantees for the personal safety and personal property of the Dutch in Indonesia—to say nothing of the anti-Republic natives. The position of the State Department appeared to have the support of the American people. That appearance was certainly strengthened if not created by a vociferous and organized few, and by very effective pro-Republic propaganda operated by a former prominent New Dealer said to be under salary from the Indonesian insurgents. Probably most Americans did not think about Indonesia at all or, if they did, based their opinions on little knowledge and considerable emotion.

The State Department's policy, so far as Angus could decipher it from its public statements, its code cables to the Hague embassy, and his own conversations with its officers, appeared simple and rational. It was based on the conviction that it was essential for America to gain the confidence and support of hundreds of millions of Asians still outside the communist curtain. To do so America must convince the watching Asians that it stood actively against colonialism and for self-determination for all Asians, and therefore on the side of the Indonesian Republicans. If this policy hurt or alienated the Dutch the State Department was sorry, but the temporary irritation of only ten million Dutchmen, who were more or less compelled to be on our side anyway, was not too high a price to pay for the permanent gratitude of seventy million Indonesians, whose earth was full of strategic materials, and the approval of other Asians from Karachi to Manila.

The policy was sound enough in theory, provided the self-appointed leaders of the Indonesian Republic were really the representative government; provided expediency and not justice was to be the first principle of American international relations —and provided the policy would work. But Angus was troubled on all three points. The defeat of communism required a demonstration of ethical elevation by the free nations that would stand in contrast to communist methods. Ethical elevation and injustice do not go together. Was justice clearly on the side of those Indonesian leaders who held the power? The right of Soekarno, Hatta, and their group to claim leadership of all Indonesians without any popular election seemed doubtful by American democratic standards. The deal these men had made with a certain American promotor of dubious motivation appeared a betrayal by its leaders of the interests of the Indonesian people, and was denounced by the State Department. Was it true, as the Dutch said, that Indonesian Republican leaders had been notorious collaborators with the Japanese and had even begun their "revolution" with Japanese guns? Was it true, as the Dutch claimed, that the Republican government was largely financed by illegal trade in drugs? If the Indonesian Republican government was strong enough to govern, why was it not strong enough to maintain elementary order in the areas it claimed to control? If it was moral enough to merit American support, how could it explain the American exploiter and the Chinese drug merchants?

The State Department seemed to Angus to be operating on expediency partly because its concern about freedom for the Indonesians was as sudden as it was vehement. If the American government was so devoted to immediate self-government for Indonesians, why had not Presidents Roosevelt and Truman ever mentioned it, or taken any action, previous to 1948? As late as July of that year the Administration had allocated Marshall Plan dollars to the Netherlands government for use in its "colonial dependency" Indonesia, and it continued to recognize the "colonial dependency" status of certain areas attached to other western European Marshall Plan nations.

If the Department of State was devoted to the principle of forcing its allies to give up their colonies, why was it not applying that policy with equal vigor in several obvious spots? The two million Chinese in Malaya, to say nothing of the Malayans themselves, were asking a voice in their own government; the natives in certain French colonies in Asia and Africa were demonstrating their dissatisfaction with French rule; not all the black races in Africa were happy under British, Belgian, and South African domination there—and in some cases that domination was far less benign than that of the Dutch in Indonesia. Could the reason for the State Department's lack of immediate concern for those other colonial peoples possibly be that Britain and France

were larger and more powerful nations than the Netherlands—
or that Singapore and Suez had greater importance as military
bases than Batavia?

Asians are not children. Would they not see behind the façade
of American eloquence in the United Nations about self-
determination for all people the structure of expediency? Would
they not wonder whether, if the United States could find today
expedient reasons for ignoring Dutch rights, it might not tomorrow find other reasons for ignoring Indonesian rights? Would
the American policy really convince them of America's high virtue and deep affection for the people of Asia, or would it merely
encourage them to emulate America's expediency at America's
expense?

Perhaps the President and Department of State thought the
Indonesians more capable of self-government than other colonial
natives. If so, had they studied the political capacity and experience of the average Indonesian? Angus had read reports prepared within the Department, and had heard conversations between some of its members, that revealed great ignorance of the
economic and political life and abilities of native Indonesian villagers. They seemed to assume that the average Indonesian
thought and lived very much like a middle-class Filipino or a
French peasant translated to the tropics, and that he understood
the meaning and processes of democratic government. One had
but to study the facts to know this was not true. The average
Indonesian of 1949 was probably less capable of intelligent self-
government than a Filipino of 1910. When Angus heard certain
"experts" in Washington talk of the Indonesian he was reminded of that romantic school of eighteenth-century literati
who called the American Indian the "noble savage."

America assured the world soon after 1898 that it would grant
full independence to the Filipinos as soon as they were capable of
self-government. No nation ever worked harder or more sincerely
than the United States to prepare a native people to govern itself.
It was a record unparalleled in history and one Americans could

be proud of. Yet it was nearly fifty years after that declaration that the United States concluded that the Filipinos were ready for independence, and granted it. The Dutch nation had assured the world that it had similar intentions regarding the Indonesians, and those intentions were officially reasserted by the Netherlands Parliament, by Queen Wilhelmina, and by Queen Juliana. Unless Mr. Truman and the State Department believed the Dutch to be insincere, would it not have been better to take them at their word, and work with both Indonesians and Dutch to prepare the new Republic to meet its responsibilities; to assist an amicable separation rather than force an immediate one? Was not the wisest expediency to make sure that a friendly and stable government, able to resist communism, controlled those strategic islands?

When Angus appeared before Senate and House committees in early 1949, to testify regarding ECA operations, his time was largely given to answering questions about the Indonesian situation. In the Senate Committee on Foreign Relations were half a dozen men who could be expected, in line of duty, to be accurately informed about the Netherlands-Indonesia issue. The questions of several of them revealed that they knew little—not even the names of the chief islands—and of two that they had accepted fantastic distortions of the facts. Only Senator Tydings seemed to be well-informed. Members of the House Committee told Angus privately, after he had talked with them, that they realized they had been previously badly misled by propaganda. But in State Department circles Angus found that to question the full justice of the Indonesian cause was to be regarded as a reactionary or a propagandist for the Dutch.

The pragmatic test of a policy is whether it achieves its end. The United States paid a high price for its Indonesian policy, by impairing its relations with the Dutch people and their faith in its fairness. Has America received value in proportion to its cost? The situation in 1955 does not indicate it. The United States does not have the support of the Indonesian Republic for its anticommunist policy; it does not have the real friendship of the Indonesian people. The Republic has in most cases refused to co-operate with the United States in the Pacific area, or even to accept American aid except on occasion and grudgingly. It has emphatically refused to join in any Pacific pact. It is extremely reluctant to give an American a visa to enter Indonesia unless his visit is clearly for acceptable routine business alone. Americans who do get into Indonesia are watched with suspicion. The Indonesian government has been barely able to subdue major revolts among its own people; as of August, 1955, general elections have never been held; the economic position has greatly deteriorated. The two million Chinese who still handle most of the commerce of Indonesia have become an ideal channel for the infiltration of communism. The effectiveness of communist propaganda is constantly increasing, and as early as 1954 American press correspondents were reporting that Indonesia looked ripe for the communist kill. It is generally agreed that if Indonesia should be taken over by communists, the rest of Southeast Asia could not long stay free.

As for the balance of the American objective—the permanent good will of other Asians—there is no evidence that it was achieved or even forwarded by the gesture toward Indonesia. China has become a powerful communist state. Nehru is leading India to what seems at best an isolationism closer in sympathy with Russia and communist China than with the United States. Only one or two small Asian nations are as friendly to America in 1955 as they were in 1948. The policy of the State Department was at the time supported on the ground that the end justified the means. Perhaps the means were excusable, provided they gained their end—but they did not. This was a lesson to Angus, who also on occasion attempted questionable methods toward worthy objectives, generally with no greater success. He hoped it was also a lesson for the State Department.

Another aspect of the education of Angus by Indonesia was still more sobering. It was clear that even a highly literate society like that of America, with endless and ubiquitous newspapers, newscasters, and columnists, can remain unaware of the issues and significance of contemporary events. Leaving out entirely the question of who was right and who was wrong about Indonesia, one of the greatest events in modern history took place there without its full implications being realized by one out of a hundred Americans. Seventy million people, occupying large islands with tremendous strategic materials, agricultural and mineral resources, and military value conducted a revolution in which America was in effect their ally. They ended with a new government the nature of which might determine whether America would undergo another great defeat by communism, or whether Asia's most crucial corner would be safe for freedom. Yet few Americans could even name the islands of this archipelago, and almost none could have given the names of the new President and Premier. Has a century of free public education, has the most extensive press and communication system in the world, achieved no more than this?

Angus returned from the Netherlands knowing that his year there had been the most rewarding in his life. The Dutch people, the Dutch skies, and his part in the Dutch recovery had made it so. Education is partly the stimulus of new friendships, new experiences, and new thoughts, and these had been given him in generous measure. But education that offers new ideas also demolishes earlier assumptions, and that is less happy. Angus' year had also given him disillusion about the wisdom and efficiency of American democratic government. It had come to him not from the enthusiastic amateurs of economic diplomacy but from the professionals of Washington.

Angus' life, it is true, had been spent chiefly in sheltered circles where men's reason is as sweet and men's motives are as generous as can be expected in imperfect humanity. But this had not made him wholly naïve, for even in academic cloisters there are confusion, rancor, and self-seeking. He had learned a little more of these during his earlier forays into the less gentle worlds of business and politics, and had taken to Washington and on to Holland the average patriotic American's mixture of esteem for the high purposes of democracy and awareness of its imperfections. He did not expect to find that the abilities of men in government service were always exceptional or their motives invariably noble. But he had assumed that in the upper brackets of Washington, and particularly in the Department of State, he would find a general level of knowledge, skill, organization, personal quality, and personal dedication superior to those in normal academic and business circles. He found the contrary.

This, too, was education, but it was not constructive or inspiring education. Holland had uplifted him about humanity and democracy; his own country had depressed him. It was not simply a matter of his disagreement with Washington about Indonesia; that was only an incident in the revelation. Whether the State Department was right or wrong in its policy in Southeast Asia; whether the Washington bureaucracy was right or wrong in its unceasing efforts to submerge Paul Hoffman and his ECA staff in the turgid sea of bureaucratic regulations, procedures, and delays; the confusions, pedantries, rivalries, rumor-mongerings, double-crossings, and inefficiencies he had seen rampant in Washington left him shocked and irritated. It was less the actual incidents than the cynical spirit of bureaucracy that disturbed him most. The situation of democratic government at its fountainhead and point of application seemed to Angus so parlous and pressing that he could not comfortably return to academic life, regarding his experience as an interesting sabbatical year, and ignoring its implications. He did not know what to do about it, but he felt that as an American who loved his country and believed in democracy he ought to do something. At last Angus had been stirred out of his chronic self-devotion, and was ready to pursue a cause. He did not guess how far it would lead him from his established life, or how futile it would be.

IX

The Oriental Mind

WHATEVER its limitations, the diplomatic mind was
at least intelligible to Angus. The mathematical techniques of the scientific mind might be Greek to him, but he could
admire the clean logic of the process and was ready to accept the
validity of its conclusions within its own area. As for the academic mind, it was no mystery to Angus for he was part of it.
But a new accident of education revealed to him, in record time,
his mental limitations. He encountered the Oriental mind; he
greeted it with genial good will and was brought up short, in-
trigued but baffled.

In December, 1949, he was one of six university presidents appointed to attend a conference in Delhi organized by the Indian
Council on World Affairs. The delegates from India represented
its intellectuals in government, education, and business. Although Mr. Nehru did not attend the sessions of the Conference,
he kept in close touch with it and entertained the delegates more
than once. Angus had several brief talks with him. In the long,
formal sessions and in the constant conversations between the

participants, expressions of opinion were decidedly uninhibited, and visits to business houses and universities added materially to the knowledge of the American presidents.

In his intensive reading in preparation for India, Angus had concentrated on its education and economics—a distinctly long-range shotgun concentration. A man who after thirty years was doubtful that he understood American education or economics was aware of the absurdity of trying to understand those of India in a few weeks, or of drawing even tentative conclusions about them. But no academician can refrain from judgments or admit intellectual frustration, and no mind can receive strong impressions without having reactions. In the case of an academic mind they are likely to be put promptly into firm generalizations, and Angus generalized as soon as he stepped from the plane in Delhi.

The reactions of Americans to the splendor of the old India and the squalor of the new are fairly uniform, a confused mixture of attraction and repulsion, and Angus' reactions were probably typical. Chewing the cud of his Indian experience in the years that followed, he concluded that the only way to bring order to his impressions would be to consider at what points they supported his earlier opinions and prejudices, and where they confuted or perplexed all his previous experience. He found that his mind had been enlarged by glimpses of ancient Indian culture but frustrated by his attempts to understand the modern Indian, and concluded that he had begun his Asian education at least thirty years too late. He was too mentally inflexible, too incorrigible an exponent of Western culture, to be able to overcome its limitations. He feared that even had he prolonged his stay for a decade he would have emerged only a little wiser about the workings of the Indian mind.

Any intelligent American knows that the passenger to India must carry humility in his baggage. The weight restrictions of air travel prevented Angus from taking with him all he needed of that unfamiliar commodity, for he was not able to listen humbly for many hours to vigorous attacks by educated Indians on American culture and integrity. He was surprised to find how strongly he was defending America against Indian strictures on its materialism, of which he himself had been critical. The Indian charges were too wholesale and too extreme, and hardly seemed sporting in view of the reluctance of the critical Indians to consider any American refutations. In trying to defend his country Angus was led to revise his own thinking about American culture. The net result of his Indian experience was to make him value the American way of life and thought a little more highly —a conclusion that would have disappointed his Indian instructors.

Angus had approached Indian culture with all the receptivity and sympathy of which he was capable, but they proved considerably less than the situation required. What was more, he did not seem to find those qualities abundant in the Oriental minds he met. He did not lose sympathy with the problems of modern India, but became a little less patient with its somewhat dogmatic representatives. Conversations with Indian leaders left him more than ever conscious of the boundaries that circumscribed his own mental process.

The tourist in Rome inevitably draws comparisons between the glories reflected in Forum and Sistine Chapel and the products of modern Romans. The possibilities of such contrasts in India did not seem to have occurred to the Indian intellects he met. They claimed all the merits of ancient Indian culture as their own, and blamed their failure to reproduce them wholly upon external adversities like British rule and Western exploitation. Aware of his abysmal ignorance of Indian culture, ancient or modern, Angus nevertheless could not avoid distinguishing between the past as represented by Agra and the Sacred Books, and what he saw in the narrow streets of Delhi or even at government receptions, where the manners and attitudes of the milling modern rulers of India were in contrast to the values of Akbar and the Taj, and to the dignity of the surrounding splendor inherited from the British Raj. He grew bored with hearing Indian spokesmen avoid any admission of present Indian infelicities by prompt and inevitable reference to their superior cultural background. He was ready to admit that the ancient art of India was finer than that of Stonehenge, Westminster, or Mount Vernon, but he could not see that the culture producing modern Indian structures was demonstrably superior to that which built the Empire State Building or even the Nassau County Court House. He was prepared to concur that Indian spiritual wisdom was more profound than that of George Fox or Martin Luther, but his own interest was in the levels of contemporary Indian thought and culture, and those were what he had been invited to India to talk about. The spiritual elevation of ancient Brahmans seemed irrelevant to what appeared to be the spiritual pride of some of their descendants, and irrelevant to the question of whether Americans overestimated the dangers of communism or whether Indians underestimated them. Such topics were eloquently detoured by most Indian intellectuals, at least in discussion with Westerners, in favor of disquisitions extolling peace and neutrality. Indian intellectuals seemed to have acquired just enough Occidental education to have become facile at Western rationalization as a tool to support their own prejudices and self-deceptions.

Hence the American Quaker, eager for international understanding, was brought up short in his intellectual approach to India, and was forced to conclude—tentatively, of course—that the Western mind alone could not travel in India beyond a fixed point. The point was reached not where prejudice appeared on either side, but where the process of joint reason or communication seemed suddenly to break down. That was more alarming, for there was no apparent solution. Neither Indian nor American, no matter how great his good will or how sound his education, could wholly overcome his centuries of different conditioning, different values, different loyalties, and different patterns of thought.

Is it possible that there are functional differences in the mental process itself, that the Eastern and Western concepts of logic, of *therefore* and *QED,* are irreconcilable in this generation? Occidental and Oriental might embark upon the same train of reason, determined to stay together, but they would arrive at separate destinations. An American scholar's concept of reason is based on his conviction of its universality, on the assumption that to all disciplined minds the process of logic is identical. But as he listened to American and Indian minds volubly hurl themselves at one another without quite hitting the target, Angus began to wonder whether efforts at full communication by the intellect alone were not futile. American and Indian seemed to lack those common foundations of unspoken mutual assumptions upon which Western discussions are based and Western agreements erected. Since the Russian mind is said to be Oriental, Angus wondered whether the same problem might not be at the root of coexistence; faulty communication and variant mental processes might be a bigger problem than ideologies or national rivalries in the keeping of the peace.

One clear cool December day Cyril James, the Principal of McGill University, and Angus were being motored to Aligarh University by one of the most cultivated and congenial of their Indian co-delegates. Angus could not have found any man in India more likely to talk his mental language or share his basic assumptions than their host-chauffeur, for he was a Nestorian Christian, a graduate of Oxford, a professor of English literature at a leading Indian university, and a leader in the all-India university council. By any standards he was a highly intellectual citizen of the world. Yet a single brief conversation revealed the barrier to communication.

As their friend M. skillfully avoided camels, oxen, water buffalo, Indian peasants, and other beasts of burden plodding along almost invisibly in the clouds of dust ahead, James and Angus observed regiments of monkeys busily destroying the precious crops in fields along the road. Angus said that he had read in the *Times of India* a day or two before that the citizens of Aligarh had suffered serious food shortages from these depredations. The *Times* reported that since their religion forbade them to kill monkeys, the men and boys of the district had, with unique collective enterprise, captured the monkeys and deposited them some thirty miles away—a gesture doubtless appreciated by the natives of the receiving area. Within a week, said the *Times,* all the monkeys had loyally returned to Aligarh. Angus mentioned, too, statements by Indian government authorities that inability to increase food production in pace with the staggering increase in population was India's greatest problem. He recalled that he had discussed, rather unsatisfactorily, with Mr. Nehru the relation of the food shortage to the population. Professor M., replying obliquely to Angus' thoughts, remarked that the new India was inducing its peasants to drop their traditional habits and prejudices and accept more modern and rational ways of village life and thought, including political rights for women and improved agricultural methods.

Angus, interpreting this as indirect assurance that something more effective would be done about the monkeys, said he understood that the children of the area were in danger of starvation or serious malnutrition because the crops were eaten by the monkeys. M. said that was true. Angus asked whether it would not be better to kill the monkeys than to let them, in effect, kill the children. M. thought it would. Angus suggested that the Indians therefore overcome their religious precept for the sake of their children, and set about destroying the monkeys. M. said that would be unthinkable. Angus agreed it might be difficult, but asked if M. did not concur that the only alternatives were the deaths of monkeys and the deaths of human beings, and that the Indian people would have to choose between the two. M. agreed that was completely logical. Then, said Angus, triumphant in what he thought was reason, which choice should the Indian people make? M. quietly replied that either choice was out of the question. "Then what will be done?" asked Angus. "Nothing," replied M.

Angus' efforts were amusing James, but he persisted. "Granted," he said, "that those Indians whose religion forbids them to kill monkeys will do nothing, and that some of them will consequently starve. You are a Christian and your religion sets a high value on human life and does not specially ban the killing of monkeys to keep men alive. Just as an abstract and theoretical question, if the decision were wholly yours, which would you elect to keep alive, the children or the monkeys?" M. said he would personally prefer to see the children live. "Then you would kill the monkeys?" asked Angus. "That would be unthinkable," repeated M.

"But," said Angus, in frustration that the horse would not drink, "if you accept my reasoning you must, at least in theory, make the choice." "Ah," said M., nearly bisecting a camel, "the trouble with Western logic is that it so often leads to a choice between two unacceptable alternatives." Angus subsided and James was generous enough not to laugh at him. Both recalled the conversation as they watched Mr. Nehru's obvious reluctance to choose between the unsatisfactory alternatives of a Western alliance and Russian communism.

Men of all races and nations side-step unpleasant issues, but when Americans do so they usually recognize that they are evading, and are often secretly ashamed of themselves. The Indian seemed to Angus to eschew logical conclusions by instinct and preference, with the inner conviction that logic is an inferior Western device unworthy of the subtleties of higher culture. The efforts of an American to hold him to a specific issue seem to the Indian a crude limitation of mind to be politely tolerated but not encouraged. Logic as the West understands it may indeed be a limitation; Angus himself had often found it inconvenient, but he could not see that the Indian mind had found a better method of arriving at truth, at least as he understood truth. In the West it is the child mind that seeks most habitually to escape an issue by refusing to recognize it; in the East it is the most mature minds that seem at their best and happiest in that evasion. Whatever the explanation, it led to a real inability for East and West to pursue a subject mutually by the same method.

That inability is a fundamental barrier between India and America, perhaps between East and West. How can diplomats or the people of two nations hope to reach understanding if they cannot talk their ways into it by a process each regards as valid? If Americans seem to Indians hopelessly earth-bound by the lack of some fourth dimension in the higher mathematics of thought; if the minds of many Indians seem to Americans inattentive to the inevitable third dimension of *demonstrandum* in the sequence of reason, then discussions, conferences, diplomatic missions, and all the explanatory work of the United States Information Service are a waste of time and words. An American academician could not accept the theory that the minds of different races work differently. Yet the discrepancy could not lie in the training, for M. and Angus had undergone the same disciplines at Oxford and elsewhere. If the explanation lies in centuries of variant conditioning, that is not a consoling explanation for the purposes of effective agreements in our time.

The conference discussions seemed to bear out Angus' feeling of mental frustration. After listening to the opening sessions, President Colgate Darden of Virginia, a man not lacking in political experience as former Governor of his state, privately predicted to Angus that nothing would come of them in the way of concrete agreements on any important problem. Time proved him right. At the end every man understood the issues and the other man's point of view a little better, and personal friendships were formed that might prove valuable to both nations. Perhaps this was all one could hope for, and perhaps it was enough. But when understanding the other man's point of view only emphasizes its irreconcilability, the discovery of an intellectual no man's land between East and West seems too much like progress in reverse. The shattering of an illusion is a dubious gain when the illusion shattered is that communication between any two well-meaning parties is only a matter of patient discussion until reason is triumphant.

It did not appear that those Indians who had studied in the universities of America had brought home with them a very balanced understanding of American ways and values, or any greater ability to accept American logic. One unhappy episode in a New York subway train had convinced a certain Indian professor of economics that race prejudice is rampant and mounting in America and applies especially to his own race. A single experience with American academic pedantry (as though there were no pedantry in India!) was magnified to the discredit of the entire educational system. In this trait at least the Indian scholar is no different from the American abroad, and it is partly the fault of Americans if visiting Indian intellectuals have a queer view of our country. Americans do little or nothing, apart from sporadic gestures of superficial hospitality, to present America to Indian visitors in any balanced way, and many Indian scholars in American cities have, as a result, consorted with frustrated or left-wing intellectuals who delight in proving their own superiority to current American values by belittling the motives and ways of most other Americans.

Whether the leaders of Indian thought have been influenced primarily by communist propaganda or by festering inherited hatred of "Western colonialism," the results are the same. India's own extreme nationalism does not seem to them relevant when nationalism is discussed; India's ardent desire for American dollars does not seem to them materialism. Nearly all the Indians at the Delhi conference asserted that India hates Western imperialism as much as it hates Russian communism. When an American delegate inquired whether the worst that British imperialism had ever done to India compared with what Russian communist imperialism is doing to postwar Poland and Czechoslovakia, the Indian delegates said they had no sure knowledge of Russian procedure in those cases, but understood there had been much exaggeration of them in the American press. They turned the conversation as quickly as possible to American materialism and discrimination against Negro and Jew, which, some of them asserted, far exceeded any mistreatment of minorities in Russia. American denials were often received as though they were merely the standard American propaganda line.

The Indian mind has its own logic, when the Occidental can detect it. When Angus read the Indian program for education he found in it many references to Russian education and almost none to American. He noted that the Indians preparing the program had visited Russia to study its educational system but had not gone to America for a similar purpose. Yet India was planning a system of free public education under a democratic government, and the United States seemed to Angus the outstanding example of a similar attempt. When in Delhi he voiced this thought to several leading Indian educators, and they explained the flaw in his reasoning. India, they said, must move from the almost medieval and highly restricted educational system forced upon it by British imperialism to a modern universal democratic system, and do it in the least possible time. Only one nation had attempted a similar large-scale leap across the centuries, and that was Russia. What more logical than that they should study chiefly Russian schools? The American educator suggested that the American system functioned in a democracy and fostered freedom, but that the Russian system did not. One Indian savant replied that that was a matter of opinion, and another added that he was not sure Russia was wholly democratic but he was certain that America was not. Russia, they added, had no racial discrimination in its schools.

There was a kind of logic, too, in the Indian attitude toward American economic aid, but it was not American logic. Indian intellectuals repeatedly asserted that India did not want large-scale economic assistance from the American government, since America would use such aid, as it had in Europe, to draw India into the American capitalistic orbit. But the same men were very critical of the American government for not having offered India aid equal in dollars to the total aid it had granted to all the nations of western Europe. Europe and India were both subcontinents with approximately equal populations; Europe might have its starvation and want, but India had more. Yet America had given Two Billion Dollars (one could hear the words capitalized as they were spoken) to Europe in the first year of the Marshall Plan, and none to India. Though India, they said, would not have accepted so large a capitalistic bribe, America's failure to offer it was a clear indication that America belittled India's place among the nations, or did not want her friendship in spite of all the talk, or was as usual discriminating against the brown races. When the obvious reasons why the economic stability of Europe is of primary importance to America were offered, the Indian mind appeared unconvinced. Taken separately, the two Indian points of view were not without reason, but taken together they reduced the American mind to frustration if not anger.

Angus' Western mind encountered what seemed another paradox in connection with proposed aid by American business to Indian "private" business. American private investment was greatly wanted but was not being provided them, the Indians complained. Americans pointed out that the terms stipulated by the Indian government for the introduction of American private capital made it almost impossible for most American companies to invest in India, much as they would like to do so. They explained why the Indian regulations would permit few if any American boards of directors to risk the money of their stockholders in private investments in India; that there was not even a dependable guarantee against expropriation. The Indians said they did not want American capital on any terms but their own, and that failure of American capital to accept those terms indicated American uncompromising self-interest. Discussion repeatedly swung this circle with no further progress.

At about that time the Indian government was endeavoring to secure some two million tons of wheat from the United States to feed its prolific people. The Indian population was increasing at one of the highest rates in the world. Many authorities in India admitted that only by a revolution in the methods of its agriculture and food distribution could India hope to feed its existing population. The new millions it was producing annually would have to be fed by some miracle beyond any estimates revealed to Angus. To many foreign observers it seemed patent that India's only economic solution lay in some form of population control. Yet when Angus raised the question in private conversation with Mr. Nehru, the Prime Minister disposed of it very quickly by the remark that the planned increase in food production should in time take care of the increasing population. The time-minded Occidental asked him to estimate the time, or the numbers who would starve in the interval, but Mr. Nehru remained vague and seemed anxious to change the subject. Angus persisted and suggested that the figures of Mr. Nehru's own government indicated that even if its rosiest plans to increase food production were fully achieved, that percent of food increase would lag far behind the percent of population increase, and that currently India was having to import food on a large scale. Mr. Nehru would say no more than that the Indian population figures were known to be inaccurate, and that the production of more food was the solution. Angus recalled his friend M.'s dissatisfaction with logic that led to unacceptable alternatives.

It was obvious that there would be much objection in India to any effective method of general birth control; it was also doubtful whether any birth control could be successful in Indian villages until public health and understanding of sanitation were much further advanced. In avoiding any mention of the possibility of birth control Mr. Nehru may have been doing no more than carrying political discretion to its utmost bourn, yet he had been surprisingly frank in discussing other issues equally controversial, and political caution need not have forced him to deny the existence of a problem and a solution known to the entire world. Some two years later he cautiously opened the door to the more primitive forms of birth control. Perhaps during the interval he had recognized the obvious, or felt that public opinion had become ready for the first move. But Angus had found public opinion, at least among intellectuals in the Congress party, in advance of the Prime Minister on that issue. Neither explanation satisfied an American in search of understanding; was this a case of fourth-dimensional logic?

No one who had given most of his life to education could accept the explanation that there are racial differences in the way men's minds work. A keen intellect is no racial or national monopoly, and disciplined minds must think by the same process and in the same dimensions, if the verb "to think" has any meaning. There is no question of the quality or subtlety of the Indian mind. Are the apparent differences in its product due to different intellectual disciplines, or does the actual process of rationality follow in some obscure way the value judgments of the individual? It did not appear to Angus to be a matter of intellectual conditioning, since the Indian mind trained at Columbia or Oxford seemed to work like any other Oriental mind. Perhaps the mental process is determined at a far earlier age, as psychologists say is the case with men's attitudes toward their fellow men. If so, then how superficial a thing is higher education, and how great the need for revaluating it from the ground up! The mind of the college president went in circles to find an answer, and no educationist or psychologist seemed prepared to give him one.

While thus temporarily abased to intellectual humility, Angus saw that India might have one more lesson to give him. Since the fruits of intellectual training appear less effective and their uses less general than he had thought, since they fail as a medium of ultimate international communication between even first-rate minds, then the intellect alone is an inadequate tool for human understanding or even for the shallower uses of diplomacy. If men of India and America are ever to gain complete understanding they will have to develop media of communication deeper and more dependable than words and logic. Perhaps America's

relations with the Orient should be based less on appeals to reason and more on mutual feelings; less on the products of the head
and more on those of hand and heart. This would call for a new
approach to diplomacy.

Conferences and protocols would be replaced by exchanges in
the creative arts and the fruits of the spirit. Working together on
simple things like crops and dams, living together in the simplicity of an Indian village or a Nebraska farm, might prove a
better road to understanding than words and reasons. Diplomats,
if they then continued to exist at all, would be selected for their
possession and cultivation of denominators common to all men;
they would join, naturally, in the work and play, the joys and
pains, the dreams and disappointments, the common efforts and
the common prayers of the ordinary humanity of the nation to
which they were sent. Their mission would be to demonstrate
that hearts and emotions, hunger and the joy of creation, have no
national boundaries. Angus later noticed that all the diplomatic
conversations of Ambassador Chester Bowles had probably been
less helpful to Indo-American friendship than the simple daily
act of his small daughter in attending happily the local Indian
school.

These mental fruits of a fortnight in a strange land were
doubtless as green and inedible as those of the most callow tourist
who generalizes about the French character from one day in the
Louvre and an evening in the Place Pigalle. They were soon to
be somewhat matured, though hardly brought to mellow ripe-
ness, by further experience with the Oriental mind during a
laboratory course of nearly a year in Asian psychology.

The Delhi adventure had widened Angus' horizons enough
to set him talking in the State Department and before the American Academy of Political and Social Science on the need for co-
ordination between American diplomatic and economic policies
overseas, and on the uses of the Point Four program. Those activities may have had something to do with an invitation offered
him in late 1951 to accept leadership of a private organization to

assist the free people of Asia to fight communism in their own countries, and this led Angus into complicated dealings with Asians in America and in the Far East. No work could have been more interesting or more frustrating.

There are wheels within wheels in Asian politics, and it was essential for Angus to avoid entanglement in any of them. But he could not keep clear of that delicate piece of machinery he had already found so perplexing—the Asian mind. It was his job to learn how it worked, and to make use of it in the interests of the Asians. He encountered again in numerous forms and individuals the problem of how to understand the mental processes of Asians and reconcile them with American thinking and values. As he attempted this, he began to suspect that so far as unity of opinion and expression is concerned, there is no more an Asian mind than an academic mind. Later that suspicion was fortified by the conclusions of others. Philip Deane commented after observing the Rangoon Conference that "the delegates from the various countries often meant different things when using the same words, and they did not have a common frame of reference, a background of common experience, or even a common sense of history."

Yet in several important respects there is unity in the attitudes of most men, from the Red Sea to the Celebes and Japan. There is a common feeling of remoteness from the Caucasian world, and a tendency to search beneath the surface of every Western idea and action for a motive more complicated and disinterested than the obvious one. And even if Asians have difficulty in communicating accurately with one another, their inability to meet the Western mind foursquare is so much greater that their minds still seemed to Angus to operate in either one more, or one less, dimension than his own. Professor G. D. Parikh of Bombay has suggested that sudden national independence after centuries under Western governments or Eastern despots has impaired the capacity of millions of Asians to face the current world on level terms. "Asia suffers from chronic negatives," Dr. Charles

Malik of Lebanon has remarked. "We reject in principle that which we practice ourselves." Asians, it seemed to Angus, were not the only masters of that trick, but he concluded that the inscrutability of the East is due less to the uniqueness of its intellectual processes than to its psychology. Whatever its causes, the practical difficulty of dealing with most Asians was their common suspicion of the Western mind.

In the preparation of a simple printed pamphlet to explain to Asians the purpose of his Committee, Angus found that no draft prepared by any group of Americans could win the approval of the Asian members of his own staff, though they were all as one in opposition to communism. So eventually he threw the job of preparing the text of the pamphlet to a committee of Asians. They were delighted at this recognition and opportunity and went to work with energy and volubility. Weeks and then months passed, but no text was produced. The Asians themselves could not agree on the phrasing of the simple statement. Burmese, Japanese, Indians, and Nationalist Chinese had very strong and different opinions about what should be said. Angus finally had to draft a text himself, and then to issue it over their halfhearted approval. This brought them back to unity in the pleasure of pointing out his mistakes and infelicities.

An illuminating criticism came from an ardent anticommunist Indian who had taken a Doctor's degree in America. The Committee had been officially incorporated as The Committee for a Free Asia, but the Indian protested the use of the article. He said it implied to Asians that there is no free Asia now, and that that implication is insulting to the free Asians of Burma, India, Thai, and elsewhere. Though Angus was not convinced by that logic, he acquiesced, and the title became The Committee for Free Asia. But the Indian again objected to the new title he had previously advocated, on the grounds that it was inaccurate. It was not a committee for free Asia, he now argued, since it did not include the mainland Chinese in its membership, and that is a free country of Asia. Angus protested to this anticommunist that the people of communist China are not free. The Indian insisted that technically they are free, since they made the free choice of accepting communism. He added that although of course the communist Chinese could not be asked to join the Committee, their exclusion from the Committee, under its new name, would be taken by the free people of Southeast Asia to mean that the Americans on the Committee were really opposed to free self-government by any Asians. The title of the Committee, said the Indian, should be changed again, though this time he would not presume to suggest a new one. Like discussions with Mr. Nehru about birth control, the matter had to end there.

Perhaps the Asian mind and that of the Western politician have something in common, for one episode reminded Angus of his days in Washington. A problem of his Committee was how to help anticommunist Chinese without taking sides in their internecine squabbles. Not all anticommunist Chinese are pro-Nationalist; the number of individual groups ready, with adequate aid from American sources, to invade communist China and turn it overnight into a democratic Utopia is determined by the number of unemployed Chinese generals at odds with Chiang Kai-shek. The policy of the Committee was to keep its hands free to aid any group that would effectively oppose communism in Asia, including of course the Nationalists. Each Chinese group, including the Nationalists, was trying to jockey the Committee into aiding it alone.

One day in his San Francisco office Angus received by appointment an important figure in the Chinese Nationalist group, well known in America as a friend and a man of integrity, but also as a politician. Angus, as an ingenuous neophyte in Chinese affairs, had been advised by old China hands on his staff to choose his words carefully and to have reliable witnesses present throughout the conversation. He did both. The guest was charming and very friendly, and the conversation proceeded according to the most exalted protocol. When the visitor inquired whether the Committee would consider aiding the Nationalists in disseminating information about the merits of democracy and the evils of communism, Angus was a little surprised. His Committee was already aiding the Nationalists in Formosa in just that way, and he knew that his caller knew it. He simply replied, however, that the Committee was giving some aid and was prepared to give more, and was ready to consider aiding any responsible group that sincerely and effectively opposed communism. The visitor appeared more than satisfied.

A few weeks later the Committee's own American representatives in Formosa reported that their work was greatly handicapped by a sudden coolness from certain high Nationalist government officials who had previously been most friendly, and that the reason was that Angus was said to have informed an important Nationalist that the Committee was opposed to the Nationalist cause and would give no further aid to it. Naturally, the Committee's representatives were baffled, and critical of Angus. The source of the misinformation was found to be, beyond doubt, Angus' San Francisco visitor.

Angus' reactions were those of any outraged American, and since he had his witnesses to the conversation, and his proof on other points, he proposed to set the position of himself and the Committee straight in Formosa and repair the damage done, even if it meant revealing the gentleman (such a devoted friend of America!) as a liar. But experienced experts in Chinese ways dissuaded him. They told him the false report was only part of an obvious Chinese game. The Nationalists thought they could get more aid from Angus' Committee by putting him and it on the defensive, and eager to prove friendship with dollars.

That was all pure politics, and perhaps no more Asian than American, though the psychology of the lie differed a little from the standard Washington technique. What seemed to Angus the Asian touch was the complete indifference to covering up the tracks. But the Asian mind was further revealed to him when he was assured that no harm whatever had been done by the false report, since none of the Chinese had believed it and were only play-acting. Angus concluded that his course in Asian psychology was too complicated, and shortly returned to more elementary studies in Washington.

These experiences made him realize how ignorant he must be of human psychology. He had more to learn about the Oriental mind than the greenest freshman had to learn about college mores, and much less chance of learning it. Thereafter he offered his thoughts on the Far East with a modesty that surprised his friends and disconcerted his critics. Though his reactions might not be in the least valuable to others, they were to him, for they set him thinking about the inadequacies of education, and particularly of his own. India, with a little help from China, had achieved what had taken years at Oxford and American universities: it had shaken the foundations of his most confident assumptions. His Oriental education was brief but it was cyclonic.

X

Political Economics

ADVENTURES in search of an education often bring it in unexpected forms. The voyager's danger is that he may take his own part in them too seriously. It is the Sancho Panzas and not the Quixotes who learn the most from tilting against windmills. Angus was about to embark on a new course in which economics was the nominal subject, but politics was the teacher and irony was the lesson. Had he been less of a Quixote and more of a Panza he would not have needed the lesson or would have left the windmills alone.

Economic diplomacy in the Netherlands had given him a taste of the rewards and frustrations of government service. It had enhanced his interest in politics and given him some claim to an understanding of applied economics. The experience had been a happy one and he was ready to serve his government again, though he made no advances to anyone connected with it.

Out of a clear sky and over a telephone less clear came the voice of Stuart Symington, then heading the National Security Resources Board and closely in the confidence of President Truman. Symington said he was commissioned to recommend an Administrator of Economic Stabilization to the President, and wanted to talk immediately with Angus about taking the job.

Angus had made no study of the Stabilization Act or of price and wage control. He knew it to be a specialized branch of economics about which there was very little tested knowledge but much strong opinion. He knew that under the best of conditions the job of the first Stabilizer would be extremely difficult and probably of brief duration. The widely variant interests of consumer and producer, wage earner and farmer, meant that any action taken or not taken regarding prices or wages was sure to bring strong criticism from some segments of society. The large staff envisaged, carrying new appointments and salaries across the nation, might make it the biggest bonanza in political patronage since the Post Office, and the fugitive educator wanted no part in that. No man in Washington was likely to be under greater pressures from both public and politicians than the Economic Stabilizer, and many of the pressures would be far from scrupulous.

Angus was not in sympathy with many of the policies and actions of the Truman Administration, and he had no confidence in its quality or character. Moreover, if the Administrator were Angus, he would have no support from the Democratic organization. Though a registered Republican, he could count on no protection from that party, to which he was a political maverick. The better a man's reputation when he went to Washington the greater the damage it might suffer; the less self-interested the more vulnerable. Everything the educator had learned argued that to accept would be foolhardy. Yet if a man wanted to serve his government, here was a chance.

Mr. Truman proved more impressive than Angus had expected, but it was characteristic of a Scotch Quaker that he insisted on stating very clearly to the President the conditions of his acceptance. He told Mr. Truman that as Stabilizer he would want the President's personal promise to protect him against pressures to make political appointments to his staff. He said that he could take no effective steps toward controlling inflation unless measures for cutting the cost of government were taken by Congress and the White House. He said that he saw price and wage levels as inextricably joined, so that action to "freeze" one would mean freezing the other, and that he interpreted the Stabilization Act to make joint action on prices and wages mandatory; that the first step must be industry-by-industry controls, and that that was where he, Angus, would start and might stop. He further said he could take the job only if the President would give him unqualified personal agreement to those terms and that he would be relieved if the President said no.

The President, perhaps more in desperation to secure a Stabilizer than in full agreement, gave an unqualified yes. Angus had used the simile of weighting down the lid of a teakettle to convey his opinion of the futility of wage-price controls without measures to turn down the flame of inflation beneath it. The President, who had probably heard the figure a dozen times, said emphatically that that was the best way of putting it he had ever heard. He added that since the beginning of the Korean War there had been no place for politics in a government agency so crucial as one concerned with economic stabilization. Angus was assured of the full support of the White House. It was further agreed that he would be directly responsible to the President; that, under Angus, the Director of Price Control should be a businessman, and that the President would appoint any good businessman whom Angus might recommend.

Angus accepted the job on those terms. Within five minutes he was in the hands of the President's press officer, and by the time he reached New York by plane, a little dazed, the story was ahead of him. For the first time in his life the cautious Quaker had set all reason aside. Instinct told him to take the risk, that no man could be choosy about the nature of his service to his government. Did he not have the President's pledged word to support him in all the matters he thought most important? So, on twelve hours' notice he set aside everything he had learned, broke his private life in half, and embarked on a new form of education, on lines he had not chosen, in work he did not know, with some men he did not admire, and with a future he could not envisage. The economic lamb was on the way to the nation's greatest political slaughterhouse, though it was not until Angus gave the new Economic Stabilization Act a thorough study that he realized all he had let himself in for. In the judgments of most men Angus' decision was his greatest blunder.

The Stabilizer brought certain economic convictions to his new office and held them unaltered when he left it. The first was that a nation's economic stability rests primarily on the attitudes, operations, and economic understanding of its people. No government can alone save its citizens from their mistakes. A government can create instability, but it cannot by itself maintain stability. It can contribute to curbing inflation or deflation by judicious management of its budget and currency, by general oversight of the national economy, and by the economic education of its citizens. But its touch must be light. By attempting mandatory controls too drastic, too general, or too circumscribing to normal business operations, government may impair the very economic stability it seeks to maintain.

In 1950 the concern of government was to restrain excessive inflation. Most of its officers thought of doing so through the dramatic but superficial method of establishing "ceilings" on prices and, if politically expedient, on wages. But to Angus any sound attack on inflation demanded that government first ask and answer the question what, under the given circumstances, constituted inflation. The level of prices was only a mirror of the economic forces beneath them, and the real question was the health of those forces and the amount of inflation or deflation that would be appropriate to assist the industry of the nation to accomplish the number one job of 1950. The economic job that had top priority was to put and keep the nation in a condition

to win a Korean war and if necessary a far larger war. That
meant the rapid production of military and strategic goods while
disturbing as little as possible the normal economy; maintaining
as much employment, public and private solvency and confidence, purchasing power, consumer goods and strength yet flexibility as the military needs would permit. The level of prices and
wages necessary to get that big job done might be quite different
from those the government should regard as proper if there were
no need for a suddenly expanded defense program. There was
no such thing as an absolute ideal level of prices, best at all times
and under all conditions.

Price levels are somewhat similar to the temperature of the
human body. A century ago the medical profession regarded
fever as something to be reduced as rapidly as possible for its own
sake. Doctors attacked the temperature directly instead of removing its cause. Modern physicians recognize that high tem-
peratures represent the body's efforts to adjust to abnormal conditions; the heart has gone to work to achieve a new, temporary
balance as the human engine accelerates to cope with the disease.
Prices are the temperature of the economic organism, the mani-
festations of its special crisis. Attempts to reduce them by direct
and arbitrary methods ignore their causes and could achieve only
superficial results. Angus was under the impression that the
government he was to serve would adopt the modern method of
getting at the causes, and that he would be only one of the physicians.

But rising prices brought rising specters to a public mind still
raw with the memory of 1932. In late 1950 the public, which
judged inflation not by what it received in wages or income but
by what it had to pay for all the things it wanted, demanded
with increasing clamor that the government hold down and even
by fiat reduce existing prices. At that point political issues entered to complicate wise economic action. A government facing
an election was eager to do all it could to please the public, even
if it knew that the public's judgment might be harmful to its own

long-run interests. The public regarded inflation as some doctors of 1800 regarded fever.

When all prices were ultimately frozen by government fiat in early 1951, they remained almost stable thereafter not because a price stabilizer, like another King Canute, ordered the tide of prices not to rise, but because the forces that made the inflation had begun to recede. Had this not been true, all the government's horses and men could not have enforced price ceilings, short of Gestapo methods.

The fact was that in mid-1950 the American people liked inflation to the extent it then existed, for although it increased the prices of what they bought it also increased the prices of what they sold, as well as their wages, their employment, and the value of their stock. They enjoyed the cake of inflation so long as the indigestion it gave them was only mild, but they wanted government to give them the panacea of price ceilings when it began to hurt too much. After China entered the Korean War, it became painful, though the indigestion was due more to nerves than to physical causes.

The Stabilization Act proved to be an almost unworkable pot-pourri of compromise between the various opinions and interests brought to bear on legislation. Congress had attempted to create an agency powerful enough to prevent inflation but not powerful enough to embarrass politicians or offend any politically important group of voters. To be effective, an agency would have to be empowered to control Congressional appropriations and the federal budget, cut down military expenditures, reduce interest rates, regulate installment buying, oversee the purchase of raw materials, and fix wages. Such an agency would step on every toe in Washington, and the thought of its creation by a Congress whose powers it would usurp was fantastic. The fact that only such a bill would permit an economic stabilizer to stabilize effectively seemed to Angus to prove how absurd was the policy of detailed federal control of economic forces in a great industrial democracy.

The Act actually passed by Congress substituted for the impossibilities of economic dictatorship the probabilities of confusion or impotence. In deference to one school of thought it authorized the Stabilizer to freeze all prices; in deference to another it made a general freeze illegal until the Stabilizer had already brought a substantial portion of the national economy under "selective" (i.e., separate) controls. But even this authority was almost hopelessly qualified. For example, prices and wages could not, as a practical matter, be controlled unless prices of meat and agricultural products could be controlled, yet Congress retained an agricultural parity support program that made it virtually impossible for a stabilizer to hold food prices at a fixed level.

To satisfy conservatives and businessmen, Congress had decreed in the Act that action on prices in a given area of the national economy must be accompanied by a comparable action on wages, and that the Stabilizer was charged to co-ordinate these actions. But it had also established separate agencies for price and wage control, independent of each other, and had made their officers appointees of the President. The Stabilizer, by law responsible for what each of them did, was thus relatively impotent to control and hence to co-ordinate them. Organized labor had declared its firm opposition to selective controls and to any regulation of wages by the Stabilizer, but shouted for a general freeze of prices. How could any stabilizer force a Wage Board with active and vocal union members to freeze wages simply because the Price Director had seen fit to freeze prices?

A third unofficial "agency" was in the picture, for in one serious wage dispute the White House took over, conducted negotiations, and approved settlements. It did this in the case of railway wages in December, 1950, without informing the Stabilizer or the Wage Board until after the fact. Angus ruefully compared himself to a circus rider mounted on two unruly horses labeled Price and Wage, which were charging off in separate directions, urged on by the cracking whip of political expediency.

In the initial interview in which the President assured Angus that he would keep political patronage out of stabilization, he made a second statement, and only later did Angus realize the irony of their juxtaposition. Mr. Truman said that he was placing one of his ablest White House assistants at Angus' disposal to help in assembling an initial cadre of skilled government workers, borrowed from other departments. Angus was glad of the help and promptly called, as instructed, on his new helper. It was Donald Dawson. Angus did not know then that Dawson's chief service to the President was reputedly the handling of political patronage. The cadre Dawson had already lined up was able and experienced, and many of them could be wholly trusted—by Donald Dawson. It was three months before Angus was certain of what he soon suspected: that some of these men had been sent not only to help him but to watch him and make sure that he kept in political line. Too late he discovered that directives he had issued had been quietly nullified or revised.

Under these conditions the best an honest economist could hope to do was to win voluntary agreements from trade and industry to hold the existing price level, using government fiat as little as possible. This, with a pitifully small staff, Angus went about as quietly as politicians and press would let him. Had he been able to assemble a staff sufficiently large, competent, and trustworthy, and had he had the support of government and public, that program would have been enough to cope with an inflation which by January, 1951, had nearly run its course.

After only a few weeks in office it was clear to the already politically unstable Stabilizer that what he was expected to do was to sit on the safety valve of inflation while government, labor, and the consumer built up more steam in the boiler. He was called upon to window-dress an administration reluctant to take sound but unpopular steps and eager to take popular ones, even if meretricious. His own term would be brief and futile and he would end it looking, to all except the most perceptive, either an incompetent or a fool.

The story of his political demise was fairly routine, but it was significant to him, and the method of his destruction was interesting. He was no match for his politically minded colleagues and stubbornly refused to use their weapons. It was revealing to observe how, when the Washington tide turned against him, it turned with unity and dispatch in the offices and corridors of White House, Congress, and pressrooms.

The President had agreed with Angus that the support of business was essential, and that able men from commerce and industry should be recruited as leaders in the Stabilization staff. But few first-rate businessmen were willing to serve, and it was easy to understand their reluctance. Most of them were not in general sympathy with the Truman Administration and its economic policies; many believed the new Act unworkable; some of them had served their government through the war and felt entitled to a few years of private life to recover; they feared the agency would be pressured into partisan politics, and they may well have hesitated to join an Administrator likely to be only briefly in office. The war was over, and the spirit of sacrifice had ended with it.

For nearly two months Angus made the search for an able Price Director his highest priority. He urged the post successively upon some thirty leading businessmen, and made personal appeals to the national business organizations and the heads of many large companies to help him find a good man. A few helped; some went through the motions; only one company head found a good man for Angus and arranged to make him available. It was the Monsanto Chemical Company, and the man was William Rand, its President. Mr. Rand indicated that he would take the job. The results were educational to an amateur economic statesman.

The President was away, so Angus forwarded the message asking for the President's approval of Rand as Price Director through Dawson, as directed. The call was made to Dawson over Angus' private wire to the White House, and no other person was at that time privy to the matter. The next morning the story of the Rand appointment broke in the New York *Times,* which refused to reveal the source of the leak. Meanwhile Dawson informed Angus that the President had rejected the nomination of Rand. Remembering his agreement with Mr. Truman, Angus indicated his shocked surprise and asked the reason. All he could get from Dawson was the comment that if Rand had come from any other state than Missouri the President would have appointed him.

The powers of Monsanto had opposed Mr. Truman politically in Missouri. Angus was never able to find any other explanation of the President's departure from his promise. Angus made every effort to find out how the news leaked to the press, and ended very certain that it had not leaked from the Stabilization office or from Rand. That left the White House. Rand had been made the undeserved casualty of a political twist and subjected to public embarrassment. As for Angus, the victim of his own misplaced confidence, he turned again with mounting desperation to the search of a Price Director. He would have to find one soon, for pressure to appoint a political lame duck was strong from Senators and national committeemen.

The gods finally decided to give Angus a Price Director and a final lesson in practical politics. The Mayor of Toledo was reported willing to resign his position to take the job. His name was Michael DiSalle. Inquiries into his qualifications were not as thorough as usual because the need was desperate, Angus was deeply involved in crucial wage problems, and few men outside Toledo seemed to know much about DiSalle. DiSalle was sent for and proved to be a baffling character to assess with confidence. If he had any knowledge of economics or price control, or any desire to learn their principles, he did not disclose it. Two men more different in background and methods could hardly have talked together about joining forces. But DiSalle emanated quiet confidence that he could do the job, and that was impressive. There was no visible alternative in the least degree acceptable. Angus took a chance.

On inquiry he found that the President who declined to appoint the head of Monsanto was ready without details to appoint the Democratic Mayor of Toledo. Angus immediately took DiSalle to the White House to recommend him to the President. The manner of their reception was illuminating. DiSalle was affably greeted in turn, as an old crony, by Dawson, by the Chairman of the Democratic National Committee (who seemed there on the purest chance), and by the President. A heavy aroma of political camaraderie hung in the air. The interview with the President was almost entirely devoted to a jocular discussion of politics in the State of Ohio, and problems of price control were hardly mentioned. Somehow the press was waiting en masse as they emerged from Mr. Truman's office, and to the reporters DiSalle was far more revealing about his plans than he had been to Angus. He told them that he would not only hold prices where they were but would "roll back" some of them. He did not say how, but the reporters were delighted by his confidence and wit, and DiSalle stayed happily in their graces for some months.

From that day Angus had a new intellectual interest, and regretted that there was not more time to study DiSalle as he deserved study. He wished that the work were less important, so that one would not have to bother about the effects of DiSalle's operations but could enjoy them as one enjoys a movie thriller. The Toledo ex-mayor's personality, values, and political methods were intriguing: Angus could not help speculating on him as a type produced by twentieth-century America, and on the ultimate effects of this type on democracy. But nothing Angus had been taught qualified him to assess or to cope with this natural phenomenon. It was as foolish to be angry at DiSalle's maneuvers as with a dog that yields to his natural instinct to chase cats.

Inscrutability and transparency, economic indifference and political shrewdness, the professional comic and the professional politician were so neatly mixed and so brilliantly utilized toward personal ends that Angus realized that at last he had found the perfect politician. As Angus watched DiSalle turn the ability to amuse into a powerful political weapon he realized he had read his Shakespeare badly, for he should have known that shrewd clowning can be more influential than cautious accuracy. And DiSalle knew what Angus was only learning: that in the Washington of 1951 no politics were too crude to work if one had the right flair and the right backing. In the weeks that followed, Angus confirmed the conclusions of Machiavelli.

From the day of DiSalle's appointment the character of the Stabilization agency changed, and its atmosphere became more political. What had been a reasonably tight economic ship began to leak information. DiSalle surrounded himself with characters that did not look or act like economists or businessmen. What they knew and thought and did, no one seemed to know; Angus never did. They kept as remote as possible from Angus and the staff he had assembled; they met behind closed doors and protective secretaries or in well-serviced hotel suites, often in company with one or two Congressmen and reporters. When Angus needed to reach DiSalle immediately he often found him at the Press Club.

These men may not have been economists but they knew and cared about what the public wanted, and the public seemed to want an immediate freeze of all prices. It was unaware of how far Angus and his staff had got in obtaining voluntary agreements, industry by industry, to hold price levels on basic commodities, or how effective those agreements would soon prove to be. Had the public known, it would still not have been satisfied; it was impatient for some drastic over-all action. By a general price freeze DiSalle could please almost everyone.

Of course the public did not know that the Wage Board could not achieve the concomitant general freeze on wages that the Act called for. Organized labor had secured sliding scale wage agreements in some industries, and to tamper with these was to court strikes all but fatal to the production of certain war essentials. By negotiation with industry and labor, progress on holding back or minimizing wage increases was being made. The public was impatient of these delicate balances even when it understood them. It wanted someone to wave a magic wand that would at once reduce the prices of what they bought, maintain the prices of what they sold, and put high wages in their pockets.

In championing before the public a general price freeze the Price Director could maneuver Angus into a position so unpopular that he would lose public support, and then the Administration could not afford to back him. This was accomplished with speed and skill. It was leaked to the press that DiSalle was drawing up an order for an immediate freezing of all prices, which he would shortly submit to Angus for approval. When the press reported this to the public, prices went up while they could still be raised, and this provided an added argument for a general freeze to keep them from going still higher.

The public applauded DiSalle's plan, unaware that neither the agency's legal counsel nor the Bureau of the Budget would recommend it to Angus for his approval. Nor could Angus find in his own staff or among his consultants a single man who would recommend it except as a matter of political expediency. Angus promptly rejected the order when DiSalle finally brought it to him, and the Democratic heavens began to fall on his head.

The sidereal descent came quickly. DiSalle and his friends demanded through the press that the Stabilizer grant full authority for all actions on prices to the Price Director, and after a sufficient public build-up made the request formally to Angus. Angus could not, under the Act, thus disclaim his own responsibility, even had he been willing to do so. At that point melodrama of the old Lyceum Hall type appeared to make the scene more colorful. The Democratic National Committee summoned the Agency's general counsel to appear before it. On the counsel's bristling return from the meeting he reported to Angus that the acting chairman of the National Committee had dramatically waved a stiletto-like letter-opener at him and sent the message to Angus that if he did not promptly grant full price powers to DiSalle he would "wake up with a knife like this in his back."

Angus was learning something about in-fighting in the Truman Administration, and it was not a game he liked. The struggle was now in the open and there was no doubt who would win, but Angus wanted to hold on until he had developed a staff and a program that would prevent in some measure the turning of the Stabilization agency into an agency of party politics and party employment. Working with the Price Director and previous heads of price control, during and after the war, he sponsored the preparation of an administratively feasible and legally sound order for a general freeze of prices on the earliest practicable date. That date must be a secret lest speculators turn it to personal profit at public expense. The date "leaked," and that fact, together with several other episodes, determined Angus that either he or DiSalle must go.

After a thoughtful intervening Sunday, Angus formally asked the President to secure the resignation of DiSalle, and stated some of the reasons in writing. He went about his business for three days, and then called to report that a general order freezing all prices could be issued in about two weeks. He also inquired whether the President would act on his recommendation regarding DiSalle. He was told the President would not, but would welcome resignation by Angus. Angus agreed, since he had already determined to resign immediately if DiSalle were kept.

The next morning Angus handed his letter of resignation to the President. The letter made no reference to DiSalle, or to any lack of support from the White House. The President was cordial, and after a brief talk handed Angus a very courteous reply. Later he asked Angus to call, but the nature of the conversation was confidential and Angus never revealed it. He resisted strong pressure from newspapers and magazines to make a statement.

The brief Stabilizer tried hard to regain detachment and perspective on an experience that hurt his pride more than it hurt him. He had made his position untenable by refusing to act until he was ready, and by charging the windmill of practical politics. He had no right to complain, for he had deliberately exposed himself. He had insisted on his own economic creed; he had ventured into a game in which he was not only a novice but unwilling to play by the professional rules, and the professionals had given him a mauling. He had taken at face value the word of a President known to be a politician, when he should have realized that any pledge given by any politician has a codicil: it is automatically qualified by the unspoken phrase "unless it is politically inexpedient." Angus had made his presence highly inexpedient to a President who had supported him longer than he might have expected. Whom could he blame but himself?

And yet, there were other matters at stake besides Angus' personal pride or welfare, and to those he could be less easily reconciled. What he had seen of the inner workings of democratic government at its highest level did not seem to him a pretty picture. It provided him with much food for thought about democracy as it is, compared with democracy as its founders conceived it and speakers describe it on Independence Day. Was his own experience typical, and if so was there no place in Washington for the kind of idealism Angus had brought there, simply because he nursed it too inflexibly? He wanted to believe that what he saw and learned was the product of that particular Administration, but was he blaming Mr. Truman and his associates unjustly for conditions that exist under every President? Angus did not know the answers any better after some years of speculation.

So far as his education was concerned, his adventures in Holland and Washington were invaluable. He had been exposed in the Netherlands to the most thorough and expensive course in international economics the world had ever offered. His Washington course in domestic economy had been less perfect but equally instructive in unplanned ways. It too had been expensive, especially to his ego. There was still much he did not know about economics, but he doubted his capacity to learn more or his chance to use what he knew. He ruled all government service out of his future, for he was unwilling to abandon a conviction he knew to be naïve in government circles—that there is a dividing line between what is expedient and what is right.

XI

The Political Mind

THE fugitive from the ivory tower had become the fugitive from Capitol Hill. Education had led him to politics and politics had led him to new education, but neither had taught him how to function happily in either environment. To both he was now a displaced person. He had no desire to be anything else, but his come-uppance in politics left him with much to think about, and a sharpened curiosity about the mental machinery of those who direct democratic government. Though he remained remote from the doings of capital and campus, he continued to speculate on the vagaries of their practices.

The practice of politics has been called the systematic organization of hatreds. Though Angus had some reasons for disillusion, he could not agree. He had not found hatred the chief ingredient of the Washington stew. The politician, as distinguished from the statesman, may not shrink from using for his purposes whatever hatreds come easily to hand, but he seldom creates or organizes them. Men who pull the wires in Washington, or in any

Middletown in the country, may indulge in sharp practices, but they have no conscious intention of dividing democratic society into separate particles mutually repelled by hate. The average politician is by instinct a placater, a compromiser, a unifier, for elections are more often won by solidarities than by schisms. Most political animosities are more conventional than deep, and exaggerated for public consumption. The politician's attitude is too professional to let him give way to emotions unless they are politically expedient, and most of his ends are better gained by friendship, real or simulated, than by hatred.

The practice of politics is the systematic organization not of hatreds but of half-truths. Specious reasons are its stock in trade, and professional politicians exploit them until they fool even themselves. They become masters by habit of the impressive non sequitur, and of selecting whatever facts support their predetermined objectives and discarding the rest. The political mind can carry expedient rationalization to a technical fantasy never more interesting than in the mental acrobatics of the writhing twenty-two Republican Senators who voted against the McCarthy censure motion of November, 1954. Angus decided that if he were ever to teach political psychology, he would make the records of the Army-McCarthy hearings and the Senate censure debates his principal texts.

The cerebral process of the politician is the reverse of the professor's. The professor begins with facts and from them tries to find a principle. The politician begins with the practical end he wishes to gain, elevates it into a principle, and then selects or adjusts facts to support it. His method is in mundane affairs the more successful of the two, but it works only when he knows in advance what decision he wishes retroactively to reach. When the issue is one in which he has no party line or personal predilection to guide him, the politician is lost. He has to start with the conclusion and work back to the reasons. As logic, his accomplishment is like reading in a mirror. When robbed of the guidance of his objective he can only await the divination of the supernatural in its modern form of the will of the people. When he wishes to pursue truth for its own sake he has forgotten how.

Angus had thought Mr. Nehru's mind must operate in some fourth dimension, but observation of the Washington mind explained the Indian statesman better than the universities or the Sacred Books. Mr. Nehru's logic was baffling because he was thinking like an American politician. Both reversed the usual process in order to make the evidence fit the time. The Indian mystic and the Missouri ex-President might be mentally closer than they knew.

It was only when Angus realized this that he understood some of the conferences he attended in government circles. There policy decisions were sometimes made and men advanced or sidetracked for no apparent reasons, or for reasons quite irrelevant to any pattern of rationality—even the rationale of self-interest. In some conferences of federal officers in which Angus sat, the decision reached seemed to him to be the exact opposite of that indicated by the facts and arguments presented. It was as though the participants were all engaged in a discussion merely in formal deference to the principle of consultation, which had nothing to do with the final conclusion someone would somehow reach and establish. The conferees seemed to be waiting for some external power or circumstance to bring them the miracle of decision.

Would a gust of air through the conference window blow from the table all the recommendations but one? Would someone's secretary, handing notes about the table, inadvertently drop a remark indicating what decision the staff of assistants expected this group of great men to reach, and thereby present them with their verdict? Would some press reporter publish an article predicting the line they would take, so that depending on their opinion of him and his paper they would know whether to accept or reject it? Would a telegram arrive from somewhere that would make up their minds for them? Would the fact that one of them had to leave for London or Miami in half an hour, and must therefore be heard among the first, make his opinion determinant; would the group grasp gratefully at the first straw of hinted opinion in some muttered aside, so that all could rush on to other important conferences and decisions, and leave it to the secretariat to consolidate their vague mumblings into rational form? Sometimes such men sat as if they were awaiting a supernatural sign or the return of a messenger sent by special plane to consult a nebulous oracle at a nebulous Delphi. Once or twice Angus had the curious illusion that most men in government were in a state of semishock, with minds dazed by the powers and responsibilities they bore or the machinery they had to serve, or drugged by infinite briefings and memoranda. Angus concluded that as Stabilizer he had been a victim of the partial coma that seizes normal men on sudden exposure to bureaucracy.

For a while he suspected that some of the top-level sessions he attended must have been held simply for window-dressing; that the decision had previously been made in a secret session and would be cautiously unwrapped here. But surely men of cabinet rank would not be taking time for such a farce, merely to fool a newcomer in their councils. Later he realized that what was being concluded, there in his presence, by a kind of mental osmosis or negative confusion, was the actual decision. He was observing the political mind in action at its highest level.

Perhaps the process was rational and he alone could not detect its rationality, like the fourth dimension of Indian logic. But in his incomprehension he was in good company. William Ewart Gladstone, himself a master of the art of inexplicable political decision, had, near the end of his career, written of his fellow statesmen: "Politicians are the men whom, as a rule, it is most difficult to comprehend. I have never . . . thought I understood above one or two."

Angus had been offered a partial explanation from a high source. After a session of the Truman inner cabinet around a table in the White House, one of its ablest and most powerful members remarked to Angus as they walked out together: "You will never understand this Administration until you realize that we are, to all practical purposes, a labor government." Angus had begun to suspect that, as he observed the dismay in White House and Congress if the Economic Stabilizer took any position that might offend organized labor, but it was illuminating that a leading cabinet member whom Angus then hardly knew would say it so tersely to an outsider. Unfortunately, it made the decision the group had just reached even more unintelligible, for it had no bearing on the interests of organized labor. When labor interests arose in that group the mental process was clear enough.

Perhaps politicians, whether from Delhi or from Kansas City, depend on some guidance higher than reason, though certainly lower than the angels. Are their minds specially attuned to some wave length of instinct that rises above the pitch of rationality? Angus thought he had learned something of human nature in various universities and less exalted way stations, but he had expected that politicians would know far more about human motivations. Perhaps this irrationality was the quality of their genius: they understood men well enough to know that reason plays a small part in human decisions, and that therefore the more irrational they are, the more likely to be at one with the majority. One could make a good case, over history, for the success of those who were guided by signs and portents. Perhaps Gallup Polls, Winchell's columns, and the aura of a labor union meeting are the modern equivalent of medicine men and Macbeth's witches. Since the better reason is often unpalatable, since half-truth is often more powerful than truth, perhaps a mind like that of Angus, painfully persisting in trying to depend on reason, is therefore disqualified for service to the democratic process. Perhaps the politician does not fall below reason but rises above it.

But the more Angus saw of these men, the more he doubted that they understood, better than others, men's motives and emotions. In their assumptions of what the people are thinking they are as often wrong as right. Like the producers of Hollywood and the tabloids, their only consistent assumption seems to be that nothing can be crude enough to offend most of the people most of the time; that the only universal motives are self-interest, sensationalism, and the desire to be amused. Only a few men in political life—the statesmen as distinct from the politi-cians—seek to elevate society; the rest only utilize it. The politi-cian may begin his career with circumspection toward truth and the higher ideals of democracy, but he soon adopts the accepted techniques. How can he help to elevate politics unless he is elected, and how can he be elected unless he plays the game—at least in a decent way? Even men of the highest personal standards and motivations are led into that syllogism. The 1952 speeches and bearing of Adlai Stevenson set a new political high in their quality and perspective, but by late 1954 he was yielding a little to the established pattern of political demagoguery. Mr. Eisen-hower, another man of exceptional standards, had made earlier concessions to the political common denominator.

The explanation of the logic of the average politician may be simpler than Angus thought. When their actions are difficult to understand it may be not because they are subtle but because they are confused. What looks like shrewdness or the wisdom of in-stinct is merely the vacillation of the unsure mind. Occasional lapses into apparent integrity or courage could conceivably be simply the desperation of the baffled man. One sees enough sim-ple crudity in some politicians to doubt whether they are at other times very subtle. Even if they have the ability to see beyond the immediate political need of the situation, they have so little time to do so. They must move on to the next legislative bill, the next request from a constituent, the next election, the next crisis.

Under those pressures all but the most external amenities of human relationships must go by the board. There may be much corridor geniality and many exchanges of mutual respect or de-votion, but they rarely go deeper than immediate interest or po-litical convenience. Political Washington becomes a place to make acquaintances and lose friends. Its dominant school is the school of expediency. Its basic tenet is that with sufficient need and ingenuity the means can be found to excuse the attainment of almost any end. There are few men in Washington, under any administration, with talent, integrity, and maneuverability, who avoid this canon and give notable and disinterested public service over many years; many attempt it but are broken or frustrated in the effort. Even if successful they usually emerge a little cynical or a little dingy from the contacts of political success.

That atmosphere is diminishing to the values the educated man has been taught to respect, for in the smoke-filled rooms of political strategy men's effectiveness is impaired by idealism and advanced by lack of it. High personal quality is swamped by mediocrity and self-seeking. Angus could not understand why American society was not more disturbed by the average quality of its public servants, since they were shaping world events and the lives of America's children. As he watched federal statesmanship it seemed a tightrope walk over pressure groups, cross-purposes, and the morass of confused or second-rate minds. There was no further lesson to be learned, except the miraculous power or luck of American democracy in surviving the mediocrity of its political middlemen.

Anything else that Washington could teach in practical politics could be learned more comfortably, and more safely, from a quiet reading of Andrew Jackson, Martin Van Buren, Mark Hanna, and Franklin D. Roosevelt. Intellectually, Washington had nothing of its own to give; it was not a capital but a mirror. Like the long pools in its beautiful Mall, it reflected whatever changes of intellectual climate were blown to it from north, south, and west. There were notable and inspiring exceptions, but they were too few to raise the spirits. As for the members of House and Senate, most of them had little to offer in ideas except the views of their constituents. Angus could not see that the collective political results of this mass of eager operators were any better than could have been achieved by a group of professors or businessmen chosen at random across the country.

His judgment was not based wholly on brief periods as Economic Stabilizer and with the Economic Cooperation Administration. He had grown up among local politicians and was familiar with their ways. When he went to Washington it was with the mistaken assumption that national politicians at the top of their profession would have greater ability and higher visions than the small-time operators of Long Island, Philadelphia, or upstate New York. He should have known better, for he had been in contact with the national scene in a variety of minor ways since 1940, when he served as Director of the National Committee of Democrats-for-Willkie. That experience alone should have disabused him of the idea that national political operators were, except in power, any different from local ones.

In the history of the 1940 campaign the work of that temporary maverick committee counted for very little, but it convinced Angus of the comparative efficiency of businessmen and even the maligned professors. He saw no political strategy in the upper councils of either national party that showed any gain in methods or objectives over that of Martin Van Buren or Mark Hanna—or as skillful as what he had observed in some faculty meetings at Yale. Here was a Republican organization presented with one of the most colorful and appealing candidates in its history, yet it did all it could to turn him into a drab specimen of party regularity and double-talk. Even in a time of imminent war, neither party seemed able to lift itself above its traditional patterns of voter appeal. The dictionary meaning of the word "campaign" connotes a planned and orderly operation, but the 1940 campaign began with party disorganization and ended with party extemporizing and recrimination. Politicians played chiefly by ear. Surveying their activities as he saw them then, Angus concluded that if businessmen and universities planned and performed no better than they, both would soon be bankrupt.

Angus realized that it was unjust and futile to waste time inveighing against the weaknesses of the operating mechanics of our democratic system. They are what democratic society has made them—what it has thrown to its surface to operate its policy. In their quality and values they represent that society, and represent it all too accurately. Their flaws are only more apparent than those of the average American because their actions are conducted under public scrutiny, and because the nature of their work accentuates them. If society's operators are mediocre, if they instinctively put expediency before principle, they do so with the general acceptance of society.

All politicians everywhere have been attracted by expediency, but in the Washington of 1950 a man could carry it to surprising lengths and get away with it. Angus remembered an interesting example from his Stabilization days. In a formal appearance before the Joint Committee on Defense Production on December 21, 1950, Michael DiSalle, the Director of Price Stabilization under Angus, stated to the Committee that he could not testify on an order, prepared in his office, establishing a temporary freeze on the prices of new motorcars, since that order had been issued before he took office. Angus, who was sitting next to DiSalle, could hardly believe his ears.

DiSalle had accepted appointment from the President on November 31, and had gone to work, full time, on December 6. He was sworn into office on December 12 and the price order was issued on December 18. He had been active in discussions of motorcar prices from the very day on which the price increases which occasioned the order were announced, and he had approved, arranged, and with the Administrator presided over the meetings with the manufacturers. He had been the central figure in the later office discussions as to what action should be taken; he had made the decision to issue the restraining order, and had stated directly to the Administrator that he approved his signing that order. Yet the official stenotype record of the Committee session verified what Angus had heard DiSalle say.*

* See the official stenotype Report of Proceedings of a Hearing held before the Joint Committee on Defense Production on Thursday, December 21, 1950, and compare with items in the Washington *Post* of December 1 to 18, 1950, and with DiSalle's statements in the official printed record of a Hearing before the Senate Committee on Banking and Currency held May 14, 1951.

Angus sent for DiSalle; sat with him alone; stated the facts and asked him to comment. DiSalle declined to do so. Angus then asked DiSalle to inform the Chairman of the Committee that he had made a mistake in his statement and wished to correct it. DiSalle smilingly refused. Angus then said that as Administrator he was obliged to order DiSalle to correct his misstatement. DiSalle quietly said he would do no such thing.

The issue was clear and Angus did not greatly care what happened from that point, but he was still trying to understand the motives of this interesting man. DiSalle had once told Angus that he would like to be a Senator from Ohio. Angus now reminded him of this and suggested that for that reason if for no other DiSalle could not afford to have his testimony stand unaltered on the record of Congress. DiSalle replied that so long as the present party was in power he had no worries, and if the party went out of power he would then have no chance of being elected a Senator. The stenotype record stood unaltered in 1955, when DiSalle, with the reported backing of Mr. Truman, was the runner-up for the Chairmanship of the Democratic National Committee.

Once the pain of parting was over, Angus' interest in DiSalle was as a striking specimen of one type of American being produced by our present education and culture. There are other types of political operators, and federal workers fall into still a separate class, though not always as separate as they should be. Federal employees are a special variation of the political mind, and of their several categories the members of the Department of State are the most distinct and interesting. Over the decade before 1953 Angus had several different opportunities to watch them in action. His personal experiences were not thorough enough to make him an authority on that unique fauna, the diplomatic bureaucrat, but he could not avoid forming opinions. He realized that in talking about the State Department he should put aside his own irritations and frustrations and stick to the facts of his experience. It would be difficult to be impersonal, but he would try.

In the foreign service and the Department in Washington Angus came upon many able and attractive men. Collectively, their knowledge and experience were impressive. Many of them put the highest interests of the nation, as they saw them, before personal ambitions. Some did not, and some others confused the larger loyalty by the smaller one, unconsciously putting the welfare of Department traditions before the welfare of the nation. There were many whose personal talents did not seem to be better than average yet who were in posts of great influence, actual if not in title.

Angus did not form as good an opinion of the Department as of its individual members. As a whole it lacked coherence and efficiency. To what extent this was due to the structure of its organization he did not know. He had neither the qualifications nor the desire to contribute one more blueprint for reorganization to those already filling the files of the capital city. Angus was satisfied that if its structure and methods of operation were not perfect it was not from lack of advice. The difficulties seemed to him to go much deeper.

So far as the wisdom of State policies was concerned, Angus was no more critical than the average American. He saw enough to know that many international problems are not as simple as they seem; that officers of State are often forced to temper their ideal policy to public opinion, the capacities of military defense, and the necessities of internal politics. There are occasions when the Department cannot make public at the time all the factors it must consider. In a few cases like that of Indonesia, Angus thought he knew enough to offer criticisms; in most cases he recognized he did not. No Secretary of State could be expected to please one particular citizen all the time. Angus' concern was not centered about the affirmative policies of the Department of State.

He was more disturbed about its occasional lack of policy. This was true in the case of Southeast Asia. The private Committee for Free Asia was eager to take no steps affecting Asia that were not in line with the official policy of the United States government. As President of that Committee Angus had many sessions with various officers of the State Department to find out what its policy was. He was always received with courtesy, and was often assured by men at its top levels that they were ready to help the Committee in any possible way.

It was not long before Angus was compelled to conclude that in the early 1950s the Department had no clear-cut policy regarding Southeast Asia. There was only a general desire to strengthen American friendships and to prevent communist inroads. Beyond that there were uncertainties and conflicts. One leading member of the Department, himself charged with the formulation of policy in that part of the world, told Angus privately that there was no clearly defined policy for the Far East, and told him why. A few weeks later Angus reported that statement to a Secretary of one of the Defense arms, who agreed there was no policy but angrily denied the reasons why.

Angus saw many incidents in his own work to corroborate this revelation. He found various policies, quite inconsistent with one another, within the State Department. He watched several different groups take independent steps in Asia that confused and damaged each other and the standing of the United States. He could never find out which policies and which groups acted with the approval of the Secretary of State, if any of them did. Each conference he held in the Department was with a different group of its experts, and from no two groups did he ever get similar opinions and advice. Sometimes men sent by the Department to speak for it betrayed complete ignorance of what their colleagues had said or done.

A typical example was the question whether, where, and on what terms Angus' Committee should set up anticommunist broadcasting in Asia. This was under discussion with the State Department for many months. Each group that Angus dealt with there assured him it spoke with the authority of the Department. Within a three-month period one group recommended abandoning all broadcasting to Asia; a second, that it be greatly amplified; a third urged the purchase and outfitting of a special ship as a roving broadcasting station; a fourth proposed an elaborate installation in Burma; a fifth, in the Philippines; another, in Japan. When all these were finally dealt with, a "final" meeting was held with a Committee of the Department, few of whose members had taken part in the earlier talks or apparently knew much about them. The new group suddenly urged the abandonment of all the carefully prepared plans and the development of a base for the Committee's broadcasting operations in India. This had been agreed impossible by all previous Department representatives, and from his own investigations Angus knew that to be the case.

The difficulty went further than inconsistencies in advice; it included contradictions in practice. A top officer of government assured Angus that his Committee's representatives in Asia would be given co-operation and free hands in certain Asian countries, and in Angus' presence called in his subordinates and instructed them to that effect. The orders were not only disregarded but were reversed in practice by some of those same subordinates and their juniors in the field. When Angus reported this to the superiors, apologies were offered but the subordinates were not reprimanded and continued to flout their orders. Angus knew of a similar case in China just before it was taken over by the communists. A junior State Department officer there deliberately disobeyed specific cabled instructions personally sent him by an Assistant Secretary of State. Since that time the man has been several times promoted, and has held an important ambassadorial post.

When Angus was Chief of the ECA mission in the Netherlands he received an official cable from the Department of State reporting that the International Bank would shortly announce its refusal of a loan requested by the Netherlands government because the Bank did not approve the Netherlands financial policy. Copies of this cable had been sent to the offices of Harriman in Paris and Hoffman in Washington, and Angus knew they would be read and believed by a large number of ECA officers. Angus was able to identify from internal evidence the actual author of the cable, though it bore the name of a very high government officer who had never seen it. Angus had talked in Washington only a few weeks before with John McCloy, the President of the Bank, Robert Garner, its Vice-President, and other officers, and they had told him in confidence that they approved the Netherlands loan and policy. He cabled back questions that brought a thorough investigation. Two representatives of the Bank flew immediately from Washington and denied categorically the statements in the cable. The loan was granted.

Angus reported the matter to his chiefs and to the State Department, where the offender was a very junior employee—an ardent supporter of the Indonesian Republic. Angus received a long personal reply, explaining that it would be inexpedient "at this time" to cashier or discipline the offender. Some months after Angus had left the government service the young man was given the unusual reward for valuable services of joining a special government mission to Indonesia. So far as Angus ever knew, the cable episode never adversely affected the young man's government career.

Many such episodes are due less to deliberate intent than to lack of co-ordination within government. Angus came on many examples of lack of effective liaison. ECA officers were instructed to explain to American businessmen that European countries should, during their economic crisis, purchase European goods with European currency whenever they could. This would stimulate Europe's manufacture and trade, and save its American dollars for the purchase of necessary goods obtainable only from America. But at the same time American consuls in Europe were, in obedience to their orders from the State Department, encouraging and helping all American businessmen in Europe to sell all they could to Europeans, and the Department of Commerce was sometimes taking the same position. Thus an American machine tool manufacturer in Holland would hear one policy from Angus in The Hague and an opposite one from the American Consul in Amsterdam.

At the time that was an important matter, but in far greater ones there was also very little co-ordination between various agencies of the American government at work in Europe. ECA was working and spending American taxpayers' dollars to re-establish the Rhine as a traffic route on its old international basis. At the same time General Lucius Clay, heading our armed forces in Germany, was, for military reasons, working and spending other American taxpayers' dollars to develop a new line of carrying trade from the German seaports by land to the Rhineland area. This contretemps was known in top Washington circles, as of course it was in every European capital, but the two mutually contradictory efforts continued for more than a year.

One department of government was in 1949 facilitating the sale of certain goods to Russia; another department was doing its best to prevent the exchange. The two departments had different lists of what constituted strategic materials, and neither would concede to the other. Later, when Angus was Economic Stabilizer, that agency did everything possible to keep the American people from a state of mind that would create further inflation of prices and wages; at the same time the Department of Defense was making purchases—including reserve supplies that would not be needed for many years—at prices that were constantly inflating the market. Various Congressmen and Senators were making, in public speeches, hints of further inflation that sent wages and prices further upward. When Angus protested this to the President at a quasi-cabinet meeting he got sympathy but no assistance.

During World War II certain government research agencies and military officers were moving heaven and earth to put certain scientists to work on crucial war weapons, and were willing to accept full responsibility for the men. Other government agencies and military officers opposed many cases on security grounds. As a result much important research was prevented or seriously delayed. In one such case Angus was told, by the officer who had refused to permit a certain scientist to undertake such work in his university, that his refusal was based on the fact that the scientist had been born in Vienna (fifty years earlier); that Vienna had been the home of several revolutions and many socialists; that as a boy the scientist must have been familiar with both; and that "any man familiar with the great revolutionary movements of history is disqualified for secret war research." Angus suggested that the officer himself probably knew something of the events of 1776, but the decision stood.

The weaknesses Angus thought he saw in the Department of State apply in varying degrees to other departments of the federal government. The abilities and judgment of their individual members often fail to coalesce into comparable cumulative wisdom and efficiency. Department policies and operations are consequently less good than many individuals who form and direct them. Sometimes there are only varied opinions instead of uniform policy; sometimes policy is so loosely defined that bureaucrats interpret it as they please. Sometimes there is a clear policy but no collective will to implement it loyally and consistently. Government seems like a basketball team of thousands of shouting and running players, in which the man with the ball will pass it only to a few of his teammates. Each player wants to make all the shots, or is afraid to shoot at all. The sweet reason and detachment of the few are submerged in the rivalries of the many. In only one respect is the State Department unique: no other organization has so many privates and corporals with the manners, and sometimes the influence, of major generals.

Whatever may be the causes of these weaknesses, the numerical expansion of federal government is certainly one of them. It makes efficient co-ordination and liaison almost impossible. The country would benefit if the number of things the government tries to do were considerably reduced, and the number of people trying to do them were cut by perhaps one third. Departments, agencies, and workers now get into one another's way. The American passion for expansion has overreached the American genius for organization. It would not be easy to reduce government functions, curb the political patronage which supports expansion, and revise the civil service so that government can both protect the able and the loyal and dismiss the incompetents and the slackers. It will always be easier to augment a government staff than to reduce it.

In any case there are flaws in our government more basic than its megalomania. Its only consistency of policy derives from the continued dominance of one political party. For the Republican or Democratic party to remain in control it must win elections. To win elections in the twentieth century it must convince most of the voters that it will maintain national prosperity. Government is forced to become first of all a machine to stimulate and increase employment, wages, production, and consumption, and domestic statesmanship must be subordinated to that end. Politics has become a contest of economic interests masquerading as a conflict of principles. Most of the rest is campaign talk.

That talk conceals a curious attitude toward democracy. There is a discrepancy between politicians' public assertions of faith in the common man and their private doubts of his political capacity. The first is shown in words; the second in deeds. Most men long in government act as though they think the public can absorb political truth only in calculated doses, usually best coated with sugar. The skill of democratic politics lies in the astuteness with which the doses are administered and the sugar is provided. There are a few cases, such as national security, where this method of easing out truth is justified, but it is also used for purposes of party politics and personal advancement. Democracy is based on the conviction of the wisdom of the common man if he is given all the facts, but it is administered by cautious purveyors of small pills for the body politic. No men are more eloquent in stating their faith in the wisdom of the people, yet

Angus came on very few who acted in practice as though they really believed in it.

The insincerity is often unconscious, for men so accustomed to rationalization fool even themselves. President Truman was a striking example of the political dual personality. He was both the honest and courageous statesman and the politician to whom party success was the highest end. Angus saw even Mr. Truman's manner and vocabulary automatically change from impressive *gravitas* at the cabinet table to wisecracking heartiness and vulgarisms of speech at a Democratic party gathering or a conference with political cronies. In this he was no different from many others; he simply played both roles better because he played both sincerely. Responsibility had turned the politician into the statesman, but the statesman could never wholly escape from being the politician his earlier conditioning had made him. When the political stakes were high, the man of the White House reverted to the political satellite from Missouri, and the shift was so natural that the President would have denied that it ever took place. However unfortunate this chameleon quality might be for statesmanship, it was an asset to the Democratic party, which could not have stayed in power after 1948 had not a President with moments of real statesmanlike vision become the "Harry of the whistle-stops," ready to "pour it on." The success of the role was its appeal to the dual personalities of many voters, who admire statesmen but cast their ballots for the men who amuse them or fortify their egos by seeming as ordinary, and hence as "human," as themselves.

The longer Angus watched the operations of democracy, the more he became convinced that it could not solve its gigantic new problems unless it could develop a society more responsible as individuals. That was a cliché, but it was less a cliché to suggest that a responsible society must be one which builds up in its members higher standards in culture and ethics as well as in material goods. America is committed to the kind of popular sovereignty in which the people determine the nation's cultural and ethical standards as well as its politics. The dominant attitude is that what pleases the majority must be good, that the judgments of fifty million purchasers cannot be wrong, whether in politics, music, literature, or manners. At present it is prepared to follow no cultural leadership except the cultural leadership of the wealthy or of the popular.

The older plutocracy no longer sets the standards, for the New Deal nearly destroyed it. But the many who now share the wealth have not set notably higher standards of social responsibility, cultivation, and conduct. As for the cultural leadership of the popular—the idols of radio, screen, and sports—it offers small promise of elevated standards in thought, taste, or ethics. As a total human organism, American society shows little by way of standards or order except what is derived from its economic functions and ambitions. There is no evidence that America is successfully developing the democratic *aristoi* advocated by Thomas Jefferson, that great champion of the common man, or that the majority of Americans really desire it; many of them condemn the idea as undemocratic. They confuse democracy with egalitarianism, which can lead only to cultural anarchy.

One way to evaluate democracy and the political mind would be to assess the society they create. So Angus turned again to Washington, whose society presumably would be the clearest social expression of the democratic mind. Since the city was built as a political center, erected on no economic foundations and dominated by its governmental society, the quality of its culture and values should be a fair measure of the standards of democracy. As the capital of the world's most powerful free nation one could expect it to offer a social life unrivaled in brilliance and in the stimulating interplay of independent and powerful minds. Where, if not in Washington, would one look for a society expressing democracy's social ideals?

Except for a few families established there for generations, who have less influence on its manners and values than they think, contemporary Washington society has the atmosphere of a resort hotel or a military camp. Its residents are mostly temporary or in fear of being temporary. Even its civil service employees, who do not in any case dominate its upper strata, are uncertain of their geographical stability. Its political society has no roots; its diplomatic society no tenure; its bureaucratic society no *esprit*. There is little civic spirit among its peripatetics, and the fact that the residents of the District have no vote is more symbolic of their psychic instability than they know. Conversation is largely local gossip, not less trivial because it gossips about big names and big issues. It is usually as limited and inaccurate as shop gossip in any other one-industry town.

Many men and women enjoy Washington's social game because they can play with important names and national issues. They feel that to sit at the same table with any ambassador or undersecretary is social distinction; that to exchange cocktail-party small talk with a certain ever-present Supreme Court Justice is the peak of cultural achievement; that to be the first to predict the fall of an old White House favorite or the rise of a new one places them among the knowing; that to babble on large subjects instead of small ones makes them intellectuals. They seldom suspect that a first-name acquaintance with the near-great has no more significance than the brief intimacies of an ocean crossing, or that all their lionizing leaves them remote from the real sources of democratic power in New York, Los Angeles, Houston, and Detroit.

To win success in such a society neither knowledge nor character is essential. A man or woman can rise to the top of a fashionable dinner table by the possession of a powerful acquaintance and a good cook. One does not even have to have political convictions or affiliations if one can give dinners so succulent that the powerful come. One need only be in constant circulation to become socially desirable, or have the power of making or breaking reputations that brings deference to syndicated gossip-columnists of both sexes. Most major Washington social events have the febrile gaiety and effortful tensions generally associated

with the imminent father of an overdue first-born or the mother
of an unattractive debutante. Cocktails help to create the illusion
of *élan,* and Washington's per capita consumption of alcohol is
notably high. In time the participants in this almost nightly round
acquire the hard glitter of strained alertness or the vague polite-
ness of self-defense, but nearly all in time develop the inevitable
infection of their years of social competition—a lack of compas-
sion for all who slip on the rungs of "success."

That kind of society has, of course, little relation to the real
work of the government or the city, or to the lives of the real
statesmen, who avoid it when they can. Washington and its sub-
urbs are full of their invaluable and socially unknown assistants,
who lead normal domestic lives, or if unmarried alternate between loneliness and sexual safaris, like the unsettled youth in
any American city. This is the real society of Washington, but it
is not thought so by those who circulate almost nightly between
Georgetown and Kalorama Drive, between the Shoreham and
the large apartment houses on Connecticut Avenue, between the
embassies and the boxes of Constitution Hall.

But no society of Washington creates any ideas or manners beyond what its members brought with them from Kansas City,
Pasadena, or Grosse Pointe. Whatever may be said against the
social structure of Pittsburgh or Chicago or Cedar Rapids, it has
reality. It is based upon the established power of the commercially
competent, and has a stability lacking from the Washington mixture of peripatetic ambitions and tame lions.

One measure of the political mind, and of democracy, is the
society they have created at the center of their operations.
Neither has advanced since the days of John Quincy Adams. If
the cultivation and tastes of democracy are expressed by those of
Washington "society," then democracy is socially the least versed
form of government, and the political mind among the least
creative.

XII

The Social Animal

THE basis of human society, it seemed to Angus, is men's need for one another. Much of that need is economic and domestic, but the human animal instinctively seeks the company of his fellows for reasons beyond food, security, and reproduction. Democratic society is founded on the premise that men's mutual dependence is happiest when it is implemented by mutual respect. That respect is effective only if it is instinctive. It is not enough for a man to accept intellectually his membership in the human race; he must feel it and enjoy it, and identify himself with the hopes and disappointments of those about him. To make mutual respect natural as well as logical should be a primary objective of society.

The first step toward liking other people is understanding them. Throughout all his schooling, only one teacher ever suggested to Angus, in concrete terms, that observation of men in action is an essential part of education. Professor Brooks of Swarthmore used to urge his students to make the acquaintance of politicians in their home towns, or of ward heelers and local bosses in the back streets of near-by Philadelphia. That advice was contrary to the cloistered spirit of the college, the cautious suzerainty of parents, and the conventionality of its students. Only two young men in Angus' time acted upon it. One was Leon Henderson, who became a powerful liberal in the Roosevelt Administration, and the other was Drew Pearson, the political columnist. But no one—not even Brooks—suggested that the same procedure is desirable in areas outside politics. Though William Graham Sumner was opening the eyes of some students at Yale to the curious conduct of men in groups, the study of society as a part of formal education had not yet been generally established. Later, when it was, many teachers of sociology would lose themselves and their students in statistics and the anthropological approach. Philosophy and literature had always been concerned with man's relation to man, but courses in philosophy were not fashionable among undergraduates, and in most cases such courses either wallowed in logic or lost themselves in the empyrean or Platonic ideals or the abstractions of Hegel and Kant. Courses in literature were left largely to the women.

During Angus' time in college America was undergoing social and economic changes that would alter the whole fabric of men's relation to those about them, but if Angus and his contemporaries had the slightest suspicion of this, it did not impinge on their thinking or their studies. If teachers were conscious of the changes and their implications, they seldom said so.

In that environment the word "society" failed to evoke any concept except the glamorous activities of America's social or financial elite—an elite remote from Angus' world. To Swarthmore boys and girls it meant dances in Philadelphia's old Bellevue-Stratford or new Ritz, pictures of the Four Hundred at Newport, or engraved invitations to coming-out parties on Park Avenue, in all of which their participation was at best peripheral. Angus and his friends, concealing a little envy under professed disdain, would have said they had no interest in society and no use for it. It did not occur to them that they too were society, or that those who lived in the new rows of identical houses in North Philadelphia, or punched time clocks in the shipbuilding plants of near-by Chester, were also society—the dominant society of the new America, and hence important people to understand—the material of education. College youths had heard of Jacob Riis, Booker Washington, and Jane Addams, but were only vaguely aware of American class problems and only remotely sympathetic with the idea of knowing something about them. The fact that their own futures depended on the interplay of the forces that had created such problems, and the forces created by them, was not known to one in a hundred of the undergraduates of Angus' time and milieu.

They were not averse to using the society they knew for the advancement of their personal ends, but only in the conventional ways of the current formula. They recognized, for example, the merits of marrying well, though most of them thought that love should take precedence over expediency. They agreed, however, with Tennyson's Northern Farmer (though most of them had never heard of him) that it is only sensible to go where money is. Love was a kind of personal lightning that might strike at any time, and it was well to be in some prosperous area when it struck. They accepted the career value of contacts with the well-to-do and powerful, and were receptive to the uses of what they called "pull." An attractive personality was highly prized, and undergraduate activities flourished as its forcing bed. The age of the salesman and of George F. Babbitt was approaching its first flowering, and Angus' college generation was preparing to pluck its blooms.

For the subtler skills and advantages of social intercourse they had little thought and less use. Had they read Franklin on the cultural value of an elderly mistress the idea would have appealed to them as pornography, but as serious education it would have seemed as fantastic as the court of Bagdad or Louis XIV. Friendship, on any basis, with an older woman was quite outside their consideration; one was fond of aunts, sisters, and female

cousins; one recognized the propriety of sentiment and polite-
ness toward women, but real friendships were with one's male
contemporaries. With younger women one did not have friendships but "cases" and "dates." If someone had suggested that social finesse as distinguished from social popularity should be added
to the skills of the American youth, he would have looked a little
blank. At the further suggestion that he could learn it best from
older women, the blankness would have turned to laughter. Instruction from women, except by mutual research in lovemaking,
was something to be tolerated only in the home and the classroom and if possible avoided there. These young men respected
women as much as any previous generation. They favored political equality of the sexes as a matter of simple justice, and they
claimed no intellectual superiority. But in spite of coeducation
and "petting parties," they probably knew women less well than
their ancestors, and they were unaware of their ignorance.

The European concept of the salon where men and women
polished their wits against each other; where small talk was
raised to a fine art and believed worth the mastery; where
women changed the course of history by conversational or amo-
rous nuances with statesmen; where a ready wit or a knowledge
of the arts could be made a political or economic asset—that
would have seemed to Angus and his classmates outdated and
decadent. Social gatherings were for amusement only, not for
practice or profit. To turn them into gymnasia for the intellect or
media for personal advancement would spoil the fun by making
artificial what should be spontaneous. Anyone who did so would
in a vague sense be cheating, like marrying a girl for money
alone. It was a curious paradox that these young men with so
strong a vocational attitude were so firm or unimaginative in
missing the opportunities to develop social subtleties that would
have been great vocational assets.

To be subtle was to be "smooth," and smoothness was hypocrisy, than which there was no greater sin to the youth of
the 1920s. It was legitimate to advance oneself by ingratiating

play with the right men on the golf course or at the bridge table, but to do so over the teacups smacked of the gigolo. As for culture and wit, they were all very well in their places, but their places were for social decoration on special occasions, like a carnation in the buttonhole. To make them important tools of self-advancement would be to exalt the decorative and thus diminish the greater virtues, which were manliness, industry, honest shrewdness, and masculine leadership. Social life was relaxation, and finesse would make it effortful and even deceitful. Young men of the twenties believed in open covenants openly arrived at; European worldliness and indirection had been the cause of all the trouble.

Of course Angus and his generation theoretically accepted the philosophy that a man was a member of society and must play his part in it. In his own school valedictory Angus had pronounced that of all the aspects of knowledge the most important was to understand other people, but this must have been something he read or heard somewhere that sounded good for platform purposes. What he said was meaningful to him only as theory, an idealistic balloon ascension appropriate to the occasion. He believed in practicing what he preached, and thought he was automatically doing so. He thought understanding others was part of the intellectual process; he did not realize that it was shallow unless it was done as a joy and not as a duty; unless it sprang from instinct and was translated into the emotions.

That was unfortunate for him, but as his personal limitation it had no importance to most other people. Its significance lay in the fact that this restriction of the spirit could lie unliberated not only in Angus but in many another intelligent and well-meaning young man and woman. The restriction was not confined to the time of Angus' youth. It is as possible in 1955 as in 1920 for a well-intentioned young American to emerge from school and college with honors, but more ignorant than an Eskimo as to how to achieve in living the more profound contacts, enjoyments, and sensitivities of human association.

An ambitious young extrovert can be superficially curious about people and remotely fond of them; he can get on well enough with those about him, like many and love a few, but still remain untouched by any close personal identification with their lives and emotions. He can be popular without winning or giving deep affection. He can play his part in the human organism called society without feeling it except in purely conventional ways. When he is thoughtful it can be only from good manners; when he is generous it can be only from high spirits; when he is perceptive it can be from the head rather than from the heart. He can grow mentally mature but still remain, in the human sense, a child.

Modern education now emphasizes social orientation, social adjustment, and social responsibility as it did not emphasize them in the twenties. But these are often only phrases, and do not dig deep enough into the relationship between one individual and another. A young man can accept them as social concepts and learn their techniques in dealing with others, but they remain relatively superficial and meaningless until the youth himself converts them into instincts of understanding and habits of the heart. Modern education's concentration on the mass aspects of human relationships distracts young Americans from deepening their understanding of individual personalities, and from forging strong bonds with a few chosen friends. The easy gregariousness and communication of modern life make breadth rather than depth of acquaintance the natural social life. The interpretation of democracy as equality, which makes every man something of a glad-hander with every other man, augments the casual nature of all human relationships.

Angus had a large measure of blindness about personal relationships, and it was fortified by his egoism and the self-sufficiency of apparent personal success. For many years life seemed to be giving him all he wanted, including the friendship of an adequate number of men and women. Why should he trouble to seek warmer understanding than he seemed to need?

He got from others what little he wanted, and was careful to give as much in return. Anything more would be demanding in time, energy, and emotions, and these were commodities of which Angus was consciously economical. If he ever admitted to himself that his friendships ended just as casually as they began, that few of them endured beyond the easy bounds of geography or mutual convenience, and that most of them were based on temporary working associations or propinquity, he would have replied that such friendships were the best, since they were sanely undemanding and could always be picked up just where they were left off. It did not enter his mind that friendships so casual and easily renewable could be had only with people like himself, who were ready to take what was conveniently offered and felt no need for more. What such friendships gave Angus was pleasant and stimulating, but added little to what he already possessed. They were only friendships of convenience and hence not friendships at all. As spiritual growth they were anemic.

In the case of Angus the cause may have been deeper than the failures of education and the myopia of success. His instinct was to keep all but one or two deeply loved people at arm's length; he rarely gave himself completely and without an escape hatch. Most of his closest relationships touched only a few facets of his rather many-sided life. It was almost as though he feared to make vulnerable by exposure some inner sensitivity that had once been badly hurt. But as Angus thought about this explanation it was not convincing. It seemed rather a romantic reason and more flattering than he deserved, for he doubted that he had much inner sensitivity. He could not identify any tender spot or remember any deep childhood wound that could have put him so cautiously on his guard. He did recall that his father and his grandmother had something of the same attitude, and wondered if heredity were as strong and simple as that. On the whole, it seemed to him that his social obtuseness was chiefly due to his pride in being able to walk alone and in being the only person who knew all about himself—as if he did! When he finally recognized his blindness it was too late to make amends for the past, and almost too late to break the habit of indifference.

Education enhances a man's ability to rationalize his weak-nesses to his own satisfaction. Angus' logic never seemed to him more conclusive than on the subject of his own social limitations, where he joyfully turned defense into attack. He regarded him-self as a man of considerable social charm—an asset to any gath-ering, when he wanted to be—but bored or frustrated by the so-cial conventions and values about him. The force with which he offered his criticisms of society's faults betrayed his awareness of the need to defend his own. Some of his strictures were specious and others exaggerated, but they have significance, if for no other reason, as the intellectual acrobatics of a nonconformist.

The test of the good society is whether it really satisfies the needs of its members, spiritual as well as temporal. So measured, American society did not seem to Angus The Good Society. In the circles in which he moved, social life was an extremely active diversion which some of its members exalted to a vocation. Its demands were almost compulsive upon those who made them as well as those who acceded to them, and its gatherings offered little opportunity for uninterrupted talk or the choice of a con-versational partner. Its nervous quality set a tempo disruptive of good conversation. Tension rather than stimulation was the fruit of most social occasions. With feverish effort at their centers and boredom at their peripheries, they resembled a night club where, if some kind of loud noise was not being made, someone should make it.

Angus was not always comfortable at these effortful attempts at organized gaiety. Even when he got into the spirit of the affair he never felt completely and sincerely himself. He sometimes watched the eyes of guests rove through the assembling gather-ing as though they were hopefully searching for some long-sought beautiful or handsome unknown, or some new and exalt-ing experience which would give the whole thing meaning; if it did not appear there was always the hope that it could be found, like Venus from the sea or Hermes from the clouds, at the next cocktail party just around the corner. Does the cohesion of such groups rest on the secret fact that most of their members are searching for some vague miracle that will give their lives zest or meaning? Certainly not entirely, since it is clear that to some the greatest miracle would be the unexpectedly early departure of the guest of honor. Meanwhile the assemblage holds together, like shipwrecked sailors in the same lifeboat, sucking their own conversational blood and searching the horizon for some rescuing sail.

For many years Angus had thought that most sensible men secretly felt as he did about this kind of conventionalized social endeavor. Some of them said so; many of them frequently displayed reluctance to yield to marital mandates that this was an invitation that must be accepted; the preprandial phrase "I'll need a stiff drink or two to get through the evening" was very familiar and often true. These reluctant revelers nearly always did go, but Angus thought he was merely more outspoken and intransigent than most of his men friends when it came to formal social functions. He came to realize that whatever might be the protests of most men of his acquaintance, they enjoyed these organized gastronomic and conversational obstacle races more than he. He tried to solve his problem by making greater efforts to give more pleasure and consequently get more, but was depressed to hear the balderdash he was talking and the parlor acrobatics he was attempting, and to think how inept and effortful they must seem to others. His attempts to pull his party weight in the overloaded boat even led him to anecdotes—that last refuge of the conversationalist without ideas, the guest ill at ease, the hostess who fears a five-second silence, and the man in love with his own voice. Since American society is largely made up of these, conversation at most upper-level social gatherings becomes a competition for an audience, and Angus never won it gracefully. His

mild discomfort left him still wondering whether the fault lay in
him or in the social formula; whether as a social iconoclast he
should wear shining armor or a hair shirt.

Angus had difficulty in being specific about what he would regard as a more sensible and rewarding social life. One cannot
define the ideal relationship between a dozen congenial people
any better than one can chart a perfect course for true love between two starry-eyed youngsters. One can only talk in principles, some of them in negative terms. Principles should be but-
tressed by examples, but each example may seem inept or trivial
and thus weaken the general case. Angus advocated less elaborate
organization and more simplicity, fewer formal dinner and
luncheon parties and large-scale assemblies and more pot-luck in
the gastronomic gatherings so favored in social exchange. He
thought that conversation would be better if it were less regimented by the rules inherent in large gatherings, and that any
dinner party of more than eight makes almost impossible the easy
across-the-table general talk that is usually most rewarding. He
would have asked for less conventionality and more private enterprise in talk and movement, and suggested that freedom of association by guests should be written into our Bill of Rights. Any
milieu in which there are no tensions but considerable mutual
deference, no straining for effects but a good deal of awareness
of the reactions of others, would be a good setting for social pleasure and profit.

At the risk of his social neck he would boldly urge women to
set a slower tempo of conversation so that the males could keep
up with it; not all to talk at once; to be less afraid of brief breath-
catching silences; to avoid constant changes of subject and disconcerting non sequiturs—though he would have added that
women are not the only perpetrators of these hazards to living-
room felicity. He thought men should talk less about business,
sports, and politics and more about topics of general interest and
knowledge; should not cluster in male knots with such obvious
relief; should avoid long factual anecdotes, familiar stories, ex-

cessive cocktails, and heavy conventional gallantries, and he put
it on the record that not all these offenses are limited to males. He
made the dangerous generalization that the best hostess is she
who governs least, and that she should assemble only guests she
likes, and not insert "pay backs" into an otherwise congenial
group. Her "duty dinners" should, in fairness to her friends, be
separate occasions limited to the necessary but unpalatable obligations. In short, Angus outlined a social system demanding the
minimum effort from him and the maximum pleasure to him,
catering to all his personal prejudices and assumed talents, and
probably pleasing only to tweedy pedants like himself. His criticisms of current social practice never seemed weaker than when
he was challenged to supply concrete alternatives.

He was mistaken in directing his diatribes against American
social practices, for what really disturbed him was the shallowness of personal relations that they revealed. He resented this
shallowness all the more deeply because he knew he shared it.
The average American is obviously better at quantitative activity
than qualitative depth of personal exchange. He tends to make
friendship little more than social partnership in the same pursuits of pleasure, which rest chiefly on the desire of several persons to do the same thing at the same time. It is a corporate, not
a dual, association, and like other corporations becomes more
impersonal as it becomes larger. To have many friends is a sign
of personal worth and even a vocational asset. This attitude is not
unique to twentieth-century American society, but many of the
friendships it creates are too shallow to deserve the name. Under
the formula two people can be "friends" without knowing more
about one another, except externally, after ten years of friendship
than at its beginning.

Such social circles, like the gangs of boyhood, are close-knit
and demanding. They require that their members be full-time
participants, and do not long embrace individuals who are willing to be only part-time associates. The man or woman who does
not accept their terms had best move on to another group to

which he can give exclusive devotion, or admit himself a hermit or a social maverick. Angus had never run with a gang in his boyhood and did not want exclusive membership in anything. He liked to be independent in his activities, eclectic in his acquaintance, private in his intimacies, and uncluttered in his life and conversations. What he wanted to do seemed to him to be entitled to priority over staying with others who insisted on doing something else—all together, of course. If he could not control a situation he either fought it or left it, not always gracefully. When others assumed his acquiescence without consulting him, he sulked or belligerently declared his independence. Since nothing is more distasteful to the American hostess than someone who does not stay in line, the more Angus was himself the less he was in demand, and his desire for fewer trying evenings was gratified by a decreasing number of invitations.

He could not think of any social life in America, at the various economic levels he knew, that was not dominated by its women. This was partly because it was the wives who issued the invitations and other wives who accepted them. If man is a social animal, woman is his tamer and ringmaster—the power behind the social machine. Angus was impressed by the wisdom of ancient societies in placing nearly all the powerful forces of nature and mankind under the control, not of gods, but of goddesses. On Greek Olympus the fertility of crops and human beings; the forces of love, justice, beauty, and wisdom; even the operations of fate itself, were presided over by the women of the Pantheon. Only a few destructive forces like war, waves, and thunderbolts were allowed the Olympian males. It was the Virgin who was worshiped in the Middle Ages as the source of spiritual power, and when liberty was personified it became a woman. The men of our own times have altered the ancient pattern by calling their hurricanes Carol and Edna, thus apparently associating woman with destructive force. Angus wondered if that change had any significance for the social historian.

Whatever one may think of the quality and techniques of current American social exchange, few would deny that women have made them and only women could change them. Angus saw that if he wanted to know what American society is about and where it is going he would have to ask women. To understand society he would have to understand them. That is generally believed to be impossible, but the nature of woman has always been a stimulating subject, and Angus found it had its rewards as well as its dangers. It gave him a sure-fire topic for conversation with any lady trapped on his right or left, and though the results were unpredictable they were invariably lively. He had to risk this uncontrolled experiment in research in any case, since he had assumed through his university some responsibility for the indoctrination of many women students. He hoped what they learned there was half as interesting as the information they dispensed.

The education college girls were offered seemed to Angus to be justified in itself but lacking in much that they would need for their own self-realization, and far from providing them with all that society would demand from them. It did not emphasize or develop their special powers as women, and often seemed to interpret equality of the sexes as meaning that there are no intellectual or emotional differences between them. Schools and colleges were giving their girls, with only slight variations, an education which in content, objectives, and atmosphere had been developed for young men. Most young women were accepting it without protest, absorbing it with apparent docility and success, and defending it because it was the same as that given to men, without considering very seriously whether it should be. Angus was constantly surprised that a sex more realistic than men was so contentedly following an educational and vocational path so unrealistic in its estimate of their potential powers. He thought that society might be able to stagger along if its men were no better educated than at present, but he doubted its capacity to flourish if it continued to be so myopic in its view of the potentialities of its women.

No man with sense could undergo thirty years of education and coeducation without a high opinion of the intelligence and competence of American women. There are few if any areas of intellectual activity in which women, given an equal chance, are not at least as capable as men. It is true that they have not yet equaled men in artistic and musical creation, but that may be because they have not yet had equal opportunity or freedom from the distractions not essential but traditional to their sex. As individuals they are superior to men in energy, speed of reaction, patience, and sense of reality.

As social animals, however, they do not appear at their best. When three or more women are gathered together their wisdom is less obvious and their weaknesses are more apparent. As for women *en masse,* they seem less sensible and attractive than as individuals. Women with other women appear uncertain of themselves and one another. They try to cover their uncertainties with unceasing chatter couched in superlatives, with excessive assurances of mutual devotion, and with rapid changes of subject in order never to be left behind. In groups they do not listen but merely exude vocal tensions. Why are modern American women so constantly in need of social restraints or social reassurance? The question seemed to go deeper into psychology than Angus could follow, but he suspected it was allied with the frustrations incident to the role of man-duplication they have elected to play.

No man is wholly objective about women, and Angus did not pretend to be. He was too much attracted to them, and like many men past forty had developed a special admiration for young women that was not purely intellectual. He became increasingly conscious of how different they were from young men, in ways beyond the obvious. Nor can any man escape his own conditioning. Angus had a background of mixed Victorian standards and literary romanticism that made his ideas of women seem absurd to his daughters, though he was rarely as adulatory or as critical as he sometimes sounded.

It did seem to him unfortunate that women had gained political and economic equality at about the same time that mechanical civilization was developing so rapidly. The world that women entered as free and equal citizens was new even to the men, and that made women's orientation to it more difficult. The new culture of scientific materialism was more remote from women's special sources of power than any previous culture in history. In their eagerness to demonstrate their equal capacities, women set out to conquer mechanistic culture, and were conquered by it. They demonstrated their competence more impressively than their judgment. Earlier women were the exponents of the humane values, but modern women accept men's values and try to duplicate their abilities. By neglecting the earlier sources of their self-realization and the more subtle forms of feminine leadership, they let humane values become trivial. Instead of complementing masculine talents with their own, they throw society out of balance, and neither sex is happier as a result.

In earlier centuries women made their sex a symbol of creative power, and in the Middle Ages men accepted the concept of the woman as the source of spiritual and cultural exaltation. Puritanism attacked that concept by frowning on sex and thus diminishing its power to elevate society and stimulate its creativity. Women achieved their new equality while the traditions of puritanism were still strong, and instead of working to regain their power as symbols of something different from the mundane pursuits of men, they conceded to the modern age as they found it. The opportunities for new achievements and new pleasures went to their heads. Some women diminished their special power of creativity by cheapening it into transient pleasures, in which occupation, as always, they had the ready co-operation of most men. Other women diminished it by regarding their part in human creation as a regrettable interruption of their normal activities, to be minimized as much as possible, making childbirth merely an uncomfortable medical event comparable to an appendectomy, and the care of their children not a deepening experience but a series of economic and pedagogical problems;

they intellectualized child care into psychological confusions. Other women were far more sensible, but many of them then diminished their own creative power by the infinite distractions of their well-meaning activities in civic and social affairs.

It is not that American women are unconscious of sex or shrink from its more obvious uses. On the contrary, sex is featured more widely than ever before, though it is not exactly glorified. Literature, entertainments, and advertisements make the female anatomy the allurement for the purchase of everything from beer to motorcars. Never before in history has sex been so commercialized, even though fewer women's bodies are now rented, bought, and sold. Never before in history have so many women spent so much time in making themselves alluring, though it is uncertain whether their motive is to influence men or impress other women. Unfortunately, their new devices attract men more effectively than they hold or uplift them. Their lures are obvious and superficial, and many men are failing to find the depth of femininity and warmth of devotion they crave and need in these smartly groomed, mentally alert, domestically competent, but always slightly distrait comrades of their work and play.

The casual camaraderie between modern young men and women reveals the gains and the losses of the new freedom. It has brought greater equality, healthy-mindedness, and mutual ease. But it has also made manners mediocre, rudeness routine, reserve unfashionable, and romantic feeling a rare victory of instinct over habit. Angus wished he knew how modern boys and girls react to Dante's devotion to Beatrice, or the passions of Romeo and Juliet, or what they think of the motivations of Hamlet, Ophelia, Othello, and Desdemona. Do such emotions seem to them real and valid, or merely anachronistic literary conventions?

It must be difficult for a young man to think of a modern American girl as a frail and precious ideal, or as needing the special gentle shielding of the male; and it must be equally difficult for the young woman to see herself thus. Men have ceased to be gallant to women because women do not call out gallantry; they prefer to demonstrate their competent independence. A young man of the mid-century can with good reason feel various kinds of admiration for these magnificent Amazons —equally competent and equally independent; equally experienced in skiing, sailing, and sex, disarmingly unaffected and devastatingly frank—but romantic exaltation cannot easily be one of them. Reserve and mystery may always have been no more than female pretensions, but they served good ends and may even be essential to man's worshipful devotion. To make a woman, simply because she is a woman, an object of automatic respect may be an outworn endeavor, but the qualities it developed in men were good for them and good for society. Somewhere between the vapors and fainting spells of the nineteenth-century virgin and the durable insensitivities of the twentieth-century debutante must lie a happier medium for women.

Whatever the losses resulting from the effortless association of modern young people, they know one another better than in Angus' youth, and that is a notable gain. But their understanding may not go much deeper than that of their parents, and it may involve some losses of the spirit in both sexes. The twentieth century is completing what the nineteenth began: it is changing the concept of woman as a conservator of ideals to a co-partner in ideas, from a conceiver of beautiful dreams to a consumer of beautiful things, from a spiritual factor to a social worker or a social problem. Women are perhaps no more to blame for this than men, for both are in the hands of forces they have not fathomed. The present situation, and the effect it will have on future generations, requires more thought from both sexes than it is getting.

Angus did nothing constructive to implement his concern, for there was little he could do, especially since most women he knew did not agree with him. Yet if he were right, or only partly right, social life and education are moving in the wrong direction. It was, he thought, a question not only of the welfare of society but of the happiness of its individuals. Many young women now vividly confident in their enthusiastic diversities are doomed to encounter, later, personal frustrations and spiritual sterilities. They are losing unity of spirit in their variety of activities and standards, and the results are beginning to show in the empty exchanges of social life. Their social lives will become as conventional or as shallow as their parents'.

As an excuse for his own maladjustment to group pleasure, Angus used to quote the statement of Henry Adams that "one friend in a lifetime is much, two are many, three are hardly possible," and to say that he was looking for a social life that developed such friendships. But it is doubtful that under any conditions Angus would ever have maintained friendships as close as those Adams claimed with John Hay and John La-Farge. Perhaps the tempo of the twentieth century does not permit it; perhaps Angus alone lacked the capacity. In his early years he had been thrown much in the company of men twenty years or more his senior, and was closer to them than to most men of his own years, but as he moved into his fifties his old friends were no longer within call. He never knew whether in the matter of friends he was richer or poorer than most men, or poorer than had he been less independent. He only knew that in his friendships he had been far luckier than he deserved and had no ground for complaint.

Nevertheless he was a little shocked, late in life, to find how often his friendships had rested on purely procedural affinities. At the time in his life when he would most have valued the understanding of many friends he realized for the first time how few he had. This seemed for a while a new poverty until he realized that it was an old one he had just begun to feel. He had not discovered it sooner because he had not previously called upon his credit in the bank of friendship. When he did, he discovered how little interest he had earned because his own investment had been so small. He was getting no less than he deserved, for he had expected little from most people and given them little. The crop he reaped was sparse because he had not cultivated it.

That was an old story, but not quite the whole story. Angus was the victim not only of his earlier indifferences and ineptitudes in friendship but of ancient attitudes of the social order. Society does not cherish the independent man. Angus had thought that his strength lay in his self-sufficiency, and had flaunted it for years. Self-sufficiency is a form of power, and power and friendship rarely flourish together; one party or the other is uncomfortable with the inequality. The independence of an individual is an affront to society, for society's strength is based on the need men feel for it, and threatened by those who feel no need. Society resents the challenge of the self-sufficient individual, and if he comes a cropper there is a general verdict, as the Greek tragedies point out, that he got no more than he deserved. Modern society in particular is too busy to pick up the man who stumbles, especially if he insists on trying to get up alone. Like nature, it wastes no time on the plants that turn brown; why should it when there are so many others? With regard to friends, the case is more simple. Most close friendships are based on a conviction of needing or being needed, and Angus had encouraged neither. These revelations he found, by some paradox, reassuring, for they demonstrated a just logic in the affairs of men, even if it was rough justice. As education, the experience had all the virtues and pains of a cold bath.

Whatever might be Angus' personal social problems, he knew that the important thing was to translate anything they taught him into uses beyond himself. Did they throw any light on the general workings of American society? What are the real structure, objectives, and influences of American society in terms of any individual trying to orient himself to it? The sociologists and statisticians did not provide Angus with the kind of answer he was searching for. Henry Adams came closer, but what Adams called society in 1890 no longer existed, as Adams himself had predicted. Those who now thought of themselves as society did not set the standards of the nation. Adams had written that one could always descend the social ladder, and by that phrase revealed that he thought of American society as having clearly established levels. By 1950 society had lost its old rungs, and it was even difficult to know what its upper levels were, or, culturally speaking, which end of the current social ladder is up.

Social prominence, as defined in the popular mind, no longer requires the benchmarks of birth, manners, or traditional cultivation; one can find them where social standing is not recognized and fail to find them where it is. An acceptable personality, capacity to adjust to whatever the environment calls for, a wide acquaintance with influential people, and funds to support social ambition can lift one from the lowest levels of social recognition to what most Americans regard as the highest. It is not easy to envisage social gradations in a country where the standards and manners of headliners on the social page are almost indistinguishable from those of the masses— except that the headliners sit in the more expensive seats.

This would remain true, it seemed to Angus, so long as popular sovereignty confused democracy with egalitarianism, and was busy admiring itself in the reflecting pool of social conformity, while democratic education, designed to elevate mass culture, was diluting it to please mass consumers. Angus sought for a flaw in his own logic, for otherwise he had been devoting most of his life to an educational system that was moving in the wrong direction. At heart an optimist, he believed in the infinite potentialities of democracy. He had no more desire to emulate Ecclesiasticus than Pollyanna, but until society lifted its eyes from its popular narcissism the critic who raised his voice would be crying from a social wilderness.

XIII

Unity and Diversity

ANGUS had spent much of his life producing tiny crops of self-satisfaction within a rather narrow garden. As time went on the returns seemed less rewarding and his work a little sterile. He had exhausted the fertility of his intellectual soil and at the same time let the larger acreage of his spirit lie uncultivated. It was late in life to attempt drastic changes, but he set out to plow more widely and more deeply, and to try to sweeten his earth with greater understanding, not of methods but of men.

It was apparent to Angus that his need for orientation was even greater than he had realized. He must have a few years in which by independent work and thought he could learn how to live more happily with himself and others. He did not try to solve his problem by becoming a recluse, for, even if he would, he could not escape the associations of earlier years or his interest in people and affairs. Besides, he could not think in a social vacuum, and to orient himself he had to understand how society was oriented. He would observe and then perhaps write down his reactions, for even if he produced nothing that anyone else would want to read, the act of writing might clarify his ideas.

When one plows uncultivated areas of mind and spirit one lays them open to the erosions of disillusion. As Angus did so he became more aware of his own unimportance, but his discovery of the distorted values of American society depressed him more. It seemed, like himself, to have grown narrow in its vision and sterile in its spiritual life. Was that conclusion a valid one, or distorted by his own malaise? He doubted that his judgment was warped by bad digestion, excessive nostalgia, or reactionary instincts, and he was not yet especially subject to the maladies of senility. He doubted, too, that those diseases had caused more profound thinkers like Spengler, Ortega y Gasset, and Toynbee to reach somewhat similar conclusions.

He doubted that they explained Henry Adams' similar concern about the course of American society. Adams had hoped that by 1938, his centenary year, the world would become one that timid and sensitive souls could view without a shudder. But 1938 found it on the verge of its greatest orgy of brutality and destruction, and events since then may well cause the brave as well as the timid to shudder at the future. Angus' own hundredth anniversary would arrive at the end of the century; he too hoped that by then society would have righted itself, but he saw little promise of that in present trends and values.

Adams found in the America of 1904 "prosperity never before imagined, power never before wielded by man, speed never yet reached by anything but a meteor," but he also found Americans of 1904 "irritable, querulous, unreasonable and afraid." To Angus, coming along fifty years later, it seemed almost amusing that Adams should have thought 1904 rich or powerful, or that man's 1904 speed of sixty miles an hour should have seemed fast. That world seemed to Angus, as he looked back at it, modest in prosperity, power, and speed, and its people placid, sensible, secure, and free of psychoses compared to America and Americans of 1950. The aspects of America that had troubled Adams in 1904 had been vastly magnified by 1950.

Adams had once reduced the thinking of his brother Brooks to the formula that all civilization is centralization and all centralization seeks economy; since all economy is the survival of the cheapest, therefore civilization will become cheap. In 1849 Lord Kelvin thought he had proved that the universe was steadily flattening, and would in time flatten out to a level where nothing could live. Darwin had called civilization the survival of the fittest, and Angus preferred that version. But it occurred to him that the difference between these three conclusions is less great than it sounds. Modern society makes the fitness of a man depend on his usefulness in the eyes of the populace. Since mass opinion invariably prefers the cheap, and the cheap approximates the dead level, the survival of the fittest becomes the survival of the cheapest, and the cheapest is the flattest. Angus was pleased that by this juggling of words he had brought agreement between Adams, Kelvin, and Darwin—at least to his own satisfaction. But he derived no pleasure from the prospect of a culture based on the cheap, the flat, or even the most fit in terms of popular appeal.

When Angus confided these disturbing thoughts to his friends, they were kind but unconvinced. Some of them said his criticisms were negative and destructive, and seemed to think that that disposed of them. Angus replied that if to suggest that society be cautious of its course is negative, then all common sense is negative; and that his criticisms were no more destructive than modern society is, on the record, destructive. Others suggested tactfully that the Cassandras and Jeremiahs had always been mistaken. Men of every generation had seen their successors charging down the primrose path, but civilization had never quite reached the everlasting bonfire. The prophets of doom, they

said, failed to see that beneath the scummy surface of social
ferment men were always generating new meliorities that looked
ugly only because they were still crude.

It seemed to Angus that his friends were whistling through
woods much deeper and darker than they realized. The forces
polluting the twentieth-century human pond are infecting the
values of society more insidiously than ever before. Most men
are becoming less and less able to distinguish between the mediocre and the excellent except in mechanical products, and more
willing to accept popular verdicts and values. The longer cheap
standards dominate, the more difficult for society to rise above
them, for it will have lost both the vision of quality and the
desire for it.

Angus granted that the worst prophecies of the Jeremiahs
have never quite come true, but he thought that fact irrelevant to the present times. History reveals periods of serious
decay and retrogression as well as of notable advance. In spite
of the teaching of his boyhood history books, and his boyhood
conditioning that man's upward progress has been continuous,
Angus doubted that the true meaning of history justified
such optimism. In any case the precedents of earlier centuries
do not apply to the twentieth. The most drastic conflicts
of history were limited in their totality of destruction; all the
power of Caesar or Napoleon did not make a single Burmese
peasant lift his eyes from his rice paddy or frighten a single
Hottentot. But the power and speed of the atomic age has no
such limitations. The contemporary Burmese or Hottentot
knows that what is decided in Moscow or Washington today
may change or destroy his life tomorrow. Modern concentra-
tions of power can shiver the bedrock of men's pursuits from
Scotland to Samoa. Modern military mass changes national collisions into world wars; modern military weapons turn local
battlefields into universal death; modern economic power can
make starvation as well as plenty worldwide; global competi-
tions can turn the intervals between these holocausts into cold

wars, and not a single man or idea can escape the results. Even rapid and universal communication can create universal animosity more easily than universal understanding. Its ability to accelerate world collisions is so great that it turns to irony the first Morse message: "What God hath wrought!" Cable, press, and radio rouse all men to peaks of emotion at the same time, and if that emotion is fear or hate, then the charged human particles may explode more quickly and universally. Nor is the danger of these new forces solely one of physical destruction. They can also demoralize humanity spiritually and culturally if it lets its values become distorted. Troubled by these dangers, a great contemporary historian, Sir Maurice Powicke, recently tried to reassure himself by the thought that "after all has been said, we are still quite safe. Nobody can abolish the past." That is true as regards future historians, which is what Sir Maurice meant. But Angus did not find it very consoling regarding society, for of what use is the past if there are no men left or prepared to learn from it?

Men, who can hardly control the new forces, cannot predict their effects. Even scientists like Robert Oppenheimer, who have helped to create them, warn that the last fifty years have brought a massive dissolution of earlier authorities, beliefs, and rituals. The discoveries of Columbus and Newton altered man's concepts and ways of life less profoundly than they are being altered by mass production, mass culture, mass domination, and nuclear fissions. Fifty years ago, when the greatest of these developments lay ahead, Henry Adams wrote: "My country in 1900 is something totally different from my own country of 1860. I am really a stranger in it. Neither I nor anyone else understands it." Any honest man would have to make the same confession today.

Since modern man is a stranger in a world he does not understand; since that world is unprecedented and chartless; since the twentieth century cannot count on a repetition of earlier regenerations such as Renaissance and Reformation, Angus believed his friends could not call on history to discount his alarms. To assume that current American society is subject to the same laws and cycles as that of 1900 is to beg the greatest issue of the century. America today is more remote from 1900 than 1900 was from the year One.

The optimism of many Americans is based on the assumption that physical improvements assure human elevation, and that change means progress. Obviously sanitation, literacy, material security, leisure, and the control of great physical power are potential aids to spiritual and ethical progress, but they do not guarantee it. They are only foundations upon which any kind of society, good or bad, can be built. They are tools, with all the limitations of tools. Power and knowledge themselves are merely instruments, and their value depends on the use men make of them.

Angus wondered whether the confusions of contemporary society were inevitable, and—this time on the side of the optimists—decided they were not. Society's spiritual anemia and distorted values are not necessary results of its accumulation of physical force. Its mistake is in failing to use wisely its new power and potentialities, by overemphasizing the mechanical methods of progress and neglecting other methods. It is trying to solve the problems of power by the devices of power, and thereby augmenting the imbalance between its physical strength and its spiritual weakness. Its ills are cultural and cannot be cured by physical and mechanical means.

Twentieth-century men are attempting to achieve world unity, for example, by applying the thought and habit patterns derived from their conquest of the physical world. In their familiar fields of economics and technology, unity is gained through organization, machinery, and regulation, and they instinctively follow that pattern when they try to gain political unity through treaties and centralization; economic unity through integration by Marshall Plans, coal and steel committees, and tariff agreements; social unity through uniformity of opinion, and cultural unity through cultural organization.

Consequently their progress is chiefly in the development of tools for progress; the emphasis is on organization rather than principles, on the letter rather than the spirit of unity. But men cannot bring unity and elevation to their minds and emotions simply by organizing and implementing their actions. One cannot avoid world collisions merely by regulating the traffic. International treaties, economic agreements, and even social legislation are little more than exalted forms of directional signs, stop lights, and traffic regulations. They are better calculated to penalize poor drivers than to develop good ones. Since the avoidance of accidents rests primarily with the drivers, the motivation of men is more important than stop lights and penalties—particularly when one collision could destroy the world.

The superficial nature of agreement without emotional unity is illustrated by NATO. America has paper acquiescence won by narrow majority votes from some of the parliaments of Europe. That acquiescence is no more durable than the governments that won its acceptance from their citizens. It is no stronger than the emotional support of the millions of Europeans who are parties to it, and many of them are reluctant or protesting members. To meet an emergency NATO is better than nothing, but it is as fragile as mass emotion and parliamentary majorities.

Yet what is called unity is often no more than that kind of agreement. The international unity of diplomacy is chiefly the elaboration of treaties aimed at keeping the peace or stimulating the flow of goods and currencies. As for national unity, it usually means acquiescence among citizens sufficient to prevent disrupting dissensions. Family unity is measured by the ability of its members to get on equably together by that reluctant form of agreement called compromise. Unity in many other matters seems to mean whatever the emergencies of the moment require, or whatever the advocates of some special cause say it means.

Is unity, then, no more than agreement on operating measures, or the preservation of a smooth surface on which no cracks show? That would make it too shallow to be worth working for. Angus turned for a better definition to the great thinkers and writers, but except for the general principles of the religions he could find no one to tell him in concrete terms what unity is or should be. Plato, Bacon, Locke, and Emerson offered him no specifics that would catalyze the variant elements in his own mind and in society. He knew that men in quest of concrete wisdom get dusty answers, but he had hoped that someone would at least help him to ask the right questions.

Everyone talks about unity as one of men's deepest and most laudable instincts. Even amid the disillusions of 1954 Isaiah Berlin said in his Comte Memorial Lecture that "one of the deepest human desires is to find a unitary pattern in which the whole of experience, past, present and future; actual, possible and unfulfilled, is symmetrically ordered." That may be true, but few modern intellectuals seem to be considering very clearly, or at least very audibly, just what they mean by unity.

Angus salvaged one idea from all this speculation. He concluded that unity between men is one thing and unity within a man's psyche is quite another. Unity between men is a social objective, and one in which every man's opinions should be considered. Unity within a man is his personal and spiritual affair, and no one's business but his own. Personal unity and social amity are allied and complementary, but they are no more identical than they are mutually exclusive. Men's efforts toward social unity should not impinge on the freedom of the individual to find his own internal unity. To do so would be to mistake uniformity for unity, and to encourage men to claim that the need for unity entitles them to insist that their neighbors agree with them. That attitude could destroy social as well as personal unity, for beneath forced conformity smolders inner dissension.

This seemed very obvious to Angus until he observed that society was confused about it, and was neglecting to set an atmosphere that would encourage the individual to find his personal unity. By concentrating on external and collective unity, society distracts the attention of each man from searching for his own self-balance. Yet, or so it seemed to Angus, successful integration among men depends on successful personal integration within separate men. No man can find unity with others until he has learned to live in understanding and amity with himself. Society cannot, of course, supply any man with personal unity on request, with a balance between his emotions and his intellect, his dreams and his realities, his social instinct and his ego. But society could help him by creating an atmosphere that makes his need for personal orientation seem his highest priority. At present society puts the cart before the horse. Placing a priority on the amity of men to the neglect of the unity of man may prove the great fallacy of the twentieth century.

When Angus looked around him he began to wonder whether men want unity as much as they say they do. One attribute of unity is simplicity, and men are deliberately moving from the simple to the complex. Paradoxically, the half century in which Americans have most ardently pursued unity at home and abroad is the same half century in which Americans have made their lives most complex. With the purpose of simplifying their own cerebrations they have developed complicated thinking machines and statistical methods; to simplify their personal political responsibilities they have delegated them to government until government has become a great web of multiplicity; to simplify their own domestic chores they have developed a life of mechanization, packaged goods, and elaborate interdependence that have made manufacture, merchandising, and their own lives in-

finitely more complicated. To achieve unity they have spawned
new complexities. Twentieth-century society is aiming in one direction and moving in another.

In international affairs unity lags far behind the machinery
created to serve it. In national politics what Benjamin Franklin
wrote in 1788 is equally true in 1955: "As soon as a party has
gained its general point, each member becomes intent on his
particular interest; which, thwarting others, breaks that party
into divisions, and occasions more confusions."

In economics the world is becoming a single organism, but
there is more unity in its methods and products than in the men
who make and use them. Mergers which look like unification
actually add complexities in organization, and magnify the rivalries between the new industrial giants they create. Full economic unity, as the history of Benelux implies, is impossible without something very close to political unification, but even those
who work most ardently for economic integration shrink from
political mergers between nations.

In organized religion there is less unity in the current Christian faith than in its first centuries; its later history has been one
of fragmentation into new sects and dissidences. It is doubtful
that the Christian influence toward world unity is as great today
as it was at the time of the Holy Roman Empire. The other
great religions offer no convincing evidence of increased unity
within themselves or between one another.

In education diversity is overwhelming unity in subject matter,
until even the ideal of unity is being lost sight of. The institution
created by society to bind men together by common knowledge
and aspiration no longer supplies them. Higher education in
America offers even more diversities than it does degrees.

In science the effort to discover basic unity in the physical
world has given way to the pursuit of the complex. There is no
area of modern knowledge in which knowledge is less secure.
The physical "laws" that earlier scientists thought absolute and
permanent have not proved so. Under the simple, scientists find

the complex, and few of them are willing to risk the assurance that it will not be forever thus. Science and psychology are giving men the impression that the individual man is no longer an integer of physical unity but a compound of chemicals, no longer an entity of free will but an accumulation of diverse impulses derived from heredity and conditioning, a battleground between biological instinct and the inhibitions of civilization. The average man feels there is no sense in searching his psyche for a unity the experts tell him is not there.

In law men have tried to unify society through juridical order, but constant new complexities bring more laws to regulate them, until law itself becomes complex and uncertain. Laymen cannot be confident what is the law, or what the courts will determine to be justice. Lawyers themselves are often unsure of their advice, and courts of their rulings, as appeal follows appeal, precedent replaces precedent, and interpretation negates interpretation. Justice peeps through her blindfold to watch public reactions, and her scales are often weighted with deference to transient public trends. As the concept of legality changes from one of absolute and unalterable justice to a flexible cognizance of current social mores, law moves away from unity.

It looked to Angus as though the average man wants unity only so long as other men will concede to it on his terms, but prefers diversity to accepting theirs. The kind of unity gained by this attitude is no more than the unity of compromises, and qualified unity is doubtful social cement. It brings into play a variation on the old law of physics: to every action toward unity there is an equal and contrary action toward diversity. Nations ally themselves for world wars, but when the immediate crisis is over they revert to nationalism with added fervor. They reluctantly reunite under the threat of a new aggressor, but the moment the danger seems to diminish they begin to fall apart again. After World War I the victors advocated a League of Nations to unify the world, but then emasculated the League to protect their diverse nationalisms. The same President that supported the League also encouraged self-determination, and that resulted in dividing Europe into smaller political fragments than ever before. In the name of self-determination the Irish Republic justified its separation from Britain, but in the name of Irish unity it protests the right of the six northern counties to self-determination. After World War II America urged integration on western Europe but retained its own tariff barriers; it advocated a European army for defense but found it had to encourage nationalistic loyalties in Europe in order to ensure the recruitment and maintenance of that army. Meanwhile nations like India preach world unity in the United Nations assemblies but foster intense nationalism at home. And in the name of proletarian world unity Russia breaks the world in two.

The physical law applies to domestic as well as international affairs. Workmen unify their interests into labor unions, and then fight the restrictions of that unity in wildcat strikes and jurisdictional disputes. The earlier mergers of church and state, and of religion and education, break down as citizens oppose sectarian influence in government and education. Even liberty itself flounders between unity and diversity. Freedom seems a simple principle, but as society grows more complex it proceeds to define, divide, and delimit freedom into an infinite number of smaller freedoms, each of which becomes more complicated as men try to live with it. The unity of freedom becomes the diversity of statutory rights.

Of the group interests of modern democracy, the most powerful is that of organized workmen, since they are the most numerous, since they are the chief creators and consumers of goods, and since they control the physical power on which American civilization depends. They can force their desires on the rest of society by applying or refusing to apply the power of their dynamos, turbines, tractors, and atoms. But the industrial machine that gave them their power is now beginning to take it back. The impersonal forces emanating from engines and productivity are becoming the real rulers of industrial democracy. As men harness the power of water, coal, oil, and iron they harness themselves to the same machine, and end not its master but its servant. Men are subject to the diverse pulls of a complex and increasingly dominant mechanical giant who must be served and fed. The machine brings unity, but it is a unity determined by a Frankenstein. Western civilization is in real danger of ceasing to be governed by acts of human will.

What is needed, it seemed to Angus, is some unity more basic than outward agreements, governmental organization, social uniformity, and economic interdependence. It will have to be a unity of the human spirit, so strong and fundamental that it can survive all the diversities necessary to human freedom and individuality, and all the disunities inevitable in imperfect man. It will have to be a unity in men's ultimate aims, which will permit diversities in methods of achieving them—yet society seems to be emphasizing unity in methods and disregarding unity of ultimate goals. It will have to be a unity in certain common values and loyalties, such as pity, kindliness, truth, and a searching for some good beyond what man has thus far achieved—yet society seems to be stressing unity in material values and ignoring the force and quality of spiritual ones.

Angus knew just enough to know he could think no further than that. Men of every generation have sought solutions to the problem of man in his relations to other men, and Angus could not add one iota to their wisdom. He could not provide a blueprint for humanity, or a formula for regaining spiritual values. Not even society as a whole could prepare a chart that would block out in various colors the areas in which unity is desirable or diversity is good—and society would not follow it if it existed. There will always be areas in which unity and diversity are at war, where men will find it difficult to know which side to take. Angus was willing to let future generations have the fun and grief of exploring those *terrae incognitae,* and finding their own working compromises for disputed territory and uncertain boundary lines. But it did seem to him that current American society would make more progress if it would look at its unities and diversities more closely. Whatever unity this generation attempts would be more productive if it were more clearly and deeply conceived.

Angus thought he saw what is putting twentieth-century America off the track in its pursuit of unity. It is seeking its unities through low common denominators and second-rate appeals, in political and international expediencies and compromises, in the economic integration of material goods and power, in acceptance of the most popular values of a rather thoughtless and not very cultivated mass society. The attractions it offers men for unity are often more mundane than exalted: physical security, material prosperity, mechanical power and comfort, and popular culture. Even the goal of peace is presented negatively as escape from war rather than as opportunity for creation and elevation. The one noble aim America holds forth is freedom, but freedom from something rather than freedom toward something still finer. Society fails to feature the ultimate goals for which freedom itself is only a way station. It neglects the basic appeal of freedom and unity, which is of the spirit.

Angus had thus finally arrived where most of the great minds began—with spiritual aspiration. The only cement powerful enough to hold society together has throughout history been the common aspirations of the spirit. The permanent bonds between men have been intangible, and the great religious faiths have outlasted the greatest empires. Those faiths, like Roman Catholicism, sometimes utilize mundane means for their advancement; sometimes lose sight of their goal; sometimes let their representatives distort or betray their ideals, but so long as they put faith and aspiration before material things they keep their power to hold men together. Different ages and different societies have interpreted in very different terms their sense of some goal higher than material ones. They have often lost their way in their quest for unity as they saw it, but belief in the importance of the search has been more effective in holding men together than the pen, the sword, the treaty, or the production line.

Men's belief in spiritual goals has not been embodied in formal religion alone. It is expressed in the ideals of the philosophers and the creators of literature and the arts. The same aspirations are felt, even if not expressed, by every mother who dreams her hopes over the child at her side. They are innate in every man's instinctive need for the company and friendship of other men. They are the motivating force of men's search for some power and wisdom beyond their own.

Modern society has by no means lost sight of that ideal, for a few men and women hold it with tenacity. But as a living force, spiritual aspiration is less powerful in twentieth-century America than in many earlier times. It has yielded its place to more immediate goals and desires. Faith exists in less exalted forms, for no society ever gave itself more unconsciously to acts of faith than contemporary America. Its devotion to democracy is a faith, for history has not yet proved it the road to human perfection. Belief in human progress, belief in the American creed, belief in the omniscience of science are also American faiths that are not certitudes. And even the wisest of Americans profess a faith in facts that is beyond any demonstrated proof of their value as the finest form of truth.

Angus read in the newspapers that Bernard Baruch told reporters on his eightieth birthday that "facts are the only criterion of my judgments and conclusions." Angus agreed that facts are essential as a foundation for most judgments, if one can ever get all of them and be sure they are facts. But to make them the only criterion of judgment, even in matters like price control or aid to Europe, is to ignore the possibility of any wisdom beyond them. It is the capacity to understand and evaluate facts, and then sometimes to rise above their more obvious implications, that distinguishes the wise man from the citizen of average competence. Human wisdom must in the last analysis be subjective, as it actually was in the case of Mr. Baruch. The quality of mind brought to bear on raw facts is the most precious ingredient of great decisions, and that quality has to be derived from understandings and personal balances far beyond anything that can be recorded as relevant fact. America needs to balance its facts with imagination, its objective analyses with instinctive vision, and its cool judgments with warm fervors. Faith in facts is not the most elevated form of faith.

Modern man has simply altered the objects of his faith from gods, kings, medicine men, and religion to science, democracy, technical expertism, facts, and the wisdom of the common man. To those mundane faiths he entrusts his life as confidently as a Greek hero to Athena or a medieval crusader to his priest. He embarks on trains and planes with automatic faith in their engines and pilots. He places his hopes of future freedom, peace, and power in diplomatic documents and nuclear theories he neither reads nor understands. No society ever achieved a greater daily act of mass faith than millions of Americans as they speed past green traffic lights, confident that other millions will halt at red ones.

The trouble with these faiths is that they do not uplift. They offer man no inspiration and seek none in God or the unknowns of nature. They do not conceive nature and humanity as expressions of divine unity, but as complex combinations of ions and enzymes, or raw material for the economic system and the speculations of psychologists. The substitution of faith in man and his implements for faith in divine origin and omniscience has not speeded progress toward the ultimate goals of man. It is true that religious faith has sometimes led to frightful excesses and denials of humanity, but so does faith in man and his works. In the earlier quests for religious unity, wars were fought and inquisitions conducted, but today wars more devastating and inquisitions more confusing are held in the name of social unity. Earlier struggles toward agreement usually demanded orthodoxy only in religious belief or dynastic loyalty, but modern men press for orthodoxy in all thought, and even in manners and acquaintances.

When earlier generations encountered the unknown, they accepted it as beyond human understanding and left it to God. Modern men, ambitious to unravel the complexities of the universe, recognize no mystery beyond their capacity for ultimate comprehension. As they transplant the unknown from Sinai and Parnassus to their own laboratories and seminars, they feel no need for spiritual unity or guidance beyond their own intellects. The change increases their mental power and self-confidence, but diminishes society's sense of the unity of all men through their common needs and ignorances. Trying to solve the multiplicity of the universe, in the name of unity, brings multiplicity and confusion to human society. If this is a transition stage, how long will it last, and will humanity survive it?

As the twentieth century magnifies the dynamo and exalts it over the Virgin, it sows the seeds of its own disunity. It is almost as though society is seeking to defend itself against its fear of an atomic Armageddon by pretending indifference to its final destination, and is using activity as an anodyne to fear and frustration. Earlier wise men knew that the one great common denominator of the human spirit is religious experience. There are men today who believe that, and plead for deeper understanding of men's spiritual unity, but their voices are weak against the noise of the machines. Unfortunately, many of the defenders of the ancient faith seem to have little to offer that satisfies the contemporary hunger of the spirit. The conventional injunctions of organized religion seem to lead no further along the road of understanding than the researches of scientists and academicians. And the opposite procedure of some men of the churches, who try to make religion popular by making it cheap, diminishes its stature as well as their own. As a result of its own sterility and compromises, organized religion is devoting less and less of its time to inspiring men, and more and more to their psychotherapy; it acts the clinician rather than the prophet, saint, or mentor. Almost untouched by the gifts of the spirit, the majority of Americans pursue security, pleasure, and the machinery of life as arduously as Socrates pursued truth, puritans pursued their austere morality, and saints pursued their God.

It is the modern interpretation of democracy, not the ideal of democracy, that has contributed to the neglect of spiritual aspiration. The founders of the Republic based their hopes for the new nation on the reason of the common man and his faith in God. Twentieth-century democracy has emphasized reason and the common man but has neglected to cultivate faith in anything beyond him. Faith in the common man alone becomes deference to whatever is popular, no matter how cheap. Faith in reason alone tends to become legalism without heart, logic without understanding, morality without goodness. Without some polestar of the spirit, democracy will become what Brooks Adams said it was: "an infinite mass of conflicting minds and conflicting interests . . . which loses in collective energy in proportion to the perfection of its expansion."

Was all this speculation about unity and diversity, Angus wondered, no more than a game of semantics, playing fast and loose with words and ideas? Words can create a false reason of their own, and they are not dependable as conveyors of abstract thought. Their limitations, their different meanings to different people, and the overtones of emotion attached to many of them increase the difficulty of using them for communication with others and even for argument with oneself. That is another reason why unity of spirit, which goes beyond words and depends on them less than reason, is essential. But even if there were no problem of semantics, it would still be impossible to define what, in a series of variant situations, is unity and what is diversity. For instance, do the wide variations in current values and standards of art and music, from their classic to their modern extremes, represent diversity, or the unity of eclecticism and support of originality? The answer is usually determined by what the speaker wants to prove.

Perhaps, after all, the last word about unity and diversity was said by Henry Adams in his two books *Mont-Saint-Michel and Chartres* and *The Education*. Their readers miss their point unless they recognize the significance of their subtitles: "a study of thirteenth-century unity" and "a study of twentieth-century diversity." Adams preferred unity, but it seemed to Angus that diversity was just as popular and sometimes just as admirable. Some of the forces that are pulling men together —like the advantages of economic co-operation, security, education, and the desire for friendship and peace—are agreed by everyone to be virtuous. Some of the forces that are holding men apart—like self-determination in government and religion, originality, freedom of opinion, and private initiative in creative art and economics—are also thought by most Americans to be good. But both centripetal and centrifugal forces, both unity and diversity, when carried to extremes, bring their dangers. When unity is carried to excessive conformity, or organized to excessive complexity, it is harmful; when diversity destroys social order or fosters rampant egos, it is harmful. Human history can be viewed as a constant struggle between unity and diversity, and civilization as society's effort to find the proper balance between them. American society has not yet found that balance, and Angus doubted it would do so by compiling lists of subversive organizations in the name of unity, or tolerating commercial vulgarity and pornography in the name of the freedoms of diversity.

After all this effortful speculation, Angus at fifty-four was almost as ignorant as he had been at eighteen of what most men think they want of life, or what motives deeper than the obvious ones determine their conduct and decisions. So far as understanding the mass mind was concerned, he could as well have spent his time accumulating dollars or breeding dachshunds or sitting in the bar of the Racquet Club. As for understanding himself, he had at long last made a real effort and an expensive one. He had learned a little, but did not seem to be able to translate it into daily living wholly rewarding to himself and those about him. It was possible that all this self-analysis had hurt him more than it had helped. When he read Heinrich von Kleist's conclusion that to understand one's own motives is to suffer a loss of vitality, confidence, and grace, he feared it had been true in his own case. Yet not to understand one's motives, or even try to, seemed to involve still greater losses.

He concluded that his cogitations had got him as far along the road of understanding as his limping mind would take him. It was not very far, and in one sense it was not even an advance. Its chief service had been to lead him back to some truths his parents and others had told him long ago, but which in the pursuit of higher education and outward success he had half forgotten and half disbelieved. That might be good, but it was one thing to regain a conviction of the importance of cultivating the spirit and another to go about its cultivation. Conscious introspection is not necessarily spiritual growth, and Angus had had enough of it. He needed to find some way to warm his heart without warming his ego.

For some years Angus had been lifting the rocks from the tiny cultivated plots of his Maine fields and his own spirit, but each winter brought to their surfaces new crops of unsuspected stones. It was discouraging work, for his earth and spiritual soil were still thin and their produce stunted. He could not build fences high enough and strong enough to keep the winds of Penobscot Bay from leveling his vegetables, and fresh blasts of egoism from blighting the fragile growths of his spirit. Was there no alternative to continuing this plodding and unpromising performance?

But in his Maine garden he found a few native plants that

survived both rocks and winds and produced edible fruits. Per-haps this same vitality was also in American society—possibly even in himself. The thing to do might be to make his roots draw up more cordially everything his native soil had to offer. He and America were not ready to lay down their tools, their illusions, and their dreams, and maybe all three were better than they looked. In the end something good might come of them. Meanwhile the satisfactions of life lay all around. Neither Angus nor his America would gain by forgoing them, like his grandmother, merely because they were enjoyable.

XIV

Angus Emeritus

THUS Angus finally brought himself round, by instinct if not by his own reasoning, to reconciliation with the world. When this happened his usefulness to me was at an end, for he had ceased to be the Angus I had created. Either he had grown beyond me or I had grown beyond him. I began by confessing him only half a man, whose sole warmly human trait was a tendency to dramatize himself. As a screen for my own ego he proved to be transparent, and by peeping out from behind him so often I merely shriveled him without adding an inch to my own stature. To tell the truth, his rationalizations began to bore me. It was time we parted company.

Yet it would be ungracious to leave him without pronouncing those kindly words customarily addressed to men arbitrarily placed in retirement. After all, he taught me much about my own limitations, and his mental autobiography should have some significance for others. The forces that made and confused him are also at work on all Americans of the twentieth century. Most of them, like traditions and democracy and nuclear energy, are not in themselves either malevolent or benign; it is how society uses them that determines their effect on its qualities and values. Angus fought most of those forces instead of trying to help channel their direction, but at least he made ardent efforts to understand them. Later Anguses can, if there is time, put the new forces of the twentieth century to happier uses and better alignment with older forces than Angus and his contemporaries have been able to do. They will need to understand old and new energies better than Angus could, and his story may help them to that understanding. It may also stimulate their elders to see that the education of younger Americans is both broader and more unified than his.

All education is either planned and organized into institutions, or accidental and largely beyond institutional control. The planned education of parents, schools, and colleges can be directed with greater vision and courage than at present. Parents and educators can do something about that, if they will assert themselves as leaders, and not trail as followers, of society's standards.

Accidental education, like that of Angus wallowing in the mud of the Cambridge game or the politics of Washington, is less easily foreseen or altered, for it is constantly at work on every boy and girl gossiping on the street or curled up beside the radio. Its influences are derived from society as a whole, and only society as a whole can alter them. The more it elevates its own standards and habits, the more it elevates the accidental education of its youth. Of the two forms of education, the accidental is the more continuous and powerful in twentieth-century America. That fact offers the greatest challenge to modern democracy. It is a challenge that can be met, for no other society was ever so free to make itself whatever it wanted.

"Society" is a general term which no man identifies with himself; we criticize it without feeling any personal responsibility for the abstract faults we condemn. It seems too large for any average man to influence. Yet society is no more than the cumulative expression of individual attitudes, and the critic condemns in part his own weakness. According to Confucius, the superior man blames himself, the inferior man blames others. Angus made society the whipping boy for his own inadequacies; other Americans need to see as clearly as he did the flaws in our social values, and then deal with them more constructively than he.

Angus was naïve to seek in Europe, or in retirement from education and government, an escape from the distorted values of the twentieth century. There is no escape. There are no islands, of soil or of thought, where he or any other men can set up private Utopias. Nowhere can the modern American escape from the conflicts between unity and diversity, for if he avoids them in society he will still find them in himself.

Gulliver's isle of wisdom was only fictional, and was inhabited not by men but by wise horses, who soon found Gulliver intolerable and sent him back to live among men, all the less happily after a brief experience with the life of sweet equine reason. Angus might have remembered that men are influenced by more than reason, and that to live happily in their society one must feel warmly as well as try to think deeply. He should have remembered John Jay Chapman's remark that lots of people cannot think seriously without impairing their minds.

And having fruitlessly tilted at windmills himself, Angus might have recalled that at the end Don Quixote renounced all foolish tales of knight-errantry and forbade his niece to marry any man who had ever read one. Sancho Panza was right that the old days can never be recaptured, and that there is no use looking for birds of this year in the nests of the last. Life requires acceptance as well as nonconformity, unity as well as diversity, and later Anguses must learn better than he how to live contentedly with all four. If, like Candide, one is to end by living as happily as it is ever possible to do, one must accept his final conclusion:

"All is not so well as in El Dorado but, it must be confessed, things do not go too badly."